Speaking with a Boneless Tongue

Ecological Pedagogy, Curriculum and Scholarship

Vol. 1

Edited by Jodi Latremouille and David W. Jardine

PETER LANG
New York · Berlin · Bruxelles · Chennai · Lausanne · Oxford

Speaking with a Boneless Tongue

David W. Jardine

PETER LANG
New York · Berlin · Bruxelles · Chennai · Lausanne · Oxford

Bibliographic Information published by the Deutsche Nationalbibliothek

The Deutsche Nationalbibliothek lists this publication in the Deutsche Nationalbibliografie; detailed bibliographic data is available in the internet at http://dnb.d-nb.de.

Library of Congress Cataloging-in-Publication Data
A CIP catalog record for this book has been applied for at the Library of Congress.

Cover Illustration ©Eric Jardine
Cover design by Peter Lang Group AG

ISBN 978-3-0343-5417-2 (PB)
ISBN 978-3-0343-5468-4 (HB)
E-ISBN 978-3-0343-5469-1 (E-PDF)
E-ISBN 978-3-0343-5470-7 (E-PUB)
DOI 10.3726/b22723

© 2025 Peter Lang Group AG, Lausanne, Switzerland
Published by Peter Lang Publishing Inc., New York, USA

info@peterlang.com   www.peterlang.com

All rights reserved.

All parts of this publication are protected by copyright. Any utilisation outside the strict limits of the copyright law, without the permission of the publisher, is forbidden and liable to prosecution. This applies in particular to reproductions, translations, microfilming, and storage and processing in electronic retrieval systems.

This publication has been peer reviewed.

Contents

The Warbling of Birds, 2024	1
ORIGINAL INTRODUCTION AND ACKNOWLEDGEMENTS (1992)	23
Prelude One: A Reading Key	29
Prelude Two: Another Reading Key	31
Prelude Three: Another Reading Key	53
CHAPTER ONE	55
CHAPTER TWO	59
CHAPTER THREE	63
CHAPTER FOUR	67
CHAPTER FIVE	71
CHAPTER SIX	75
CHAPTER SEVEN	83
CHAPTER EIGHT	99
CHAPTER NINE	107

CHAPTER TEN	119
CHAPTER ELEVEN	121
CHAPTER TWELVE	129
CHAPTER THIRTEEN	137
CHAPTER FOURTEEN	145
CHAPTER FIFTEEN	149
CHAPTER SIXTEEN	155
CHAPTER SEVENTEEN	157
CHAPTER EIGHTEEN	163
CHAPTER NINETEEN	165
CHAPTER TWENTY	173
CHAPTER TWENTY-ONE	177
CHAPTER TWENTY-TWO	179
CHAPTER TWENTY-THREE	181
CHAPTER TWENTY-FOUR	183
CHAPTER TWENTY-FIVE	189
CHAPTER TWENTY-SIX	193

Contents

CHAPTER TWENTY-SEVEN	197
CHAPTER TWENTY-EIGHT	201
CHAPTER TWENTY-NINE	203
CHAPTER THIRTY	207
CHAPTER THIRTY-ONE	211
CHAPTER THIRTY-TWO	215
CHAPTER THIRTY-THREE	223
CHAPTER THIRTY-FOUR	225
CHAPTER THIRTY-FIVE	233
CHAPTER THIRTY-SIX	245
CHAPTER THIRTY-SEVEN	249
CHAPTER THIRTY-EIGHT	253
CHAPTER THIRTY-NINE	255
CHAPTER FORTY	261
CHAPTER FORTY-ONE	263
CHAPTER FORTY-TWO	265
"She Unnames Them"	267

"She Unnames Them"	269
A Postscript: *Ganesha's Kiss,* 2022	271
A Postscript: *Ganesha Kissed,* 2024	273
References	275

The Warbling of Birds, 2024

> "Put all the songs together and it's certainly an autobiography," he once declared, "but not necessarily mine."
>
> Lewis Reed (cited in Zoppellaro, 2014, p. 38)

First, a Playground Secret and An Ecological Reverse

> The beautiful captivates *us*. *It* has asserted *itself* and captivated us before we can come to ourselves and be in a position to test the claim … that *it* makes [on us]. We are drawn into an event. (Gadamer 1989, p. 490, emphases added)

The purpose of those citation emphases is simple. It is an ecological and pedagogical point which reverses a common and current tendency towards focussing on *me* attending to this oh-so-commonplace birdfeeder moment, my story about it, my perspective, my "take."

We've all have our own experiences. Reading this old book you have ahead of you reminds me all over again about how inadequate and banal that "insight" is. How, over decades, I've more often been *had* by "my own experiences" — outwitted, proven inadequate to the matters at hand, proved insightful in ways I never imagined, and overwhelmed by time and circumstance.

I wanted to show this photo to you and wait and listen. I'm not up to it all by my lonesome. This is not a personal failing but is, I suggest, *in the nature of things*, our nature, Raven nature, sunlight nature. Put altogether, it is in the Earthly and mutual *nurture of things*.

That fiery beak "arrests motion. You draw in your breath and stop still" (Hillman, 2006a, p. 183). This old book was one of my first gatherings around this ecological reverse and try to follow it along. It formed by smashing together several slightly older pieces of writing that erupted in the late 1980s. Smashing them apart, because the formality of their published versions still held too fast to holding the beasts at bay.

This book is an old arrest of attention. It is ridiculous, exaggerated, lively, pretentious, empty, self-aggrandizing, over-stated, and cool. And exactly what's what and who's who in this regard is just about to be decided all over again.

Enjoy.

Even me reaching for a letter in the upper-case for Raven can momentarily intercede and stop to visit a while. My spell-check is full of resignation. I witness an old hand in this memory of upper and lower cases, the old whap of keys against inks against paper. Type setting. It took me a long while to figure how whiling figures in all of this. I had sensed this firsthand for years, but this was never quite enough. I started to study and take seriously the beckons of pathways that wound off in the distance.

I was so relieved to find that this whiling time had been expressly expressed with a good warranty attached. Whiling time (Gadamer, 1970; Ross, 2004; Jardine, 2008; Ross & Jardine, 2009) opens the eyes and heart and mind. It can take your breath away and give it right back full blown. Good warrant? Simply this – in paying it its due attention, it came to something, made a place, revealed some secrets.

This sort of thing has become lovely old news these days. Ancestors, trails, stories told and suppressed, stuff animals wired to fenceposts, there for all to see (Jardine, 2024). James Hillman and Sonu Shamdasani (2013) repeatedly flirt with an image of allowing the dead to speak, allowing the mixed, shared and contested ancestral memories that bears us to perhaps yield wisdom and counsel and not just haunting. If they are treated properly and not just used as erudite hammers. Without them, we feel uprooted, unanchored, untethered, and adrift—a modern lament so gracefully articulated by Lois Lowry in her novel *The Giver*, wherein the young boy Jonas attempts a conciliatory response to his teacher:

> "The Old like to tell about their childhoods, and it's always fun to listen."
>
> The man shook his head. "No, no," he said. "I'm not being clear. It's not my past, not my childhood that I must transmit to you."
>
> He leaned back. "It's the memories of the whole world," he said with a sigh. "Before you, before me, before the previous Receiver, and generations before him."
>
> Jonas frowned. "The whole world?" he asked. "I don't understand. I thought there was only us. I thought there was only now."
>
> "There's much more. There's all that goes beyond, and all that goes back and back and back. It is how wisdom comes. And how we shape our future."
>
> He rested for a moment, breathing deeply. "I am so weighted with them," he said. (Lowry, 2011, p. 79)

And right there lightening gravities. Recollecting that I'd known *something* of this before, sought it out for decades before this old book coalesced into what seems, now, a rather quaint shape:

> When any of us think of those things in the world that we dearly love–the music of Duke Ellington, the contours of a powerful novel and how it envelopes us if we give ourselves over to it, the exquisite architectures of mathematical geometries, the old histories and stories of this place, the rows of garden plants that need our attention and devotion and care, varieties of birds and their songs, the perfect sound of an engine that works well, the pull of ice under a pair of skates, and on and on—we understand something in our relation to these things about how excessiveness might be basic to such love. We do not seek these things out and

explore them again and again simply for the profit that we might gain in exchanging what we have found for something *else*. What we have found, in exploring and coming to understanding, to learn to live well with these things is not an arms-length commodity but has become part of who we are, and how we carry ourselves in the world. We love them and we love what becomes of us in our dedication to them. And, paradoxically, the more we understand of them, the better—richer, more intriguing, more complex, more ambiguous and full and multiple of questions—*they* become, and the more we realize that gobbling them up into a knowing that we can commodify, possess and exchange is not only undesirable. It is impossible. We realize, in such knowing, that the living character of the things we love will, of necessity, outstrip our own necessarily finite and limited experience, memory, and exploration (Jardine, Clifford & Friesen 2003, p. 208).

And the earthly progenitors hidden in the plain sight of the animal body's tracing of places and footfalls. The dogs sniffing old piss trails as the snow melts. "Transforming according to circumstances, meet all beings as your ancestors" (Hongzhi, 1991, p. 43; see Jardine, 2016, p. 75-78). We "are always already everywhere inhabited" (Smith 2006, p. xxiv). (cited from Jardine, 2024, p. 367)

The particular Cartesian legacy of my own people that picked these matters apart, and in so many ways spread their pick-aparts far and wide are not my only kin. They haunt school hallways, good-hearted teachers' exhaustions. On and on, right into the soils.

There were five Ravens at the feeder out back this June 2024 morning. Another cascade of young'uns, noisy, frantic, unkempt compared to steady old dada, feeding a baby almost his size. I'm now surrounded by two grandsons – one be one in two weeks, one three in six — and that makes reading this old book quite different than it might have been before. More noisy, more frantic, more settled, more bewildered:

> After this recognition – the image as ancestor – there is the experience of the claim that images make upon me.
>
> . . .
>
> We do not make them up, so we do not make up our response to them but are 'taught' this response by them.
>
> . . .
>
> Our way . . . does not interpret the image but talks with it. It does not ask what the images means but what it wants.

. . .

> How do we know whether they mean well with us or would possess us? (Hillman, 1996, p. 60, 61, 93, 75)

Not "what does it mean?" but "what does it *want*?" We still. We giggle and gather our wits over beans coming up. I look at these old pages from 1992 and giggle and try to gather what it wanted from me back then, or now.

Still not sure.

With my grandsons in tow, us stilled for these few seconds of recognizable Raven wing winds overhead, the elder boy turning to me, finger on his ear and that do-you-hear-it? look, and me to him, agape at Ravens turning to us, my own ear touched, smiles, hushed a bit.

What a lovely mess. What lovelies to have at all in these ecologically sorrowful times (Jardine, 2024). The sorrow increases. The beans just now poking up makes it better and worse, all in one overhead swooping.

Second, A Pause for a Moment

I need to stop for a moment, because I'm finding, re-reading this old thing, that *I want to change every single sentence*. I want to add everything I've ever thought ever since. It hurts in an old familiar way. I want to confess how it traced lines more beautiful, forgiving and joyous than me and my old temperaments.

We each and I too, of course, inevitably and persistently suffer the poverty of our own experience as being *necessarily*, not *accidentally* inadequate to the fullness of things themselves. This is the beautiful, empty spotting spot. A simple truth:

> The real challenge is to face the truth that no one tradition can say everything that needs to be said about the full expression of human experience in the world and that what the global community requires more than anything else is mutual recognition of the various poverties of *every* tradition, now revealed by globalization in

unprecedented ways and in new degrees. The search to cure the poverty of one's own tradition works in all directions at once. (Smith, 2006, p. 55).

Yet, of course, not so simple a truth when we look at who gets to say what about what in all these matters, who has been silenced, who not, and on and on. And all this including the society of Raven babies' noisiness, my own tongue and bloodlines, the water running downhill.

All of it all at once and how that huge and ungainly insight lights a'perched *there*.

. . . my grandson's muttering over the feeder-wars with red squirrels *adds itself* to the overfullness of Ravens, as do tales of Odin's Ravens, or that Raven photo with a bloody beak back from a kill (Jardine, 2024).

. . . this one here:

FIGURE TWO BLOOD BEAK

And having had a dog ripped up by a cougar but not quite killed adds itself every time I see flocks around a roadkill feasting. And then the five black huddlers this morning.

How we each find our guts wrenched and cooed by moonlight.

My luck at having had a life of ease increases my desire to write about glimpses:

> "And the Raven, never flitting, still is sitting, *still* is sitting"
> Edgar Allan Poe, from "The Raven," final stanza
> (https://www.poetryfoundation.org/poems/48860/the-raven)

Is sitting *still*.

Or this from the *Prose Edda* chapter entitled "Gylfaginning: Here Begins the Beguiling of Gylfi":

> The ravens sit on [Odin's] shoulders and say into his ear all the tidings which they see or hear; they are called thus: Huginn[1] and Muninn.[2] He sends them at day-break to fly about all the world, and they come back at undern-meal; thus he is acquainted with many tidings. Therefore men call him Raven-God, as is said:
>
> > Huginn and Muninn hover each day
> > The wide earth over;
> > I fear for Huginn lest he fare not back,—
> > Yet watch I more for Muninn."
> > (https://www.sacred-texts.com/neu/pre/pre04.htm, p. 51)

The footnotes in square bracket indicate that Huggin means "thought" and Muninn means "memory."

I fear for thought lest it not come to me. It is difficult to remain alert in the clustering gatherings that classrooms can be. There are worthy companions who've written about their work in schools (see Seidel & Jardine, 2016, which contains writings of classroom teachers pondering and practicing this sort of work).

I watch out for memory traces in that Raven's arrival. I know there will be doors, ajar, if I can sit, still. (Jardine, 2024, p. 357)

Memory and thought. Two familiars shouldered by Odin who tied himself to Yggdrasil, the Ash Tree axis of the world, and awaited wisdom.

Tied to a tree. Sounds, well, familiar. Every single utter makes all the others shiver outwards at the site of relations. And how a two-minute search hints at Raven and "The Box of Daylight" (Parenteau, 2022, n.p.) – a whole bloodstream streaming over Norwegian memory and thought, a whole lifetime:

> "Do not open the lid, Grandson!" instructed the Chief. The boy, who had his own mind, opened the box and released the stars into the sky and gazed in wonder at the lights in the Heavens. (Parenteau, 2022, n.p.)

This, of course, is all too easy to do these days, just flirt by and cite. It is too easy to note that the reference refers to Ravens tales taking flight across generations.

My apologies. My poverty felt lifted a bit when I read this.

How much reading of it would be enough to let this apology take good hold?

. . . to not be appropriating?

. . . to not have even *mentioned* appropriation when quoting Tsong-kha-pa or Hongzhi above? A lovely and important mess, all this.

Apparently, there was a Raven sent from the ark as goes another tall tale.

And warnings to not open lids echoes an old Greek name meaning "the love of all." Pandora.

There is only bristling new oxygen to be gained in letting each entangle and loose the other, letting go of hold on, letting arisings arise. Whiling over it. Admitting the pleasure to be had in finding out you've been had. This is the entangle we're all in every step of the way *anyway*.

In the face of this odd ecological insight about interdependence and dependent co-arising and all the other adages that are swirling around, "subjectivity is a distorting mirror" (Gadamer 1989, p. 276). It is not up to the task. This is why overcoming the inventions of epistemological and experiential "possessive individualism" (MacPherson, 2010) is such a vital ecological act of recover and healing and why I am so wary of many current currents of thought that seem to be deepening this error. One does not overcome Cartesianism by simply democratizing it. Nor is it overcome by turning one's back on it and skipping giddly elsewhere where others identify differently. This would only work if identity were the solution. Instead, it indirectly affirms and simply proliferates all the woes of the Cartesian legacy and its agonizing analogies to colonialism, as this old book lays out a bit.

Here be at least the aspiration of hermeneutics and a hint at why I followed it up over the intervening years. One of my European ancestors: "It is not at all a question of a mere subjective variety of conceptions, but of *the work's own possibilities of being that emerge* as the work explicates itself, as it were in a variety of *its* aspects" (Gadamer, 1989, p. 118, emphasis added):

FIGURE THREE THUNDER UNDERFEATHERS

Each glimpse, each voicing, each story, each breath-halt murmurs towards all the others and each one bears its own poverties and richness all at the same time. And in case this is seeming all too woozy, consider this. A Ruffed Grouse hit our patio window full force. A notice:

FIGURE FOUR PECTINATIONS

Photo by the author.

Ready? *Bonasa umbellus.*

> Notice all the narrow pectinations (meaning comb-like) growing laterally from the scales on the toes. Those pectinations are actually extensions of foot scales so they're not feathers. Ruffed Grouse are non-migratory and typically prefer higher-elevation forests in the lower 48 states (or boreal forests further north), so they spend a lot of time in deep snow. The pectinations act to significantly increase the surface area of the feet so they function like showshoes. Interestingly, the pectinations of Ruffed Grouse in northern areas where there's typically more snow are twice as long as those in more southerly regions. The three forward toes are also slightly webbed to increase the surface area of the feet even more but that slight webbing cannot be seen here. One of several reasons very few people ever see these

"snowshoes" is that they're not permanent. They begin to grow each year in the fall and drop off in the spring. (Dudley, n.p., 2019)

Grade Five science anyone? Surface areas. Weights. Snowshoes. And summers hearing wings drumming air. Boreal forests. A whole world of relations unfolds. Treated well, any student's voicing of notice or concern adds itself to the myriad of this place. Linnaeus is nearby. The *12th Edition of Systema Naturae*, and the whole urge to classify – kinds, families, species, genera, and on and on.

Everything is like this. *Everything*.

This is the sort of mess that this old book stepped into and that I have been scraping off the soles of my shoes ever since. It guided my working with teachers and student-teachers in schools, encouraging curriculum topics to become topographies, locales of rich relations to be explored, adored, learned. *The Earth itself is multivocal not univocal, multilingual not unilingual, multicultural, not monocultural, multivarious not invariant, human and far, far, far more than that.* Each one of us most truly stands *there*, in the full, agonizing "breaking forth as if from a centre" (Gadamer, 1989, p. 458) poverty and overwhelming richness of that insight. Every single curriculum topic entrusted to teachers and students in schools is a living field of relations. And we ourselves are not a collection of myriad self-contained identities (cultural or individual or otherwise) that somehow "afterwards" have relations to the whole bloody earth. Relations are not *post hoc*. That is not how I *am*. It is not how a Raven *is*:

> *Everything* points to some other thing. ["everything is dependent on something else, and because that in turn is dependent, it is not autonomous" (Tsong-kha-pa 2004, p. 162]. Nothing comes forward just in the one meaning that is offered to us. Only because the universal relatedness of being is concealed from the human eye does it need to be discovered. (Gadamer 2007c, p. 131)

Of course I quote Gadamer; he is one of my own intimate ancestors, a long-standing companion. And of course I quote Tsong-kha-pa. He, too, is one of my own intimate ancestors that I have dwelt with ever since discovering how re-reading Gadamer with his 1406-Tibetan insights made Gadamer better and vice-versa – each made them each more forgiving of each. A tough proposal, then, that it may be that the deepest error of colonialism is *not* the violent imposition of European identity on the world to the exclusion of other identities, but, hidden deep inside this horrible imposition, the *importation and spread of the very idea of identity itself*, leading to its invasive-species proliferation as a proposed *cure* to that original univocal imposition, as if it was the Euro- that was the key problem, not the -centrism indigenous to the very idea of identity itself. As if well-intended carving off of multiple identities can avoid the wars that then often ensue. Somewhere in this old book, Wendell Berry talks of how the very act of putting up a greenhouse wall … hmm. Even Samuel Huntington (2003, p. 266) talks about what happens when, under real or proposed threat, identities *harden*. What is an understandable refuge from harm can become misunderstood as the cure of harm, not its wound.

And, of course, I hadn't read Tsong-kha-pa or Huntington when I wrote this book. So the urge to *save this book from itself*, poor thing, is hard to resist. I will resist. One more eco-convolution in the ways of ideas and words and cultures and the like. Like this particular chapter title: "'A Hubris Hiding from its Nemesis': Why Does the Affirmation of Diversity Tend Towards the Proliferation of Multiple Identities, and to What Consequence?" (in Jardine 2024, pp. 141-156).

Yikes, eh? Time for the hot-potato toss. Time to walk on thin ice. Time to avoid cliches like the plague. To walk on gilded splinters.

This is why this old book plays around so squarely with thoughts of analogies, likenesses, family resemblances, kinds, kins, kindnesses, healing, health, wholeness, and how these ideas themselves were suppressed under the dominate logics of identity and difference in various threads of Western thought.

Thank You for your Patience

Whew, okay. So much for my own night-tremors that you'll see more of rattling through this old book. Thank you for your patience.

So, just imagine, here, re-reading and writing about a book I wrote 32 years ago. There is an old hermeneutic adage: "We can entrust ourselves to what we are investigating to guide us safely in the quest" (Gadamer, 1989, p. 378). And yet here I am, warbling. And I've even added two postscripts. Forgive me. As I say to *every second old line* that I *will not* edit. Feels like facing a beak full of blood. Whose, well . . . .

I do get to rest in the repose that comes from knowing that this old book itself has been read and read over the years. This is why I read. This is why I write (Jardine, 2014):

> March 1, 2019, 2:50 pm. Text exchange:
>
> > **Jodi:** *Lesley, there is a word in Cree you have called me before. I wonder, do you remember?*
> > **Lesley:** *nitotem?*
> > **Jodi:** *YES! That means friend, right?*
> > **Lesley:** *Yes. ni. Meaning my. kitotem meaning your friend. But t's sounds like a mix between d and t.*
>
> March 10, 2019, 5:32 pm. Text exchange:
>
> > **Jodi:** *Lesley, mulling over some things.*
> > **Jodi:** *Do you see the email thread with David? Lol. feeling all tangled! overwhelmed by the limits/possibilities.*
> > **Lesley:** *No stress. We will figure it all out.*
> > **Jodi:** *I'm not stressing, it's just very interesting. Lol. [...] Using your first name doesn't give you proper credit, but it doesn't "protect" you adequately either ... and from what? From publishing a book together?*
>
> ... whose story?
>
> And then, from Thomas King (2013), read so long ago together:
>
> > Take [this] story, for instance. Do with it what you will. Tell it to friends. Turn it into a television movie. Forget it. But don't say in the years to come that you would have lived your life differently if only you had heard this story. You've heard it now. (p. 61)
>
> And [Jodi's] own note, scrawled in the margin, years ago:
> ethical responsibility towards the research
>
> > **Lesley:** No stress, nitotem. We'll figure it all out.
> > **Jodi:** Sometimes the sweat takes my breath away.
> > **Lesley:** Heat, darkness, sacredness

> **Jodi:** Sometimes my voice wavers. I just can't finish what I started.
> **Lesley:** Don't worry, nitotem, you were perfect.
> **Jodi:** My breath returns. My body breathes for me.
> (Latremouille, Tait, & Jardine, 2024, p. 123-4)

So, take this, if you want. The blossoms are phototropic. My own attention is far flightier than this. But I have been sitting outside in this early spring sun, facing it. I did so once even during an eclipse (Jardine, 2017; see also Jardine, 2024 [p. 31-60] under the chapter title "Meanwhile, Saints Graze on the Begonias"). I wrote about it, of course, because it summoned something about the very same pathways tread in this old book.

"So, Here We Are"

Driveway rivulations dammed and undammed, wet boot toes. Flushes into ditches that slowly become frogsonged into spring:

> You [can easily become] like the leading edge of water running downhill—you go anywhere you are led, taking anything said to be true, wanting to cry when you see others crying, wanting to laugh when you see others laugh. (Tsong-kha-pa 2004, p. 222).

This here thing was originally self-published in 1992. In part, it coalesced a few papers that got written all in a rush in a rush in 1990 (Jardine, 1990, 1990a, 1990b) and exploded them from the insides. Up spun James Hillman's *puer* and *senex*, matters ecological, and breaths held and drawn. Uprose Wendell Berry, and Thich Nhat Hahn, and Keiji Nishitani, and more Gary Snyder than I knew existed. Even the Second Council of Nicaea (c.787 CE) came arising, leading later to ponderings about images and words in children's books (Bastock & Jardine, 2005) and pauses over issue of Protestant and Catholic musings on the relation between words and images, and how picture books, at least back in 1992, would fade from view in schools ASAP. Images became a means. This book became an early trove in unforeseen ways. The current image-laden-ness of handheld devices and the rampant spellbinding-Ness (this was my spell-check's only resort!) that they seem to have makes me wonder about re-reading those Nicaean warnings. About all that talk of the *Biblia Pauperum* and so on.

And now, about having young grandchildren rising up in the midst of all that – screens flickering in all directions at once. Mysterious visions.

I gave the press the name *Makyō Press* in line with a passage I had found in Robert Aitken's work:

> "*Makyō*, mysterious vision" [is] a deep dream experience. Certain religious traditions place great importance on *makyō*. Visions and heavenly voices are seriously considered to be signs of enlightenment and salvation. These phenomena may be of general interest, for they reveal the rich potential of human experience, but they reveal little of the true nature of the one who experiences them. If you do experience it you can recognize that you are walking near your true home [but] no matter how interesting and encouraging *makyō* may be, they are self-limited. (Aitken, 1982, p. 46)

In reviving this old book, I've since discovered how alluring the letting loose of writing can be, how lovely, how foolish, how occasionally insightful and blasting with sunlight. How necessarily potentially misleading. Visions, voices, emotions, swept-up-nesses. All for the good in its joyous rides. How its visions and voices *are always signs* but precisely *of what* is always and everywhere yet to be decided by how it is read, by whom, for what, for why. It is thus for me, even all these years later, let along for anyone else reading this autobiography of someone, something.

Writing is always and to unretrievable and varying degrees "open for the future." (Gadamer 1989, p. 340). This book was deliberately written in an attempt to make that sort of open-future as palpable as I could manage. It is as if I tried to take the experience of reading a text and insert it into the text itself. A wonderfully pretentious exercise. More mundanely, I'd become tired of the moribund character of academic language and protocol and poise. I'd read things that could allow my own thick scholarly weight of ideas and images to expand and loosen and thus become more "readable" in a way:

> All reading involves application, so that a person reading a text is himself part of the meaning he apprehends. He belongs to the text he is reading. The line of meaning that the text manifests to him as he reads it always and necessarily breaks off into an open indeterminacy. He can, indeed he must, accept the fact that future generations will understand differently.
>
> ....
>
> In this way he keeps [both himself and the text] open for the future. (Gadamer, 1989, p. 340)

In case this all sounds a bit too arcane, just consider how odd and notable it is these days to read the relentless masculine usages in this citation. When I hit them now, the weight of their noticeability seems lighter. They *show themselves*, these translators' decisions.

Again, a pause.

Dreamstates: A November 30th 2013 Parable

> I pull up this collar of skin
> Yet it chills.
> Cold and hollow bones inside a relentless
> clock of meat. That last image one
> of Allen Ginsberg's I can no longer quite trace. His one of
> many deaths I've had around me, in the air. Of the many
> witnessed coming this way. Mine.
> How it is that them taking their time in coming takes my time, all this is
> a bit of a growing mystery.
> Part, I guess, of the terrible and elongated conceit of inevitability.
>
> The arc from light to air to water to wood to stone
> is a parabolic curve that never touches an axis.
> Just ever-nears it. No. There is no it. More like a corpse momentarily
> caught

in the happenstance orbit of warm and temporary breath.
Evidence. See?
There is no axis, only nearing.
Tree copses are full of airborne exhalations steamed out
into the dark
iron bells of the coming storm, the minus forty.
Into the wrings of hands,
Tolling fret and patience,
Both, in breath, stilled. Ice-fog.

Oh this silly fire is such a blessed thing.
Sleeping dogs nuzzled like summoned
Angels warming with no forethought.
There, in dreams of furry, feathered wings.

This is why I searched anew for this term *makyo* (魔境 *makyō*) to make the warnings to readers, and my own self-warnings, more open-wounded and a touch less sweet:

> The term *makyo* (魔境 *makyō*) means "ghost cave" or "devil's cave." It is employed in Zen as figurative reference to the kind of self-delusion that results from clinging to an experience and making a conceptual "nest" out of it for oneself. *Makyo* is, in other words, essentially synonymous with illusion, but the word is used especially in reference to experiences that can occur within meditation practice.
> *(https://tibetanbuddhistencyclopedia.com/en/index.php?title=Makyo)*

But there it is again, something showing itself because of the circumstances of our reading it. Just imagine this these days, with the blooming and bursting of autobiographical writing and talk of place and other matters ecopedagogical, that clinging to an experience and making a nest of it *just might be delusional*, beckoning the need all over again for the trick:

> "I am Christopher Columbus. I am sailing the ocean blue looking for India. Have you seen it?"
> "Forget India," says Coyote. "Let's play ball." (King & Monkman, 1992, p. 9)

I get swirled up in words so easily that the pretty surface charms can be-spell too easily. It is so easy to mix dictions – ghost caves, little *kleshas*, demons that trip me up as I waft through the forest, tricks that can break the heart open. Warnings. My family-ghost motto, *Cave Adsum*, "Beware, I Am Here" and this old book the first glimmers of worries over the be ware of "I am."

The dark of caves having a certain be wary to them. Caveats. All that.

Ah, yes, there is such an important way in which there is no "other" nest. My fullhearted response begs a little cite:

> At the very beginning of the [now around 2600] pages of [now five] volumes published thus far (2004, 2005, 2008 [, 2016, 2017]), Geshe Sopa (2004, p. 1) starts thus: "So, here we are." (Seidel & Jardine, 2014, p. 1)

With this book, here we are all over again. A strange experience.

"Whether Life Itself has a Chance": And Ode to 500 Lives

Was I ever? This
Written waiting for an other father's
Day.
What we hand along, what the river gives and takes
For good or ill.
A child. Two grand boys,
And old book. A closeup of a butterfly.
Like a mescaline dream character
Cartooned.

FIGURE FIVE A BUTTERFLY TAIL

Welcome back, then, to an old book. And to a thought back as to why I right myself around writing. A relatively new companion's suggestion:

> *Bill Callahan*: I was thinking about this yesterday. I had a really positive day yesterday. I felt really good. I think when my life is good, I want to have 10 lives, I want to have 500 lives. I want to experience everything. I think that's why people write novels and make up characters, because then that [person] has another life now. They can do that again and again. Songwriting is a kind of the same. This little story is a life I'm setting free into the world. I want 500 lives, but I can't have them. But I can write 500 songs. I think that multiplicity is in me.
>
> *Bill Callahan (2022, p. 37)*

I was 42 when I wrote this book. I am no longer 42. My son who drew the cover image will be 42 years old this 2024, under the Scorpion's signature.

I used to deliberately read specific authors when starting a new piece of writing, to help remember certain rhythms and cadences and songlines. They were my wardens of warinesses, and music teachers, helping compose my ability to compose. Like, for example, David G. Smith, this written back in 1999 as part of a Preface-paean to his work, and, as you'll come to see, a hint at one of the updrafts of this old book itself, his writing, his example, his friendship and trickeries:

> Of course, we are all living under the newly fashionable education jargon of "community" that has already ruined these words before they even had a chance. The lamentation continues: jargon is rooted in an old Welsh term *iargoun*, which means "the warbling of birds." At least the warbling of birds is done with some tilting pleasure at the sun and the airblue arch that holds David's and my life together, this broad Chinook sky and the prairie abyss and the wind, and oh, the cold that cracks your bones, Alberta. This is the sort of incident I've come to expect from David Smith's work - painful fits of often bloody-minded healing, unavoidable because their bearing is always slightly unanticipated. It is never quite clear from where the "calling" might call and just what might be at stake in such calling. (Jardine, 1999, p. xviii)

With grandchildren now around, this sort of incident, this sort of reminder, is legible now in a way it could not have been at the time. And at the time, well, a deep note of gratitude Paul Ernest, University of Exeter. He read "The Humility of Mathematical Language" (Jardine, 1990) and send me a lovely hand-writ note. It is hard to say in words exactly how much difference that made to someone at the start of such a weird venture. He even wrote a lovely introduction to an on-line version of this text which graciously introduced others to is strange ways (Ernest, 2002) Many thanks.

And here is the passage from David G. Smith's work that I would give my own student teachers back then and long afterwards:

> It is as if young people ask for, above all else, not only a genuine responsiveness from their elders but also a certain direct authenticity, a sense of that deep human resonance so easily suppressed under the smooth human-relations jargon teachers typically learn in college. Young people want to know if, under the cool and calm of efficient teaching and excellent time-on-task ratios, life itself has a chance, or whether the surface is all there is. And the best way to find out may be to provoke the teacher into showing himself or herself. (Smith, 1999, p. 139)

You'll find this passage cited with great affection in what follows. And this be the dedication of this new edition, to David, brother. We breath, us, and still wonder if life itself has a chance.

And here's thanks to Eric Jardine who, back in 1992, drew the Celtic Knot that adorns the cover. It reminds me of why I used footnotes back in '92 – something of sources living encurled underground.

The surface screens of videos and messages with no flesh swirl around my family and me. The surface is not all there is. My grandson touches his ear at the sound overhead. Seems that yes, young people ask, and they watch and wait, but not forever.

I stop and touch my ear. Life itself does have a chance.

ORIGINAL INTRODUCTION AND ACKNOWLEDGEMENTS (1992)

This book is akin to a family gathering or collection that turns around several interrelated themes —pedagogy, generativity, interpretation, ecology, feminism, narrative/story and questions of the language appropriate to such themes. It is written in a peculiar fashion. The reason for this is that this nest of themes poses a challenge *to the nature of writing itself.*

Ecology, for example, presents us with an image of our lives and the life of the Earth as involving a vast, vibrant, generative, ambiguous, multivocal, interweaving network of living interconnections. We are living *in* this web of interrelations and these interrelations are always already at work *before* the task of writing *about* those relations has begun. In this sense, therefore, if we take the example of ecology seriously, it is not enough simply to write *about* these interrelations. This sense of vastness and vibrancy and generativity and ambiguity and multivocity and interwovenness must somehow inform the character of the writing itself.

Ecology tells us that there is no center or foundation to this web of living interconnections, just small, lateral, interlacing relations of this to this to this, splayed in moving patterns of kinship and kind (wonderful terms for pedagogy to consider). If this is taken up as a challenge to the nature of writing, the question becomes one of how to write in such a way that the writing gives up the notion of having a center or a foundation. In an earlier version of this book, I wrote in a typical academic-narrative form, but I found that this form of writing was actually writing against what the book was about. This form of writing presupposed the very thing that the book then went on to critique as ecologically and pedagogically dangerous — univocity, closure, representationalism, essentialism, foundationalism.

The present version of this book is written in small, interlacing "bits" or "chunks" which relate laterally and generatively to all the other bits. Very often, the "flow" of the text is interrupted by the eruption of something new. Some new connection, another thread, another similar voice that resembles what went on before without exactly replicating it, will appear as an "aside"

> [like this one, which is actually pushed over to the side of the page and which is often accompanied by an aside to the aside]

in the text. Because of these textual interruptions, the reader's options multiply: the reader can "read on" in the main, left-margin-justified text, or can drop down into and out of the aside, or down into a footnote to the main text or, in fact, into the footnotes to the asides.

But this means that the experience of trying to read this book is inevitably one of constantly "losing the thread" and finding it again, looping back and forth. We have all been trained to believe that this "losing and finding" way of reading (and writing) indicates either a mistake in the text or a mistake in ourselves. We are not accustomed to such "comings and goings," and the first response to this book may well be one of deep frustration. However, it is precisely something akin to such interlacing, lateral "comings and goings" that ecology suggests is essential to our Earthly lives. It is precisely because we have forgotten how to live well with such "comings and goings" that describes our current ecological troubles.

In reading this book, therefore, it is necessary to allow yourself the luxury and the risk of getting lost in this huge forest of text — and then suddenly noticing something vaguely familiar, or glimpsing something moving out of the corner of your eye, or following a rocky side trail of traces and footprints that stop at the sheer edge of a cliff. Without such luxury and such risk, this book will not fit together.

It will be difficult at times to decide which is the main trail and which is the aside, for all of the threads do wind together in an interweaving web of interdependencies. It will depend, in part, on where you want to go and on where you have been. But it won't depend only on this.

Sometimes the trails will lead to places that are connected to where you want to go or where you have been, but that are more difficult or more complicated and convoluted and dangerous than any of us might wish to admit — the text may draw you, as it has (often painfully) drawn me, into implications of meaning that point to culpabilities beyond our wanting and willing. Sometimes, in writing this book, I have stumbled on things I wish I had never seen — toxic products of my living that I did not intend, but that implicate my living nevertheless. However, just as often the text stumbles out into the wide open air and has given me breathing room and made my life and my culpabilities more meaningful, more connected, more understandable and thus more bearable than they might have been borne as a private burden.

I can't help but recall the poem by Rick Fields that so eloquently expresses the lovely agonies of this sort of interpretive writing and ecological insight, where the bad news somehow turns out to be the good news, where he speaks about his heart being broken *open*.[1] Of course, whenever we lose the thread and find it again, things are never exactly the same as they were before. We inevitably "pick up the thread" from a place slightly different from where we left it. And we pick up the thread with a hand and a heart that are themselves slightly different. We bear a memory or trace with us of the places we have passed through, the experiences we have undergone. Reading marks us in a deep sense, if we allow it and if the text leaves room for our wanderings. Again, ecology challenges the nature of writing (and reading) itself.

There is thus something very important about the spaces between various pieces of text the "jumps" or "gaps" are, in a sense, longing to be filled and there is no single, prescribed, "proper" way to fill them. They are gaps in which something just might unexpectedly *happen*. The gaps are invitations for the particular reader to speak, to write, to generate meaning out of the empty, unfilled space. The gaps are like the fecund margins between forest and field or between ocean and beach and, as deep ecology suggests, "life erupts at the boundaries." Not all of these gaps will work for everyone. And no one will fill any one gap exactly the same way as anyone else. And certain gaps will haunt or frustrate or resist or provoke. All of this places a particular burden on the particular reader of this text, but it also makes each particular reader an irreplaceable thread of the whole. Parts of this book are exhausting, too steep a climb, or too frightening a

---

1   Cited in the Introduction to Catherine Ingram (1990). *In the footsteps of Ghandi: Conversations with spiritual social activists*. Berkeley: Parallax Press, p. xiv.

headlong crashcascade, too fast for sure-footing. Some passages or trails that are tightly closed early on in the text may only open later, once you have read the whole book. Some themes or concepts are introduced too early or too quickly, only to be filled out later. This, too, is not an error. This is what ranging a rich and varied eco-system is *like:* we never have it all at once as a possession that we can fully master. We always find ourselves *in* it as an ongoing, emergent nest of ways we must somehow pass through in order to understand.

This ongoing process is something that happens for me as well — the "author" of the text whom you might presume should know best what the whole thing is about. This is another presumption that ecology is putting into question — the presumption that there is someone left over, over and above the ecological web of interrelatedness, someone who might save us the trip or rescue us ahead of time from the traps and pitfalls, someone who has every thing under control. As feminism has shown us, in this sort of family gathering that is our real, fleshy, Earthly life, there is no such patriarch (over-arching pattern / pater / father) who will speak or read or interpret this text(ure) on my behalf or on your behalf. Ecology tells us that this way of living (and writing and reading) can only be taken up by each one of us, starting from the life we actually live and not from some grand fantasy of "the Whole Earth." Each of us must face our own, living cuplabilities in the face of foreboding ecological rumblings in the distance. And, once questions begin to revolve around the lives we actually live and the real, Earthly conditions under which life can go on, children have already arrived and pedagogy begins to dovetail with ecology in a strong and vital and fleshy way.

This book is a cold plunge, and, in places, the water is deep and forbidding.

It picks away at our desire for an easy, clear and simple text.

But again, ecology is reminding us that there is nothing easy, clear and simple about the Earth's textures and the ways we are culpable for and implicated in this "text."

I hope that the reader can read what follows knowing that this introduction is not a list of apologies for uncorrected mistakes but that it is somehow indicative of an urgent necessity to speak and write differently

ORIGINAL INTRODUCTION AND ACKNOWLEDGEMENTS (1992)   27

than so much of our inheritance has allowed. It aspires to the ways of the voice and the hand and the heart that embody the generativity and wildness and interdependence and ambiguous kind-ness that is also its topic.

....

Portions of this book have appeared in a radically different form in various journals. I would like to acknowledge and thank the editors of those journals for their kind permission to re-work the following essays for this text:

Jardine, David W. (1988) Piaget's clay and Descartes' wax. *Educational Theory. 38*(3), 287-298.

Jardine, David W. (1990) On the humility of mathematical language. *Educational Theory. 40*(2), 181-192.

Jardine, David W. (1990) Awakening from Descartes' nightmare: On the love of ambiguity in phenomenological approaches to education. *Studies in Philosophy and Education. 10*(1), 211-232.

Jardine, David W. (1990) "To dwell with a boundless heart": On the integrated curriculum and the recovery of the Earth. *Journal of Curriculum and Supervision. 5*(2), 107-119.

Prelude One: A Reading Key[1]

Poetry turns everything into life. It is that form of life that turns everything into language. It does not come to us unless language itself has become a form of life. That is why it is so unique. For it does not cease to work on us. To be the dream of which we are the sleep. A listening, an awakening that passes through us, the rhythm that knows us and that we do not know. It is the organization in language of what has always been said to escape language: life, the movement no word is supposed to be able to say. And in effect words do not say it.[12]

"[Poetry is]
a tool,
a net
or trap
to catch and present; a sharp edge; a medicine or
a little awl that unties knots."[3]

---

1   Taisen Deshimaru (1983). *The Ring of the Way.* New York: E.P. Dutton, p. 43.
2   Henri Meschonnic (1988). Rhyme and life. *Critical Inquiry. 15* (Autumn 1988), p. 90.
3   Gary Snyder (1979). Poetry, community and climax. *Field. 20* (Spring 1979), p. 29.

Prelude Two: Another Reading Key

> All we can do is try to speak it, try to say it, try to save it. Look, we say, this land is where your mother lived and where your daughter will live. This is you sister's country. You lived there as a child, boy or girl, you lived there — have you forgotten? All the children are wild. You lived in the wild country.[1]

Ecology does not require *going back* but rather *going down* into the still-pertaining flesh of our lives, going down into what has never ceased to be in effect. We *live* in the wild country if our living is understood as fully embodied.

> ... not "this is that" but this is a story about that, this is like that.[2]

In Buddhism there is a profoundly ecological and pedagogical notion called "circumsessional interpenetration" or "dependent co-arising" (*pratitya-samutpada*) and a tale is told about this under the name "The Jewelled Net of Indra."

This tale must not be read as a piece of exotica — like the colonial crusts of "orientalism"[3] — but as directly and intimately and lovingly

---

1   Ursula Le Guin (1989). Women/wildness. In Judith Plant (1989). *Healing the Wounds*. Toronto: Between the Lines Press, p. 47.

        Ecology faces a danger of becoming a form of "longing for old times," times *before* the ecologically disastrous turns of Eurocentric Rationality and its subsequent logics. This makes ecology into a form of romanticism.

2   James Clifford (1986a). On ethnographic allegory. In James Clifford & George Marcus, eds. *Writing Culture: The Poetics and Politics of Ethnography*. Berkeley: University of California Press, p. 100.

3   Edward Said (1978). *Orientalism*. New York: Penguin Books:

> In discussions of the Orient, the Orient is all absence, whereas one feels the Orientalist and what he says as presence; yet we must not forget that the Orientalist's presence is enabled by the Orient's effective absence. (p. 18)

addressing the assumptions we can barely utter, the assumptions we bear in our flesh.

This long-standing assumption, arced here from René Descartes back through Scholasticism and Thomas Aquinas to Aristotle:

"A substance is that which requires nothing except itself in order to exist."[4]

In the Jewelled Net of Indra, the whole of the Earth is not envisaged as populated by isolatable substances each which needs only itself in order to exist. Rather, the Earth is envisaged as a:

> "net,
> not a two-dimensional one, but a system of
> countless nets
> interwoven in all directions in a
> multidimensional
> space." [5]

In each criss-cross of the net is a Jewel which, in each of its infinite facets, reflects all of the other Jewels and all of their facetted relations.

Each Jewel thus empties out into all the others, bearing in its heart the whole of things in the midst of its very particularity. [6]

What is so breathtaking here is that we are presented with *just this* wheelbarrow of which the poet speaks and yet, in the midst of that presentation of exquisiteness the whole Earth crashes in. It is offered in such meticulous particularity pared to the barest necessities and mysteries, that the insight is unavoidable:

---

4   René Descartes (circa 1640/1955). *Descartes Selections*. New York: Dutton and Sons, p. 255.
5   Thich Nhat Hahn (1988). *The Sun My Heart*. Berkeley: Parallax Press, p. 64.
6   Consider the point of the title of Bronwen Wallace's (1989) (sadly) last book of poetry, *The Stubborn Particulars of Grace*. Toronto: McLellan and Stewart.
    Or see William Carlos Williams' (1963, p. 3) point in *Paterson* (New York: New Directions Books): "To make a start out of particulars...", like a red wheelbarrow, glazed (see William Carlos Williams [1991] *The Collected Poems of William Carlos Williams*, Volume 1, 1909-1939. New York: New Directions Books).

> *everything* depends
> on this
> rusted red
> wheelbarrow, bright with rain,
> water.

Better (but much more difficult to envisage), in each "criss-crossing, interweaving"[7] of the net is a Jewel which *is* all the other Jewels and all of their faceted relations, because it *is* its bearing to all its relations.

There is no "it" (no "substance") left over which is somehow subsequently "in relation" and which could therefore be saved / severed / understood / encountered / known free from its multiple interdependencies.[8] The difficulty with such an ecological understanding is that the logical understanding in Kantianism is more commensurate with our common-sense notion that this object before me —this pine tree out the window— is *not* the blue spruce beside it, nor is it me or the ground out of which it has erupted, or the oxygen it produces which sustains my ability to see it, now, yellow green with reddish bark, lodge-pole. Ecology is suggesting that, although there might be a certain practical exigency to such a common-sense notion, one must be careful to not take such common-sensicalness too literally, nor must we allow this notion to become a systematic course of action as it has been in the sciences (where objects are considered as separate entities bumping into one another in causal relations which are exogenous to the being of the entities in question). It is interesting to note how this antiquated notion of science/substance is being replaced.

Each "individual" thing "in itself" *is* the whole of things.

---

7   Ludwig Wittgenstein (1968). *Philosophical Investigations*. Cambridge: Basil Blackwell's, p. 32.
8   Immanuel Kant (1964, p. 27) suggested that such a "thing-in-itself" is *thinkable* in the logical sense — that is to say, there is no *logical* contradiction in *thinking* of an object out of all relations with all other entities. In spite of the lack of logical contradiction, it is becoming apparent that there is an *ecological* contradiction in thinking of objects this way, out of relation to all other entities.

This is what makes up the exquisiteness of this mossy spot, tucked in the heat curve rock face south sun deep drum water-captured air-pocket Elbow river run, because no other thing bears just these relations to the whole of things in just this way.

Nothing holds still.[9]

Every thing is what it is not:

> "All things in the world are linked together one way or the other. Not a single thing comes into being without some relationship to every other thing."[10]

> "Even the very tiniest thing, to the extent that it "is," displays in its very act of being the whole web of circumsessional interpenetration that links all things together."[11]

Erotic Wholeness,
yes,
and all the images of healing and
the hale of the breath, images of Earthy holiness.

> "The concept of health is rooted in the concept of wholeness. To be healthy is to be whole. The word *health* belongs to a family of words:

---

9   "Myth is the language of ambivalence; nothing is only this or that; the Gods and dancers will not stand still." (Hillman, 1987, p. 37)
    And further to this:

    Ambivalence, rather than being overcome. . .may be developed within its own principle. It is a way in itself. *Ambivalence is an adequate reaction to the whole psyche*, to these whole truths. Thus, going by way of ambivalence circumvents *coniunctio* efforts of the ego, because by bearing ambivalence one is in the *coniunctio* itself as the tension of opposites. (p. 15)

10 Nishitani Keiji (1982). *Religion and Nothingness*. Berkeley: University of California Press, p. 149.
11 Nishitani Keiji (1982). p. 150.

Prelude Two: Another Reading Key

> *heal, whole, wholesome, hale,*
> *hallow, holy.*"[12]

But always lived *just here,* in place, "arguing the stubborn argument of the particular, right now, in the midst of things, *this* and *this.*"[13]

"*All* is a miracle,"[14] blade by blade by blade of grass, irreplaceable, not just the ghostly visions of monotheism which drain away the life of the Earth to "elsewhere."

> [As in "This is a representation of that."[15] The Earth as a mere shadowy representation of God's beneficence, *ens creatum,* and therefore not holy in itself, not full of its own spooks and spirits demanding our attention.]

This luscious release into the stubborn particulars of a life actually lived, with all its kin abounding — this is one of the deep haunts of phenomenology a *life*-world and the deep love of the particulars of the Earthworld wormed down, fleshbound.

The "yellow eye[ed] and ridged horn[ed]"[16] goathead turned sidelong. The heat and the howl of loving suspicion as the core of interpretation.[17]

Reading the world and its pungent signs and marks left on trails and on faces and etched in soft underbelly utterance and hiss of living texts.

I suspect the interpretive disciplines may be Pagan.

This book is not simply *about* this net of Earthly interdependencies.

---

12 Wendell Berry (1986). *The Unsettling of America*. San Francisco: Sierra Club Books, p. 103.
13 Bronwen Wallace (1989). p. 111. And see how Martin Heidegger ([1971] The nature of language. In *On the Way to Language*. New York: Harper and Row) places "in the midst of things," (p. 68) *inter esse,* at the heart of the interpretive gesture.
14 Thich Nhat Hahn (1986). *The Miracle of Mindfulness*. Berkeley: Parallax Press, p. 12.
15 James Clifford (1986). p. 100.
16 Ursula Le Guin. *The Wizard of Earthsea*. London: Penguin books, p. 4.
17 see Paul Ricouer (1970). *Freud and Philosophy*. New Haven: Yale University Press, p. 32 and following where he discusses "interpretation as an exercise of suspicion."

PRELUDE TWO: ANOTHER READING KEY

This book and its crawling in-sections must also be read as an *instance* of this net.
Each
section below tell(tale)s and retell(tale)s a (tell)tale told
in all the others.
Each
can be read as the kin of all the others and to know the whole
is to read each into
each
into
each,
threads, interweaving.

Each *must* be so read if this book is to fit together.

It fits together laterally, not from
above and not ahead of time and
not just from *here* ("the author" can
not save the helpless multivocity of
writing[18] Inherent in the living metaphoricity of language (p. 428 and

---

18   The task of understanding is presented with particular clarity when we recognize the weakness of all writing. We need only recall what Plato said, namely, that the specific weakness of writing was that no one could come to the aid of the written word if it falls victim to misunderstanding, intentional or unintentional. In the helplessness of the written words, Plato discerned a more serious weakness than the weakness of speech. (Hans-Georg Gadamer [1989]. *Truth and Method*. New York: Continuum, p. 395.)

But Gadamer goes on to say that this weakness of writing is also its freedom:

What is fixed in writing has detached itself from the contingency of its origin and its author and made itself free for new relationships. (p. 395)

In a sense, then, the helplessness and weakness of the written word is also its strength, for in such weakness, writing retains an irreducible "porousness" and "openness."

Prelude Two: Another Reading Key

following), is that the written word does not have the author available to close down the inherent multiplicity of what is written. The helplessness of the written work, its weakness, could also be its *interpretability* and *generativity*, turning the "weakness" of reproduction into an ecological strength. with some foreclosing "authoritative" reading. Reading and writing as "following the movement of showing"[19] for author-reader-text alike.

Textus: "that which is woven, web, texture."[20]
Spinning tales.[21]
Spiders' webs.
Fairy tales.

This way works at wholeness not in halves but through wholeness from the start. The way is slower, actions is hindered, and one fumbles foolishly in the half-light. This way finds echo in many familiar phrases from Lao Tzu, but especially: "Soften the light, become one with the dusty world."[22]

---

19 Martin Heidegger (1972a). Time and Being. In *On Time and Being*. New York: Harper and Row, p. 1.
20 Following the *Oxford English Dictionary*.
21 For metaphors of "spinning" see Mary Daly (1985). *Gyn-Ecology*. Boston: Beacon Press. Consider also the mere titles of Judith Plaskow & Carol Christ (1989). *Weaving the Visions*. (New York: Harper and Row) or Irene Diamond & Gloria Feman Orenstein (1990). *Reweaving the World*. San Francisco: Sierra Club Books.
22 James Hillman (1987). Puer and senex. In James Hillman, ed. *Puer Papers*. Dallas: Spring Publications, p. 15.

Each particular, each foolish fumble, bears the whole, but the whole is never given.[23]

This is one of the profound and disturbing effects of Martin Heidegger's analyses of the deep temporality and historicity of human experience. (read here an implicit critique of the reliance of phenomenology on "givenness").

> [a critique of how the phenomenological urge to remain faithful to what is *given in experience*.[24] This focus on what is given in experience, what presents itself in experience, curbs phenomenology into a reliance on the fixity for which the *Wesenschau* is the solution. is *already*

---

23 Everything that is experienced is experienced by oneself, and part of its meaning is that it belongs to the unity of this self and thus contains an unmistakable and irreplaceable relation to the whole of this one life. Thus, essential to an experience is that it cannot be exhausted in what can be said of it or grasped as its meaning. As determined through autobiographical or biographical reflection, its meaning remains fused with the whole movement of life and constantly accompanies it. The mode of being of experience is precisely to be so determinative that one is never finished with it. (Gadamer [1989], p. 67).

The whole of one's life, of course, is never given but always coming, so very often we will find that we are precisely mistaken about our experience and its place. Over the course of one's life, experiences are shuffled and reshuffled as the emergent whole emerges ever wider. I cannot exhaust this experience through saying or grasping, not simply because the whole is too large, but also because the whole is always yet-to-be-given.

24 from Edmund Husserl (1970b). *The Idea of Phenomenology*. The Hague: Martinus Nijhoff:

> Absolute and clear givenness, self-givenness in the absolute sense. This givenness, which rules out any meaningful doubt, consists of a simple immediate 'seeing.' (p. 28).

> Our phenomenological sphere of givenness, the sphere of absolute clarity, of immanence in the true sense, reaches no farther than self-givenness reaches. (p. 8).

> a form of essentialism which, added to Edmund Husserl's deep faith in a "unity of one meaning,"[25] steps phenomenology up from lividness to givenness to essence to a ghostly version of monotheism]

> [the post-modern critique of *presence* and its inherent foundationalism has its entrails here. Post-modernist philosophizing as the dis-tension of the bowel from Husserl through Heidegger]

To avoid these ascending steps (which are the steps of our current ecological crisis)

> [What (Gregory) Bateson called "the pattern that connects" and the Buddhist's image as the Jewelled Net of Indra can be construed in lay, secular terms as our deep ecology.[26]]

---

25 Edmund Husserl (1970). *The Crisis of European Science*. Evanston: Northwestern University Press, p. 70.
26 Joanne Macy (1989). Awakening to the ecological self. In Judith Plant (1989). *Healing the Wounds*. Toronto: Between the Lines Press, p. 209. For the notion of "deep ecology" see George Sessions & Bill Devall (1985) *Deep Ecology*. Salt Lake City: Peregrine Books. See also Bill Devall (1988). *Simply in Means, Rich in Ends: Practicing Deep Ecology*. Salt Lake City: Peregrine Books.

each particular must be "unnamed"[27] outwards, like exhaled breath, innumerable in its meanings[28] and kin.

"This is like that."

Each section of this book is a story about every other section. Each section is *like* every other.

It is a nest of familiar tales told by many kin.

Along such a way, working at wholeness, bloodlines will appear and disappear and reappear.

No one section offers the whole.

> [Although each section does *precisely this,* from *here,* a tale t/issued out into the Whole, red wheelbarrow]

There is no patriarch in this flow of bloodlines, just figures that come and go, some of large and some of little influence and generativity, some notable in brief, some notable at length.

> [No
> *one*

accounts for the whole cascade. This is a rejection of fundamentalism and representationalism. It is a rejection of the possibility of making this generative cascade a *given,* something *present.* Patterns, figures, come and go in kind, but kinds are never given but are always right in the midst of ushering in new yet-to-be-given kin who *add themselves* to the kin(d), transforming it]

---

27 After the title of Ursula Le Guin's (1987a). She unnames them. In *Buffalo Gals and other Animal Presences*. Santa Barbara: Capra Press.
28 Bunno Kato, Yoshiro Tamura & Kojiro Miyasaka, eds. (1987). The Sutra of innumerable meanings. In *The Threefold Lotus Sutra*. Tokyo: Kosei Publishing Company.

Prelude Two: Another Reading Key

[Representationalism and fundamentalism always arrive
too late
and then make up for their tardiness through reprimand, finding
that the children have been fiddling and fooling, full of vibrancy.]

No one section is the representative section that can stand in on behalf
of all the rest.

None has the moral right to represent all the others.

["representative" ("this is that") or "narrative" ("this is like that, this is a
story about that") structure in writing is a *moral issue* and a *moral choice*
— this "untypical" written format is a moral choice and the difficulty a
reader {myself included} might face in reading this text hints at a moral
dilemma.]

    The placement of the

        line on the page, the horizontal white

            spaces and the   vertical

                                                        white
                                                        spaces

are all
    s
      c
        o
          r
            i
              n
                g

forhowitistoberead and howitistobetimed.
Space   means   time.
The marginal in
            den
                ta
                    tions are more an indication of VOICE emphasis,
                    breath emphasis — *logopoeia,* some of the d
                                                                a
                                                                  n
                                                                c
                                                              e
                                                            s
of the ideas that are working within your s-y-n-t-a-c-t-i-c-s-t-r-u-c-t-u-r-e-s.[29]

    [Literacy is, among other things, a moral issue. Literalism and its courting of univocity — its banning of multivocity or seeing such multivocity *pathologically* as something to be fix(ated) is a form of moral blindness which flattens discourse and severs etymo-ecological reliances, kinships and family resemblances in favour of the brutality of isolated substances which need nothing and stand in no *ethos*. This means that not only is literalism linked to colonialism. It is *pathetic* in its attempt to understand language out-of-relation, with no horizon (pathos being the opposite of ethos).]
    [Breakdowns in the fabric of language are ethical breakdowns].

[This is like that: break
downs in the fabric of lan
guage are ecolo
gical and ethical breakdowns.[30]]

---

29   quote from, with apologies to Gary Snyder (1980). *The Real Work*. New York: New Directions Books, p. 31.

30   see David W. Jardine & James C. Field. (1992). "Disproportion, monstrousness and mystery": Ethical and ecological reflections on the initiation of student teachers into the community of education. *Teaching and Teacher Education*.

Prelude Two: Another Reading Key

The whole is never given, never utterable, never writable.
This book is essentially a self-contradiction.
It has no essence.

It has no normative center even though there is an old and kind and familiar way to it:

> "The universe is a dynamic fabric of interdependent events in which none is the fundamental entity."[31]

Even this prelude, with its grey and precise tone of excuse for and clarification of what follows, even this prelude is what it is not.

> [We live in a world in which we never completely know what will follow, so we can never fully know what this particular, stubborn thing now before us essentially is, because we never fully know what will be made of it, what will come of it. The future has a fecund relation to the present. (Breath continues). In the future, the present will no longer be what it used to be. This is why Martin Heidegger linked up *Being and Time*.[32] *This* is "The end of philosophy and the task of

---

31   Thich Nhat Hahn (1986). p. 70.
32   Martin Heidegger (1962). *Being and Time*. New York: Harper and Row.

thinking"[33]: Heidegger's critique of presence as a critique of the primacy of what presents itself, a critique of the primacy of givenness in the history of philosophy of which, as Husserl plainly states, his transcendental phenomenology is the *"final form."*[34]]

[These notions of fecundity and the accretions of temporality. [35]This is why the attack and love of the work of Edmund Husserl is so vehement in this book. He is the one who disappointed me the most, sun-struck as I was by the completeness of the transcendental-ide-

---

33   Martin Heidegger (1972). The end of philosophy and the task of thinking. In *Time and Being*. New York: Harper and Row.
34   Edmund Husserl (1970). p. 70.
35   To be true to one's puer nature means to admit one's puer past — all its gambols and gestures and sun-struck aspirations. From this history we draw consequences. By standing for these consequences, we let history catch up with us and thus is our haste slowed. History is the senex shadow of the puer, giving him substance. Through our individual histories, puer merges with senex, the external comes back into time, the falcon returns to the falconer's arm. (Hillman, 1987, p. 35)

alist aspirations of phenomenology in its beginnings are what distinguishes phenomenology and hermeneutics. Hermeneutics bespeaks a "self" (and an understanding of the world) which comes and goes like the breath, *this* breath, and therefore bespeaks the Whole of which that fleshy self is both part and apart[36], this *belly* of a paradox.[37] Phenomenology bespeaks an immutable *presence* of "I am" which understands itself to be Whole of itself without its Earthly countenance as that entity *to which* the Earth must present

---

36 David G. Smith (1988). Children and the gods of war. *Journal of Educational Thought*. 22(2A), p. 176.
37 David G. Smith (1988). p. 176.

itself. Saying that the life-world is constituted by immutable essences is an attempt of this "deluded", "put out of play"³⁸ "I am" to make the world in its own image].

Non-representational writing. To write about this paradox is to write *out of* this paradox. Writing must take on the heat of its topic. It must *lend itself* to the generative patterns it bespeaks.³⁹ It is not simply a challenge to *write about different things*. It is a challenge to *write differently*. For phenomenology to fulfil its promise of a turn that cracks open the hegemonic logics of foundationalism, writing itself must be transformed.

---

38 *Precisely* Edmund Husserl's description of the reflective transcendental subject. See Edmund Husserl (1969). *Ideas*. New York: Humanities Press.

39 Being without a fixed beginning, middle and end, this book is not only about postmodernism, it is also postmodern; it is devoid of metaphysical closure. This is not to say that it is devoid of meaning, or that its meaning is undecidable. Unlike a lot of postmodern narratives, it most definitely does have a story to tell — and there is a plot to it. This, though, is a plot without dénouement, since the story does not have an end, being, as it is, the story of our times, whose outcome or *sens* (meaning/direction) is as yet undecided.

> Gary Madison (1988). *The Hermeneutics of Postmodernism*. Bloomington: Indiana University Press, p. ix.

The challenge that winds through from phenomenology to hermeneutics to postmodernism and from here out into the fleshy an-archisms of ecological mindfulness is not simply a challenge to change topics of interest and intent. It is not simply a change in how we imagine human life and its fully Earthly countenance, out from under the dichotomous epistemologies of Cartesianism and the other entrails of modernism (focusses on method, on epistemology, on foundationalism and the like [Madison (1988), p. x and following).

Prelude Two: Another Reading Key   47

Read each section as if it were a tale about all the rest. Re-read this section.

Read after what is below, this prelude will never quite read the same again.

This prelude is (not) what follows. (*This is not metaphysics,* nor is it peculiar and occult, nor is it an invocation of something we don't always already know. The ingested accretions of experience are transformative of the past. This prelude is *porous.* It calls for re-reading).

In reading this or any text, prepare for loss and gain, coming and going.

The text will age over such readings.

It will lose and gain in such aging.

It will never read the same again.

[Longing, sad heart, to have it read ever the same again is the nostalgia of Essentialism and of phenomenological pedagogy.[40] It is dreams of Heaven or recollections of perfect knowledge held fast beyond the failing flesh, unfading.]

It will never read simply differently.

            [The post-modern love of novelty-items: the desire to unanchor the sign altogether and simply have our way with it is the licentiousness that comes from the first adrenalin rush of the fall of the old foundations. Post-modernism too easily confuses a critique of foundationalism with a proof that *nothing* sustains us. Our culture is easily confused between the loosening of signifier and signified and their severance.]

                [Consider: post-modernism as the toxic end-product of Cartesianism, out at the numb extremity. This text is post-modern, numbing in its cascade. Re-reading post-

---

40 see David W. Jardine (1988). On phenomenology, pedagogy and *Phenomenology + Pedagogy. Phenomenology + Pedagogy* 6(3), 158-160 for a consideration of the nostalgia inherent in a phenomenology bent on essentialism.

> modernism: it clears away the old representationalisms and makes visible the livid lateral cascade and anarchy of our Earthly lives.]
>
>> [Consider: post-modernism as the cultural and linguistic and philosophical and literary versions of our current ecological crisis Re-reading post-modernism: it is the portal through this crisis].

Read after what is below, this prelude will be kind-of familiar.

Perhaps this book is about re-reading and re-membering and how the text(ures) of the Earth each read into each other, so you never have the whole story and you can never be done with any piece of the story, because it always needs re-reading into the ongoing generosity of things — the Earth keeps coming, children keep coming, and the task is to keep open the possibility of re-reading.

> [this "keeping open of the possibility of re-reading" is an *ecological task*.]

>> [this keeping open of the possibility of re-reading is a critique of literalism and a suggestion about the nature of reading/writing/literacy that cracks open "the helplessness of the written word."[41] Literacy/reading/writing as freed from the letters "reading the ways of things" in all its agonizing multiplicity, more literate than word-surfaces:
>>> "As we become more literate we become less literal, less stuck in the case without a vision of its soul."[42]

---

41   Hans-Georg Gadamer (1989). p. 431.
42   James Hillman (1983). *Healing Fiction*. Barrytown: Station Hill, p. 28.

Prelude Two: Another Reading Key

Our reading of the letters of texts — this text — must be more helpless, must be more allowing of the helpless, intended or unintended kinships that are born(e) out of written language. The weakness of this text is its strength. It is premised on the absencing of the Author as someone who might save us all. Reading must become interpretive and each stubborn particular is responsible, not only for his or her "own(ed)" reading, but for the Whole *of which* it is a reading — that *to which* my "own" reading belongs as something profoundly *dis-owned*.

> [*Everything* depends on the red wheelbarrow, and this ought to make such a barrow seem *less* self-important in its very irreplaceability, because that irreplaceability is responsible to and for the Whole which depends upon it to be just itself *in* (not isolated from, like some autonomous "author") its full relatedness]

Literacy as interpretation beyond the letter, emptied out.

> This phenomenon of being "less stuck in the case without a vision of its soul" especially includes my own case — the "compulsive fascination with my own case history"[43] that passes for so much of "teacher narrative" is so *literal minded* about "my story" and "my voice" that it is on the verge of being an ecological disaster. Most "teacher narrative" material is little

---

43   James Hillman (1987). Puer and senex. In *Puer Papers*. Dallas: Spring Publications, p. 7.

> more that Democratic Cartesianism
> + "sharing."]

This statement of the task is (not) the essence of pedagogy (read "ecology") in the same sense that this book is (not) about the fact that pedagogy (read "ecology" — this instruction will henceforth be repeated only in passing)

> [The function of memory in spinning text.
> This book is an exercise in memory as much
> as it is *about* memory. Note: this memory
> is not just "housed" in the author, or in the
> reader. *Language itself* stores memories that
> we find ourselves suddenly *in*:
>> ". . .to be the dream of which we are
>> the sleep. A listening, an awakening
>> that passes through us, the rhythm that
>> knows us. . ."[44]
> Every writer knows this peculiar fact].

does (not) have an essence.

This statement (un)names a way that *is* not-Utterable.

The heart shrieks at this implosion of the logic of emptiness, full of the fear of the spilling of blood and the shallowing of breath.

It is the suddengasp Wound of the *living,* unhealable.

At the heart of pedagogy is an agony,[45] not an essence, *lived-through,* not envisaged (*Wesensschau*)[46].

> It is the coming and going
> of the young.

At the heart of ecology is an agony, not an essence, *lived-through,* not envisaged (*Wesensschau*).

---

44 Henri Meschonnic (1988 p. 90).
45 James Hillman (1983). p. 73.
46 Edmund Husserl (1969), p. 70 and following.

Prelude Two: Another Reading Key

It is the coming and going of the Breath.

Our essences will be taken to pieces and eaten, crawling intersections, consumed, transfigured and re-borne out into foods for others.

The cats crunch at the hard eyes of dragonflies metalgreen lighting on the compost heap above the puffypink wetgreen droop of watermelon rind shell egg hot sunwhite horseshit smell the ahhhhhhhhh of summer heat and flybuzz bristle.

Essentialism mourns this eventuality.

This ambiguity, this denial, this convolution, this folding in, this logical inconsistency, this self-contradiction, this affront, this anarchaic inessentialism, is the deep courage and consequence of ecological insight.

It is also equivalent to madness and the drooling of the body drooped down below the moist pink eyecorner blinking, *thinking* that it is.

Prelude Three: Another Reading Key

The urge to introduce and re-introduce is a form of cowardice. Always timid, moving back, repairing wounds that might inflict, hedging bets and covering hunches that might just not work out, wanting to have the first word before which no other words need to be said — the large groan of God's utterance of the world. There is danger ahead:

> But there is another dialectic to the word, which accords to every word an inner dimension of multiplication: every word breaks forth as if from a center and is related to a whole, through which alone it is a word. Every word causes the whole of the language to which it belongs to resonate and the whole world-view that underlies it to appear. Thus, every word, as the event of a moment, carries with it the unsaid, to which it is related by responding and summoning. The occasionality of human speech is not a casual imperfection of its expressive power; it is, rather, the logical expression of the living virtuality of speech that brings a totality of meaning into play, without being able to express it totally. All human speaking is finite in such a way that there is laid up within it an infinity of meaning to be explicated and laid out. That is why the hermeneutical phenomenon also can be illuminated only in light of the fundamental finitude of being.[1]

---

1   Hans-Georg Gadamer (1989). p. 458.

CHAPTER ONE

My ancestors talk to me in dangling myths. Each word a riddle each dream heirless. On sunny days I bury words. They put out roots and coil around forgotten syntax. Next spring a full blown anecdote will sprout.[1]

Language itself contains sedimented layers of emotionally resonant metaphors, knowledge and associations, which, when paid attention to can be experienced as discovery and revelation. It is to inquire into what is hidden in language, what is deferred by signs, what is pointed to, what is repressed, implicit or mediated. [*Not* simply what is given. Full, rather, of ambiguity and darkness and suggestion half-implied, full of potency and absence]. What thus seems initially to be individualistic autobiographical searching turns out to be revelations of traditions, re-collections of disseminated identities and of the divine sparks from the breaking of the vessels. These are the modern version of the Pythagorean arts of memory.[2]

This book both is and is not autobiography:

> "We are witnessing the inevitable outcome of a logic that is already centuries old and which is being played out in our own lifetime."[3]

and when I move down into my hide, I find myself living out this logic in hidden ways.

> [Not just hidden in what I think or in the forgotten syntax of what I say, but hidden too in the oxygen-depleted cells eco-biologically consequent of the car-driving carbon monoxide entrails I imagined left behind me in my wake to drive me out here to these woods and these foothills to gain the quiet and peace needed to write against such consequence. Scored on the walls of residential schools]

---

1   Diana DeHovanessian, cited in Michael Fischer (1986). Ethnicity and the post modern arts of memory. In Clifford & Marcus. (1986). p. 199.
2   Michael Fischer (1986). p. 198.
3   Morris Berman (1984). *The Reenchantment of the World*. New York: Bantam Books, p. 8.

What I hold to be mine, what is faceted here, winds out into hidden corners.

This book is an (auto)biography of the *bios* I am *in,* and the *bios* I am *in* is more than just this one, more than just me. This presumed-to-be isolated autobiographical self gets pulled to pieces in the act of self-understanding, emptied outwards.

> [Self-understanding, not as self-possession
> but as an unanticipated,
> unwilled[4]
> and often unwanted[5]
> "self-loss"[6]
> and unanticipated "recovery" from unanticipated places.]

"And so the great poet does not express his or her self, he expresses *all* of our selves. And to express *all* of ourselves you have to go beyond your own self. Like Dogen, the Zen master, said, 'We study the self to forget the self. And when you forget the self, you become *one* with all things.'"[7]

> "The inescapable rooting of poetic language in personal sensibility doesn't have to mean that the poet no longer explores an order beyond the self."[8]

And pedagogically:

> "Interpretive pedagogy tries to show the way the specificities of our lives, while in many instances unique to each person, are also

---

4   Hans Georg Gadamer (1989). p. xxviii.
5   Hans-Georg Gadamer (1989). p. xxviii.
6   Hans-Georg Gadamer (1977). *Philosophical Hermeneutics.* Berkeley: University of California Press, p. 51.
7   Gary Snyder (1980). p. 65.
8   Charles Taylor (1991) *The Malaise of Modernity.* Toronto: House of Ananasi Press, p. 89.

> participant in the full texture of human life as a whole."⁹

"The grain of the voice"[10] is surely undeniable, given a growing familiarity with the timbre and pitch and breath pitter pat(t)er(n)s. This writing is recognizably *mine* even though *I* am not its *topic*.[11]

9   David G. Smith (1988). Children and the gods of war. *Journal of Educational Thought.* 22(2A), p. 11.
10 following Roland Barthes.
11 See Charles Taylor's (1991) important distinction between two different senses of "authenticity" in discourse: there is a fundamental difference between feeling a deep and profound connection to what I am writing about and writing *about myself*. Writing "authentically" need not necessitate that I am the topic. This is a central mistake of much work in "teacher narrative."

CHAPTER TWO

> I need to remember my stories not because I need to find out about myself but because I need to found myself in a story I can hold to be mine. I also fear these stories because through them I can be found out, my imaginal foundations are exposed. Repression is built into each story as the fear of the story itself, the fear of the closeness of the Gods in the myths which found me. Thus the art of [interpretation] requires skilful handling of memory, of case history, so that it can truly found. Hence the importance of introducing the great myths into [interpretation]. They are ways of reading personal history in the foundational mode of fiction.
>
> James Hillman, from Healing Fiction.[1]

What is thus found(ed) disperses outwards in the saying. Personal history becomes a grand living out of more than just personal history.

I do not have *in* my life and the wrapped boundaries of my skin the means to understand —to *live* — that life, because I am living (in and) *out* more than I (can) contain.[2]

---

1   James Hillman (1983). p. 42.
2   This is why so much personal narrative can become so pathological unless the deep moments of our lives are allowed to be lived *out* in the public sphere. Hence the increasing recent interest in notions of ritual and ritual space. Consider:

> The transformation of the Self...is a universal human phenomenon. This development takes place in a specific human environment and is dependent upon it. [It] is so dependent on the collectivity that we find rituals [marking it] in almost all human groups. They make possible and facilitate the transition from one phase to another. As long as these transitions between phases are accented as necessary developments by the group's rites of initiation, fulfillment of [a particular person's] specific predisposition is provided for.
>
> In modern man, where collective rites no longer exist, and the problems relating to these transitions devolve upon the individual, his responsibility and understanding are so overburdened that psychic disorders are frequent. [Such transitions] were formerly numinous points at which the collectivity

My life is not a container with certain things unequivocally contained inside of it.

<blockquote>
Autobiography porous like
skin webbed in deep
Earthwater pushripples.
</blockquote>

[Interpretation — *world*-reading[3] — as the ecolinguistic parallel to the porousness of the skin and the passages of the body.

> "to hear the messages in whatever is said. This is the hermeneutic ear that listens-through, a consciousness of the borders, as Hermes was worshipped at borders. Every wall and every weave presents its opening. Everything is porous"[4]]

I find myself *in the world* as part of the world's story coalescing just here and nowhere else.

> [I am thus irreplaceable in a way that is the reverse of self-aggrandizement. Rather than becoming grander, the self in this case empties]

And *that* world story is never told and then done with: it goes on, threads of it come and go, like bloodlines, etched on the skin, relentless.

> [when I read Ludwig Wittgenstein, I read him for signs of my own pain and joy. I read him into my life. But *he* also reads *me* out into the world beyond my life, confronts me

---

intervened with its rites; today they are points of psychic illness and anxiety for the individual, whose awareness does not suffice to enable him to live his life.

From Erich Neumann (1990). *The Child*. Boston: Shambala Press, p. 185-6.

3   See Mary Sheridan (1992). The teacher as a reader of the world. Unpublished doctoral dissertation, Department of Curriculum and Instruction, Faculty of Education, University of Calgary.

4   James Hillman (1987a). Notes on opportunism. In *Puer Papers*. Dallas: Spring Publications, p. 156.

with kin I did not know I had and for whom and to whom I find that I am responsible — to understand, to care for, to teach, to make strong and well and whole, to allow to teach me and care for me and show me the painful underbellies of my living. (Literacy as an ecological task, exploring what sustains me and fecundly "giving back" in such exploration, thus creating new threads of sustenance). I cannot understand myself without understanding my "relations."

[Interpretation as healing the world. Interpretation as self-healing. These are not different tasks, although each of us may need to bear upon one rather than the other].

"The last 3000 years of mankind have been an excursion into ideals, bodilessness, and tragedy and now the excursion is over... It is a question, practically, of relationships. We *must* get back into [a] vivid and nourishing relation with the cosmos. The way is through daily ritual, and reawakening. We must once more practice the ritual of dawn and noon and sunset, the ritual of kindling fire and pouring water, the ritual of first breath, and last."[5]

[Interpretation belies the notion of self-understanding as self-presence, because I am never fully present to myself — kin keep coming, keep peeping out unexpectedly, telling me of this "self" I might have (falsely) considered settled and possessable].

— "ownership" of "my story" is a peculiar notion if considered ecologically.[6]

---

5   Dolores LaChapelle (1989). Sacred land, sacred sex. In Judith Plant (1989). *Healing the Wounds*. Toronto: Between the Lines Press, p. 167.

6   The *reasons* for such terminology, however, are not so peculiar. They erupt in response to representationalism: the colonial compulsion to *speak on behalf of*

others and all the consequent white-noise silencing that accompanies such compulsions. "Ownership" is a way of re-claiming one's identity from its dispersion in the world and from the silencing, oppressive ways that that identity has been defined and voiced by others. "Ownership" is a term of re-clamation of those who have been "disowned" from the sphere of public discourse (and it is *also* a way to require those in power to accept responsibility for *their own* discourse as *theirs*, and as therefore perhaps *not* representing others).

The paradox re-erupts, however, for there is an inherent "othering" to language (please excuse this peculiar formulation). My identity is held in the embrace of the Earth and its etymologico-semantic webs, and sometimes this holding is oppressive and silencing, and sometimes it is a moment of profound self-transcendence. In this way, if we claim "ownership" too brutally, it can become equivalent to the very removal from public discourse in response to which it began. (This is the sort of "critical immunity" of "teacher stories" that is all too common in educational discourse).

CHAPTER THREE

Instance: the off-hand comment of a student-teacher speaking about the otherworldliness of her University education and her passion for the *practice* of teaching:

> "Piaget is just a name to me that I memorized in my courses. I don't care about all of those theories. I just care about where the child is at and how to get him to the next stage."

The wonderful, innocent, unintended irony. So good.

Right in the very heart meat of this student-teacher's heart-felt words, in the very moist innards of her autobiography, she bespeaks as-yet-unnoticed relations of kind, murmured echoes of the bios she is in and the memories her language contains.

> [There are kin of yours out there in the world that you haven't met yet and who know family tales — tales of *your* family, tales of *your* family resemblances, tales of what winds and binds your words out into the flesh of the Earth.
>
>> Hermes provokes us to read this off-hand comment for signs of self-transcendence, self-loss and recovery (for *both* the interpreter *and* the author — there is no one left over who is not "it" in the (inter)play and foreplay of interpretation).
>
> Language ... is by itself the game of interpretation that we all are engaged in every day. In this game nobody is above and before all the others; everybody is at the center, [everybody] is "it" in this game. Thus it is always his turn to be interpreting. This process of interpretation takes place whenever we "understand."[1]

---

[1] Hans-Georg Gadamer (1977). p. 32.

Potential horrors of the white-noise silencing and the stealing of the voice of others. In interpretation, *nobody* is above and before all the others, not even the "author" of the text.

Hermes is cunning, and occasionally violent: a trickster, a robber. So it is not surprising that he is also the patron of interpreters.[2]

> When Hermes is at work...one feels that one's story has been stolen and turned into something else. The [person] tells his tale, and suddenly its plot has been transformed. He resists, as one would try to stop a thief...this is not what I meant at all, not at all. But too late. Hermes has caught the tale, turned its feet around, made black into white, given it wings. And the tale is gone from the upperworld historical nexus in which it had begun and been subverted into an underground meaning.[3]

> There is one further aspect of Hermes that may be worth noting, namely his impudence. He once played a trick on the most venerated Greek deity, Apollo, inciting him to great rage. Modern students of hermeneutics should be mindful that their interpretations could lead them into trouble with the authorities.[4]

---

2   Frank Kermode (1979). *The Genesis of Secrecy*. Cambridge: Harvard University Press, p.1
3   James Hillman (1983). p. 31.
4   David G. Smith (1991). Hermeneutic inquiry: The hermeneutic imagination and the pedagogic text. In Edmund Short, ed., *Forms of Curriculum Inquiry*. New York: SUNY Press.

And one of the authorities that Hermes can especially get in trouble with is "the author" who claims ownership of his or her text. The sort of "robbery" that Hermes can do is premised on the multivocity and helplessness of written language. But, as already stated, this weakness can be its strength. It can certainly allow for the possibility of violence and silencing and oppression. It also allows for the freedom and playfulness and self-transcendence of language. It allows for fluidity and the prevention of the oppressions of literalism.

Thus, in attempting to "liberate" the individual's voice from oppressive representationalism, we must avoid (if and when possible) *self-representationalism*, where the author becomes the new literalist who takes their own story literally — and, because of "ownership," demands that everyone else do so as well — and who wallows in compulsive fascination with their own life history.

It is admittedly rather frightening and disorienting to first discover that the incidental story we might tell can have implications of sense and significance that we did not anticipate, that our words might mean something more or something different that we could ever anticipate alone[5] *This violates the fabric of language itself.* Certainly, this student-teacher's tale can support many differing interpretations. But this means that *the tale itself is a multivocal nest of potentialities and possibilities of meaning.* Attempting to resolve this multivocity by locating a univocal reading in multiple readers ("this is *my* understanding," "this is *my* understanding") (and then giving precedence to the "author" as the "authoritative" reading) is simply *democratized oppression* which destroys the freedom (and *danger*) of language itself, of *life* itself., that they may be full of ironies, winding around forgotten syntax, sprouting anecdotes other than those we might ourselves tell — that I, *right in the very heart of my words,* may facet long buried memories and tales that are not precisely *owned by me.* But to say that Hermes is a trickster and a thief is not to say that the interpreter of the tale is Hermes and the student-teacher cited above is the sole "victim" of the theft of meaning and subsequent transformation of understanding that ensues. The interpretation is not so much about the autobiography of this student-teacher, but an (auto)biography of the etymologico-semantic *bios* she is *in*, the logic she is *living* out and not necessarily the logic she might explicitly or implicitly claim as her personal, practical *knowledge.*

What is "at play" in this student-teacher's "bios" is also something "at play" in me. I dwell there, too. That is why I can recognize her tale as *telling* (and not just "telling" about her, as if *she* were the sole topic of her words, *even in this case,* where she is expressing her heartfelt beliefs about children and theorizing and the like) is more than she might cite as her own "personal knowledge."

---

5 It is not enough in such a case to simply "locate" the differing interpretations in each of the interpreters, as if the multivocity of the tale *itself* (and *because* of the character of language as a living system) can be removed by simply locating each interpretation in each interpreter ("each person must take ownership and responsibility for their own interpretation").

Hermes makes the heart-meat restless, ready to beat again, bloody
valves opening and closing — the "ethnographic ear"[6]
bent sidelong
rushpulse pillow sleep.

6   Clifford (1986).

CHAPTER FOUR

Re-membering persists:

1. "not forgetting"
2. "gaining new members"
3. "putting back together"

Children keep coming (the text goes on). The chickadee's songs have changed for spring, familiar, yet needing this one to re-tell, re-membering what is passed and fluttering in kind, kin to what came before but just this one here.[1] What will be added to this point below is that, in a peculiar sense, humans can choose to do the impossible.

The world is different now with this child in it, fluttering in kind, song changed for spring.

This is Edward Lorenz's Butterfly Effect, each stubborn particular cascading outwards away from an empty center, infinite in its eventual effects.

---

1   What we call nature is, in a sense, the sum of the changes made by all the various creatures and natural forces in their intricate actions and influences upon each other and upon their places. Because of the woodpeckers, nature is different from what it would be without them. Humans, like all other creatures, must make a difference; otherwise they cannot live. But unlike other creatures, human must make a choice as to the kind and scale of the difference they make. If they choose to make too small a difference, they diminish their humanity. If they choose to make too great a difference, they diminish nature, and narrow their subsequent choices; ultimately, they diminish or destroy themselves. Nature, then, is not only our source but also our limit and measure.

   Wendell Berry (1987a). Getting along with nature. In *Home Economics*. San Francisco: North Point Press, p. 7.

["*The center is everywhere.* Each and every thing becomes the center of all things and, in that sense, becomes an absolute center. This is the absolute uniqueness of things, their reality."[2]]

In 1961, Edward Lorenz created a computer program which allowed him to graph cyclic variations in the weather. When he ran these programs:

> "the orderliness of it, the recognizable cycles coming around again and again but never twice the same way, had a hypnotic fascination. The system seemed slowly to be revealing its secrets to the forecaster's eye."[3]

As the story goes, Lorenz decided to re-examine one of the graphic simulations and, instead of beginning the program anew, he re-entered the data from a point midway through a particular run. Instead of beginning with the full decimalized data (.506127), Lorenz rounded off this number to save time and space, changing it to .506.

In effect, he had dropped 127 *millionths* of a degree in temperature from his re-running of this particular simulation — a speck of dust.

Nothing grand. Nothing spectacular. He was operating under a rather non-descript assumption that "approximately accurate input gives approximately accurate output."[4] Or, more generally put:

---

2   Nishitani Keiji. (1982). p. 146.
3   James Glieck (1987). *Chaos: The Making of a New Science*. New York: Penguin Books, p. 17.
4   James Glieck (1987). p. 15.

CHAPTER FOUR   69

> given an *approximate* knowledge of a system's initial conditions and an understanding of natural law, one can calculate the *approximate* behaviour of the system.[5]

He ran his "rounded off" computer simulation and:

> within just a few months [of simulated patterns], all resemblance [to the first, "unrounded" run] had disappeared. He might as well have chosen two random weathers out of a hat.[6]

Small — in this case, *very* small — perturbations in the system had, as Lorenz later named it, "cascaded upward" in their influence, eventually causing "spectacular" differences. Lorenz's "hypnotic fascination" with rounded off, generalized, spectacular systems and their approximate properties and grand cycles lead him to overlook the intimate and small and meticulous ways in which each seemingly unspectacular element held a profound and irreplaceable place in and relation to the whole.

> [In this sense, each individual thing is fully sacred as that around which all other things are ordered in kind. Each thing is (not) the whole of things, and to understand this individual thing is to read it out into this as-yet-to-be-(un)given whole which it is (not).]

This realization came to be known as the Butterfly Effect. If one has predicted the weather by taking into consideration every possible element and, deep in the boreal forest of Carmanaugh Valley, an unconsidered and unspectacular butterfly flutters its wings and creates a moment of turbulence in the air, eventually, *everything* changes.

---

5   James Gleick (1987). p. 15.
6   James Glieck (1987). p. 16.

[A Vietnamese
Zen monk
once said
"If
this
speck of dust
did not exist,
the entire universe could not exist".⁷]

Everything depends upon this red wheelbarrow, glazed with rain water which passes from mystery, through pattern, back into mystery.⁸

7   Thich Nhat Hahn (1988). p. 65.
8   Rainwater moves from mystery through pattern back into mystery. To call the unknown "mystery" is to suggest that we had better respect the possibility of a larger, unseen pattern that can be damaged or destroyed and, with it, the smaller patterns. What impresses me about it is the insistent practicality implicit in it. If we are up against mystery, then we dare act only on the most modest assumptions. The modern scientific program has held that we must act on knowledge. But if we are up against mystery, then…the ancient program is the right one: Act on the basis of ignorance. Acting on the basis of ignorance, paradoxically, requires one to know things, remember things — for instance, that failure is possible, that error is possible, that second chances are desirable (so don't risk everything on the first chance), and so on.

   Wendell Berry (1987). A letter to Wes Jackson. In *Home Economics*. San Francisco: North Point Press, p. 4-5.

CHAPTER FIVE

As in spinning a thread, we twist fibre on fibre. And the strength of the thread does not reside in the fact that some one fibre runs through its whole length, [This is the "moral fibre" of Christian/normative/essentialism.] but in the overlapping of many fibres. Don't say "There *must* be something common"...but *look and see* whether there is anything common to all. For if you look at them you will not see something that is common to *all*, but similarities, relationships, and a whole series of them at that. To repeat: don't think but look! [This is *exactly* Husserl's invocation in phenomenology — see both his *Cartesian Meditations*[1] and his *Idea of Phenomenology*[2]]. We see a complicated network of similarities, overlapping and criss-crossing: sometimes overall similarities, sometimes similarities of detail. I can think of no better expression to characterize these similarities than "family resemblances." (*Familienahnlichkeiten*).

from Ludwig Wittgenstein, Philosophical Investigations.[3]

Consider, then, that Wittgenstein's critique of univocity in his *Philosophical Investigations* — wherein he speaks of "kinships" and "family resemblances" as metaphors for the living integrity of language — is an implicit critique of a world conceived as populated by "all that is the case"[4] in his own *Tractatus Logico Philosophicus*. Echoes, here, of the Scholastic notion of substance taken to its logical extreme and the complete inverse of the Vietnamese Zen Monk's remarks about the speck of dust. In a world

---

1   Edmund Husserl (1970a). *Cartesian Meditations*. The Hague: Martinus Nijhoff.
2   Edmund Husserl (1970b). *The Idea of Phenomenology*. The Hague: Martinus Nijhoff.
3   Ludwig Wittgenstein (1968). p. 32.
4   Ludwig Wittgenstein (1961) *Tractatus Logico-Philosophicus*. London: Routledge and Kegan Paul, p. 7.
    Consider:
       The world divides into facts. (p. 7)
       Each item can be the case or not the case while everything else remains the same. (p. 7)

where everything simply is what it is, the elimination of any one thing — its being the case or not being the case — makes no difference: everything else remains the same when the red wheelbarrow ceases to be. In the world conceived ecologically, if this speck of dust ceases to be, *everything* changes, however "insignificantly" (but, then again, remember Edward Lorenz and his "insignificant" 127 millionths of a degree centigrade)

In the *Philosophical Investigations,* everything that is the case, each stubborn particular, is not simply the case ("a substance is that which requires nothing except itself in order to exist"[5]).

Each case is what it is not. Each case is *fecund,* kin to this and this and this. Alike. Bearing a "family resemblance." This is like that. Each thing *bears* a likeness (note the generative metaphor here)

> [This case of a student-teacher's tale bears likenesses that this student-teacher *does not own*. It changes how I might talk about Piaget himself. But neither are they possessed by some *one* else who can say what this tale means *instead of her*. Rather she (and I) are owned by this tale. Gadamer's ideas on application rise up more vividly than ever. We both find ourselves living "in" an analogic of family resemblance.]

Wittgenstein's shift from the *Tractatus Logico Philosophicus* to the *Philosophical Investigations* is not simply a shift in a *theory of language*.

Or, better, Wittgenstein's shift in a theory of language bears a family resemblance to a deep shift in our ecological understanding of the Earth from univocity (belief in human dominion or the belief in a single Logos) to multivocity (proliferating/sustaining relations of kind).

This shift has a bearing on how we inhabit the world and on our images of the world we inhabit.

5   René Descartes (1955). p. 255.

Ecologically considered, the world is not populated by separate, substantial, self-existent univocal objects but a nest of interweaving, ambiguous kinds. Each object in the world is connected (ecologically, everything is intimately connected), insubstantial (unable to stand by itself; ecologically, nothing stands by itself), existent-in-relation ("All my relations"[6]), multivocal (familiar [but never self-identical] tales told and retold *here* and *here*).

> [This student-teacher's tale is *exquisite* and *irreplaceable*, but not in isolation, only "in place," a place made vivid by the place of its telling and re-telling.]

Wittgenstein's work prepares a way for understanding what ecology requires of us on the level of language, of inquiry — the deep, non-univocal, non-centered (or, "centered everywhere," each thing radiating out in kind, this like that, parallels), anarchaic discipline of ecosystems.

So: Wittgenstein's work is readable as a tale about ecology, about eco-systems.

His metaphors of "family resemblance" and "kinship" are also genealogical metaphors.

And ushering the young into the world is the task of pedagogy.

[This is not "child-centered pedagogy," nor its opposite.]

---

6   Cynthia Chambers (1992). "All my relations." A paper presented at the American Association of Colleges of Teacher Education Conference, San Antonio, Texas, February, 1992.

CHAPTER SIX

The logic we are living out is centuries old. Figures come and go.
Bloodlines.
René Descartes as a patriarch known through his kin.

> [Reverse: Descartes is not the enemy, the grand daddy who is to blame. He is not the *arche*. Rather, the inherited logic he enacted and that we live in the midst of is the object of this critique. Turning him into a patriarch turns us into victims who are somehow less responsible than he and who need not take up the task of unwinding this logic with loving suspicion.]

Descartes lived in a desperate world full of witches burnt outside the doors.
Cartesianism. The philosophical question, in the 1640's, of how to establish the newly emerging sciences on a solid footing: slippage of the Church as the authority of understanding, old suspicions of ambiguous Earth lore as the authority of understanding, suspicion of the frail senses, suspicion of the seductive dream, fear of bleeding women and wild-eyed children.

> ["... what the Dominants call animal, bestial, primitive, undeveloped, unauthentic. Their

                                                                fear of it
                                                                is ancient,
                                                                profound
                                                                and
                                                                violent."¹
                                                                I snake
                                                                these words
                                                                down the
                                                                margin.]

The process of methodic doubt: in order to establish the newly emerging sciences on a solid footing, all features of our experience of the world that are potentially dubitable should be methodically doubted.

The moist and dubitable and fruitful ambiguities that link our lives to the Earth and make us dependent upon the Earth — "the juice and the mystery"² — must be *put out of play*.

A severance of reliances of dubitable descent.

A denial of the Fleshy comings and goings of the Earth except insofar as they can be placed beyond doubt, beyond the cutting edge.

[...the aimless blade of science.³]

We must put out of play our dependencies.

This is the Enlightenment notion of *founding*:

> *Enlightenment is man's emergence from his self-imposed immaturity. Immaturity* is the inability to use one's understanding without guidance from another. This immaturity is *self-imposed* when its cause lies not in a lack of understanding, but in a lack of resolve and courage to use it without guidance from another. *Sapere Aude!*: "Have courage to use your own understanding!" — that is the motto of enlightenment.⁴

---

1   Ursula Le Guin (1989). p. 47.
2   Margot Adler (1989). The juice and the mystery. In Judith Plant (1989). *Healing the Wounds*. Toronto: Between the Lines Press, pp. 151-154.
3   Neil Young (1979). Thrashers. From *Rust Never Sleeps*. Reprise Records.
4   Immanuel Kant (1764/1983). What is Enlightenment? From *Perpetual Peace and Other Essays*. Indianapolis: Hackett Publishing Company, p. 33.

CHAPTER SIX

Forfeit all guidance from the Earth as unreliable, dubitable, tenuous, finite, unclear, ambiguous, untrustworthy, shifting, livid, frail, becoming, coming to be and passing away:

> It is now some years since I detected how many were the false beliefs that I had from my earliest youth admitted as true, and how doubtful was everything I had since constructed on this basis; and from that time I was convinced that I must once and for all seriously undertake to rid myself of all the opinions which I had formerly accepted, and commence to build anew from the foundations, if I wanted to establish any firm and permanent structure in the sciences.[5]

To recover a sense of firm and certain ground, Descartes instigated what he named a *methodical doubt* of every possible ground he had heretofore taken for granted:

> How could I deny that these hands and this body are mine, were it not perhaps that I compare myself to certain persons, devoid of any sense, whose cerebella are so troubled and clouded by the violent vapours of black bile, that they constantly assure us that they think they are kings when they are really quite poor, or who imagine that they have an earthenware head or are nothing but pumpkins or are made of glass. At the same time, I must remember that I am...in the habit of sleeping and in my dreams representing to myself the same things or sometimes even less probable things, than those who are insane in their waking moments.[6]

> I resolved to assume that everything that ever entered my mind was no more true than the illusions of my dreams. But immediately afterwards I noticed that whilst I thus wished to think all things false, it was absolutely essential that the "I" who thought this should *be* somewhat, and remarking that this truth, "*I think therefore I am*" was so certain and assured that all the most extravagant suppositions brought forward by the sceptics were incapable of shaking it. And then, examining attentively that which I was, I saw that I could conceive that I had no body, and that there was no world nor place where I might be; but yet that I could not for all that conceive that I was not.[7]

---

5   René Descartes (1955). p. 89.
6   René Descartes (1955). p. 90.
7   René Descartes (1955). p. 29.

Makyo.

Descartes' work had intended to free inquiry from unquestioned obedience to any unfounded assumption to knowledge. He methodically doubted each of the ways in which he could claim to know.

> through his senses, [the five Wounds of Buddhism]
> through the words and texts of others,
> through his own ideas,
> through the established traditions of thought passed down to him by his teachers,
> through the entrails and exigencies of the flesh,
> through Earth lore
> through all forms of "guidance by another."

One by one, he refused these forms of knowledge because of their inherent dubitability — because, for example, the evidence of the senses *can* be doubted (i.e., it is sometimes misleading), it cannot provide the foundation of any secure science, any secure inquiry.

Beginning, for example, with the evidence of the senses, any further steps would participate in the dubitability of that first beginning.

> [like all kin have come to fear the stain of the flesh which, if not renounced through purifying water, is borne on and on. Methodical doubt as renouncing the inherited stains and sins of the flesh]

All such potentially dubitable connectedness to things had to be cut.

> [note how the metaphor of "connectedness" is found in the interpretive disciplines, in ecology and in feminism. It is no coincidence that all three of these have gained ascendancy at once, and all three act laterally out into *textus,* not hierarchically to Heaven or inward to a brutally over-lit "epistemic subject"[8] It is

---

8   A distinction must be at once drawn between the individual subject, centered on his sense organs and on his own actions — and hence on the ego or egocentric

> obvious in the work of Piaget that this decentered subject is in fact *recentered* on logic and mathematics — a center *from which* it then imposes its "schemata" on the world. that blisters in its isolation]

But *this* cannot be doubted: the fact that I am doubting. Descartes discovered that this truth — *cogito ergo sum,* "I think therefore I am" — could be thought with such clarity and distinctness that it *could not possibly be doubted*. Because doubting is thinking.

> [within a *logic* intolerant of self-contradiction]

Here was the secure ground from which to begin: the clarity and distinctness of the doubting subject's presence to itself:

> I came to the conclusion that I might assume, as a general rule, that the things which we conceive very clearly and distinctly [of which the *cogito* is paradigmatic] are all true.[9]

This methodical severance of our relationship to the Earth and to each other, done with the noble intent of establishing the emerging sciences on a firm and unshakable foundation, ends up being accomplished at what is slowly turning out to be a nightmarish cost. All of the moist and dark and ambiguous connections of our lives on Earth, to each other and to

---

> subject as a source of possible deformation or illusion of the "subjective" type in the basic meaning of the term — and the decentered subject who coordinates his actions as between them and those of others; who measures, calculates and deduces in a way that can be generally verified; and whose epistemic activities are therefore common to all subjects, even if they are replaced by electronic or cybernetic machines with a built-in logical and mathematical capacity similar to that of the human brain.
>
> Jean Piaget (1973). *The Psychology of Intelligence.* Littlefield, Adams and Co., p. 7-8.

9   René Descartes (1955). p. 30. Note the whiff of colonialism already at play. I have the rule to rule in advance of anything I then meet.

the lives of our children had to be *severed* and could be re-achieved only to the extent that such re-connections moved within the parameters of the clarity and distinctness won by the methodical doubt of everything that could be doubted.

The Earth henceforth had to live up to our demand for clarity.

Those features of the Earth that are not renderable into such clarity are shunned or ignored as unreliable.

Clarity and distinctness (of which the subject's self-present "I am" is paradigmatic) would henceforth decide which re-connections were warrantable and which were not.

> [This is nothing new, this precedence of the "I am" as that from which all things must then issue. Consider the affirmation of Yhwh "I am that I am," which, in a sense, leaves the Unutterable Being first as the foundation of the world.]

> [Descartes' *cogito* as the epistemic foundation of the Earth. Ecological crisis, because the univocal *cogito* makes demands upon the multivocal Earth that it cannot sustain.]

> [Habermas' "monologic" of scientific discourse.[10]]

In Cartesianism, self-identity is put at the core of the "I am" — A=A. This puts univocity and the principle of identity at the core which puts mathematics at the core. Mathematics thus becomes the portal for the isolated subject to get back out into the world because "pure" mathematics participates in the clarity and distinctness that our methodic doubt has won. But this portal has a point/prick: the isolated subject gets back out into the Flesh of the Earth by *mathematizing* what comes to meet it.

The Earth and all its lives must henceforth be obedient to mathematics conceived after an image of self-sufficient univocity itself conceived

---

10 Jurgen Habermas (1972). *Knowledge and Human Interest*. Boston: Beacon Hill.

CHAPTER SIX

after the univocity of the "I am." Of course, this will *work* up to a point, because the Earth *does* bear a kinship to the *themata* of *ma themata*. Better, mathematics *does* bear a kinship to the Earth, even if it forgets this kinship. Mathematics *is* "Earthly." Cartesianism forgets this. Univocity as memory loss and, as well, a losing of a sense of place. The interpretive task is to *re-place* mathematics back on Earth. This is covered below in great detail in a reflection on the "humility of mathematical language" as evident in the talk of young children. Pedagogy reminds mathematics of its Earthliness.

> Civilized Man says: I am Self, I am Master, all the rest is Other — outside, below, underneath, subservient. I own, I use, I explore, I exploit, I control. What I do is what matters. What I want is what matter is for. I am that I am, and the rest is women and the wilderness, to be used as I see fit.[11]

Descartes took the first steps towards making the Earth suffer the tyranny of a subject able to contact anything outside of itself only within the methodical parameters of its own methodically established self-presence and self-security. Able to contact only through subjection.

As we sever our living connections with the Earth,

> [which God wishes us to do as well as Descartes — the renunciation of the Flesh and the systematic elimination of Paganism and the spooks of the world are both forms of methodical doubt]

the bios we dwell *in* ceases to be our abode and becomes a meaningless objective mechanism which is at the disposal of our whim and consumptive fantasies.

The Earth is no longer a patient and generous guide of our understanding which we deeply *require* to be who we are. As the Earth loses its *humus*, the subject loses its humanity by losing the connectedness with the humus out of which it has emerged. One might say that the subject loses its humility, its Being-in-the-world, its sense of having a place on

---

11 Ursula Le Guin (1989). p. 45.

Earth, and becomes, in the logic of Cartesianism, a disembodied and worldless self-presence to which the Earth must henceforth submit. Since we no longer owe anything to the Earth — that is, this "I think therefore I am" operates quite well even if we doubt the Earth's very *existence* — we cannot help but be drawn into thinking that we can "make ourselves masters and possessors of nature,"[12] rather than remembering that the debts are owed the other way around.

> [Again, an old story. Human dominion over the Earth is sketched out from near the beginnings of Genesis. Cartesianism, bent on starting anew, is in fact a profound recapitulation of an old tale. But its dangerous pretense is that it cannot allow itself to re-member that it is an old Earthly tale, part of a place and a genealogy. Starting anew demands purging ourselves of the others, becoming pure. Old story.]

Our lives, the lives of our children, the life of the Earth, become well-lit, enlightened, presentable, clear, univocal, like thin veneer whose surface is unambiguous, shiny/reflective, clean, without depth — bodiless, sexless, ghostly, empty, shallow products of what Alfred North Whitehead called "the celibacy of the intellect"[13]

---

12   René Descartes, cited in Morris Berman (1983). p. 13.
13   cited in Matthew Fox (1983). *Original Blessing*. Santa Fe: Bear and Company, p. 24.

CHAPTER SEVEN

The logic of Cartesianism may also be heard as a deep lament for a sense of connectedness that has been lost, a lament for a relation to the Earth, to our lives, to the lives of children. It is, in a rather perverse form, a desire to get back in touch.

But, as Mary Daly[1] points out, all of this is also a set of undeciphered signs pointing to the ways that male children seem to (perhaps *must*) establish a sense of who they are by beginning with *not* fully identifying with the one who gave them life.

This giver of life then becomes one from whom they feel somehow cut off, severed. And in such severance, it becomes unclear and indistinct how this one could have given me life, this one with whom I cannot fully identify. To re-attain identity in the face of this, methodical doubt of everything that can be doubted is required, and I doubt this mothering Earth with whom I have an ambiguous relation.

The Cartesian subject must become engrossed in logico-mathematical notions of self-identity because that subject can no longer "find itself" on Earth.

To understand itself, it must master itself through withdrawing the tendrils that attached it out into the Earth's flesh.

> [parallel between mastery of the Earth and self-mastery. Mathematics as a form of self-mastery. Mathematics as a *discipline*. Understood this way, however, mathematics suddenly has ambiguous kin, for example, the discipline of meditation. But now it has found itself back on Earth, wound ambiguously around forgotten syntaxes.

---

1   Mary Daly (1985) *Gyn/ecology*. Boston: Beacon Books.

> But mathematics wishes to have its syntax *unambiguous* and *fully remembered and unforgettable*. It's pride lies here in having kin only of its own explicit choosing. This knot won't untie.]

Descartes *intentionally* left the southern part of France for the cold and dark of Amsterdam to pursue his meditations. He withdrew "indoors," inside [himself] and resolved to proceed *alone*. To understand anything other than itself, this now isolated, fleshless Cartesian subject must use only its own pristine self-understanding as guide.

To then understand the Earth after having achieved self-mastery (Kant's "overcoming of immaturity"[2]) is to master the Earth and to deny that we get any life from it. For to *accept* this is to give away part of our mastery to a sense of indebtedness that we cannot have mastery over; to believe that the Earth *gives* us life is to deny the possibility of knowledge-as-mastery.

Consider a passage cited by Susan Bordo from Karl Stern's *The Flight from Woman:*

> [I]f a kind of Cartesian ideal were ever completely fulfilled, i.e., if the whole of nature were only what can be explained in terms of mathematical relationships — then we would look at the world with that fearful sense of alienation, with that utter loss of reality with which a future schizophrenic child looks at his mother. A machine cannot give birth.[3]

And consider the title of Bordo's book in relation to Stern's: *A Flight to Objectivity*.

Such a flight from the Earth-Woman and to objectivity produces a fearful severance and a relentless unfolding logic of severance and fragmentation:

> Not only is [such] fragmentation a disease, but the diseases of the disconnected parts are similar or analogous to one another. Thus, they memorialize their lost

---

2   Immanuel Kant (1983). p. 33.
3   cited in Susan Bordo (1987). *The Flight to Objectivity*. Albany: SUNY Press, p. 97.

unity, their relation persisting in their disconnection. Any severance produces two wounds that are, among other things, the record of how the severed parts once fitted together.[4]

Two wounds of severance and fragmentation: As the Cartesian subject loses its humanity, the Earth loses its humus and therefore loses that living integrity which might give us pause in our violent attempts to understand — to demand *object-ion*. The ensuing violence against the Earth by this Cartesian subject who can no longer identify with it hides both analogues and realities of a violence against women. Once "'she' becomes 'it'"[5] 'he' can decide for himself which objections will be heard and which will not (like Kant's judge, compelling the witnesses to answer questions that he himself poses).

This is where an even deeper violence begins to ensue. This systematic severance and the pain and wounds that it objectifications cause are bad enough.

But the violence of such objectifications does not have a lament for connectedness and an attempt to re-connected as its excuse.

The violence of objectification does not come from its fumbling and indelicate and inconsiderate attempts at re-connection.

The violence of objectification is aroused at the very suggestion of connectedness, for such a suggestive connectedness denies objectification its totalization.

> [A self which conceives of itself as isolated *is* violated at the suggestion of inter-dependence. What is violated here, however, is an *imaginary, ecologically disastrous* concept of "self." This sense of inter-dependence must, however, be distinguished from the violences of one person's oppression and silencing of another and from the pathologies of co-dependency. This is an untieable knot.]

---

4 Wendell Berry (1986). *The Unsettling of America*. San Francisco: Sierra Club Books, p. 110-111.
5 Susan Bordo (1987). p. 108.

And here is the grand turn around.

Connectedness — even the suggestion of it — violates objectivity, not the other way around.

Objectivity does not wound connectedness. Connectedness wounds objectivity (it "despoils" it).

This not only says that objective research must methodically and relentlessly ensure itself against any pre-existing connections to the subject that might violate its hard won sense of control. It also says that if such dis-connectedness is "despoiled," if one's results are "contaminated," if things get "out of control," that which caused me to get out of control gets what it deserves. I must dominate in order to reassert my control. The connection must be violently cut in the name of understanding, in the name of knowledge, in the name of Reason.

She wouldn't listen to reason so I had to teach her a lesson. The violence? She was just "asking for it."

> The paradigm that tells us we are apart from and above this earth is not simply an intellectual response to Nature. It is instead a deeply fearful attitude. And the fear that lies under this thought, like all fear, turns into rage.[6]

Thus, the grand and inevitable turn around works itself out in our lives:

> The "wound" of separateness is healed through the *denial* that there ever "was" any union. There is nothing to mourn, nothing to lament. Indeed... epistemological

---

6   Susan Griffin (1989). Split culture. In Judith Plant (1989). *Healing the Wounds*. Toronto: Between the Lines Press, p. 10. Regarding this "rage," see David W. Jardine (1992). Immanuel Kant, Jean Piaget and the Rage for Order: Hints of the Colonial Spirit in Pedagogy. *Educational Philosophy and Theory*.

   Susan Griffin continues to name the emotional knot of scientific discourse:

   > The pursuit of scientific knowledge in our civilization is beset by an emotional dilemma. In order to control Nature, we must know Nature. But just as we are seeking to know, there is a knowledge we fear. We are afraid to remember what we, in our bodies and in our feelings still know, but what, in our fragmented, civilized consciousness we have been persuaded to forget. That, like the forests we destroy, or the rivers we try to tame, *we* are Nature. (p. 10).

anxiety is evoked, not over [the] loss [of], but by the suggestion of *union*; [such a suggestion of union] obscures objectivity [and] muddies the clear lake of the mind.⁷

[Parallel: Descartes' methodical doubt is akin to a ancient purification ritual and thus suddenly has unforeseen kin.]

We are all familiar with the dominant Cartesian themes of starting anew, alone, without influence from the past or other people, with the guidance of reason alone. The specific origins of obscurity in our thinking are the appetites, the influence of our teachers, and the "prejudices" of childhood. The purification of the relation between knower and known requires the repudiation of childhood, a theme which was not uncommon at the time. For Descartes', happily, the state of childhood *can* be revoked, thorough a deliberate and methodical reversal of all the prejudices acquired within it, and a beginning anew with reason as one's only parent.⁸

Unclarity and uncleanness are bound together and there is an archaic linkage of philosophical clarification and philosophical essentialism to purification:

> Dr. Mary Douglas has recently advanced the very interesting and illuminating view that the concept of "pollution" "is a reaction to protect cherished principles

---

7 Susan Bordo (1987). p. 108.
8 Susan Bordo (1987). p. 97-8.

and categories from contradiction." She holds that, in effect, what is unclear and contradictory tends to be regarded as unclean. The unclear is the unclean.⁹

> Purification, when linked to unclarity/clarity becomes a process of methodical doubt which banishes anything dubitable, anything doubtful.

Christian parallel of the uncleanness of the Flesh.

> See also its parallel to academia and the hoarding of the old in vaults.¹⁰

> Each unclean thing is taken up anew from the point of
> view of pure self-presence.
> The flesh of the Earth can re-enter,
> but only insofar as it renounces its Earthly character and
> admits its uncleanness –
> it can re-enter, but now only as *object*.

The parallels in transcendental phenomenology are striking. In the case of Husserl's "pure phenomenology"[11], we wish to operate in the realm "pure evidence"[12] beheld in the "pure seeing"[13] of "pure experiences"[14] in their "pure givenness"[15] given in "pure reflection"[16] as a "pure phenomenon"[17] to "consciousness, considered in its *'purity'*."[18] And,

---

9   Victor Turner (1987). Betwixt and between: The liminal period in rites of passage. In Mahdi, L., Foster, S., & Little, M., eds. *Betwixt and between: Patterns of masculine and feminine initiation.* La Salle: Open Court, p. 7.
10 Bruce Wilshire (1990). *The Moral Collapse of the University.* Albany: State University of New York Press, especially chapter seven "Academic professionalism as a veiled purification ritual."
11 Edmund Husserl (1972). Husserl's inaugural lecture at Freiburg im Briesgau. In L. Embree, ed. *Life-world and Consciousness.* Evanston: Northwestern University Press, p. 5.
12 Edmund Husserl (1969). p. 49.
13 Edmund Husserl (1969). p. 82.
14 Edmund Husserl (1969). p. 140.
15 Edmund Husserl (1970b). p. 8.
16 Edmund Husserl (1970b). p. 50.
17 Edmund Husserl (1970a). p. 18.
18 Edmund Husserl (1969). p. 155.

parallel to the search for purity is the search for *the beginning,* for that *from which* all things issue: phenomenology is the work of unearthing and fixing *beginnings*.[19] Phenomenology was to be "a science of Beginnings; a 'first philosophy'."[20] As a "first philosophy," it is the philosophy of the Initiate, the Initial, as characterizes the one undergoing purification: the new-born re-born into the spirit, with no blood. Husserl sought over and over again for a *"radical beginning"*[21], posed over and over again *"the question of the beginning"*[22], the question of the *"absolute beginning"*[23] In each cited case, the emphasis belongs to Husserl: *Beginnings*. Phenomenology will always admit that we have always already begun, living fully in the flesh before the work of phenomenology begins. But phenomenology still demands that this "fully living in the flesh" be transformed by *"a new way of looking at things is necessary,* one that contrasts *at every point* with the natural attitude of experience and thought."[24] Our fleshy life must be purified into a phenomenon and cast with the fixity of essences. Its essence must be "fixed once and for all."[25]

[Struck by the fear of the Gods which found me: this is a *fear of the Wound* — the age-old fear and disgust at the mysteries of menstrual blood as unclear and unclean – fleshmarks. Struck by finding a god-replica in fixed essences that do not perish or bleed.'

---

19   Edmund Husserl (1970a) p. 4-6. See also Edmund Husserl (1965). Philosophy as a rigorous science of being. In *Phenomenology and the Crisis of Philosophy*. New York: Harper and Row, p. 140-147.
20   Edmund Husserl (1969). p. 28.
21   Edmund Husserl (1969). p. 27.
22   Edmund Husserl (1970a). p. 14.
23   Edmund Husserl (1969). p. 92.
24   Edmund Husserl (1969), p. 43.
25   Edmund Husserl (1970). p. 139.

Healing the Wounds: The Promise of Ecofeminism.[26] This title of a wonderful collection of essays edited by Judith Plant evokes what is in the air these days: a joyous and hopeful interweaving of ecology, feminism and the profound disruptions that the interpretive disciplines are making to the old, vicious and static edifices of the patriarchy. Such disruptions are revealing small glimpses of the delicate net of interdependencies that house and embrace us — no grand and clear and final vision "from above," but small, lateral glimpses, here and here and here, joy at this unanticipated whiff of pine couched in a sunny spot, sheltered from the wind and echoed by the whistle of an Evening Grosbeak whose yellow flash hollers in the newspring green of the trees.

But the Earth has become no longer our home, and we have become homeless. Over and over again we hear tales about the deep wounds of separation and disconnectedness and the tearing of the flesh of the Earth in the name of ethereal notions of Rationality and brutal logics. We are called to "heal the wounds," to mend the severances from the Flesh, the Earth, the *humus,* that this logic has played out in our own lifetime.

The Wound, read as an act of severance, is envisaged as the origin of our isolation from the Earth, an isolation we can "repair" through "healing," "reconnecting."

But the Wound names something age-old, far older than the "wound of severance" that is the outcome of the logic of Cartesianism and Enlightenment Ascendancy (buoyed up as it was by the Christian vision of a soul detached from the Earth and stained through attachment to the Earth: "borne into the sin of the Flesh").

An older reading of the Wound is that it is not ours to repair, nor is it a Wound of severance and isolation. This older reading requires envisaging the Wound as an "opening," a "portal," an "opportunity."[27] The link

---

26   Judith Plant (1989).
27   James Hillman (1987a). As Hillman notes, *Poros* "according to Plato's *Symposium* (203b-d), is the father of Eros." (p. 152). Openness gives birth to Desire.

> What comes through the hole (*porta*) has its source beyond the wall and cannot easily be detached from the gap (chaos) of its entry. Opportunities are not plain, clean gifts; they trail dark and chaotic attachments to their

of weakness and wounds to Hermes, the bearer of messages belies the hard-edged, heroic strength of most research. — the Wound can be read as the gateway to the Earth and to our own Earthliness, an opening-out.

In the former, isolation must be "overcome" by "healing" the "wound" of severance. In the latter, isolation is "overcome" by keeping open the Wound-as-portal.

The Wound-as-portal or opening bespeaks a tale of agony at the heart of all this reverse, of how the gut bursts open and winds its entrails around trees and burrows down into the pungent, rooted Earth and its crawling intersections. It is a tale of how our humanity, our *humus,* will inevitably be pulled out into the Earth in death and decay. In blood:

> Our blood will detoxify the phosphates and the PCB's. Our blood will feed the depleted soils. Our blood will water the dry, tired surface of the earth. We will unknown backgrounds, luring us further. One insight leads to another; one invention suggests another variation — more and more seems to press through the hole, and more and more we find ourselves drawn out into a chaos of possibilities. (p. 154)
>
> Here, mythology shows Hermes knowing the ruse and deception that opens the way until the constellation shifts. Hermes here is like Eros, whose father was Poros, "resourcefulness," "way-finding." Since situations require this opportunistic knowing about where the openings are and when the time needs voice...in an encounter, the lacuna, the weak place...gives the opportunity. *Perception of opportunities requires a sensitivity given through one's own wounds.* Here, weakness provides the kind of hermetic, secret perception critical for adaptation to situations. The weak place serves to open us to what is in the air. We feel through our pores which way the wind blows. We turn with the wind; trimmers. An opportunity requires...a sense...which reveals the daimon of a situation. The daimon of a place in antiquity supposedly revealed what the place was good for, its special quality and dangers. The daimon was though to be a *familiaris* of the place. To know a situation, one needs to sense what lurks in it." (p. 161.)

The cascade here is unbearable: the Nicean denial of daimons is a denial of the familiarity of places.

bleed. We will bleed. We will bleed until we bathe her in our blood and she turns slippery new like a baby birthing. [28]

Our lives are Earthly, fragile, wound up with all things in generative, transfiguring inevitabilities of the rhythmed breath rhymed to day and night, shortened when exhausted, just like the shortened days of winter hint at exhaustion and repose ("family resemblance").

These inevitabilities hint at a way of understanding language. They are not some fixed deep transformative grammars that can be pictured "from outside" because new instances are of a kind, i.e., fecund and we are *in* language, *being* transformed. These inevitabilities thus pertain, but what now pertains is a generative and propulsive *relation of kind* that has no *fixed* boundary, but a delicate, porous, ambiguous nature— an "open" boundary — that lures and allures.

Poros and Eros.

It is the Wound of the Navel full of green shoots splitting the innards outwards.

It is the Wound of Birth full of bright red blood, healed only at our peril.

This Wound can be read, not as a sign of severance but as a sign of the interdependencies of all things, a pain, not of severance and isolation but of connection.

It can be read as a deep phenomenology-mythology of the flesh Wound as a sign of the experience of and connection with the whole.

It is not the wound of a substantive subject methodically severed from the Earth (the wound of severance is *imaginary*, for being severed from the Earth is not actually possible; it is an albeit powerful, dangerous, potent and efficacious *illusion*), but the Wound of the connection of non-substantive "the subject" to all things.

> [Hermeneutic "self-understanding" begins at this Wound: the place of weakness and pain — the place of "openness" and "porousness"

---

28 Ellen Bass (1989). From Tampons. Cited in Judith Plant (1989). *Healing the Wounds*. Toronto: Between the Lines Press, p. 53

and "connectedness." Self-understanding in Descartes began at *the other wound*: at the wound of severance (producing a correlative 'wounded' — severed, object-ing — Earth which no longer houses).]

This reading of the Wound reminds us that our children are of our flesh and that our pedagogies must not pathologize the pain of the living and the coming and the going in the embrace of the Earth.

[At the heart of pedagogy is an agony, not an essence.]
[At the heart of pedagogy is the Wound of the Living: the coming and going of the young]
[At the heart of ecology is an agony not an essence.]

[At the heart of ecology is the Wound of the Living: the coming and going of the Breath].

Perhaps it is not so much the pain of the Wound itself, but its pathologizing into a dis-ease that we might fix that is the most brutal logic we are living out. Understood as a living, Earthly relationship, the paradox of our lives with children – "both part and apart"[29] —is not struggling to resolve itself into well-drawn, unambiguous, unequivocal declarations. Rather, being mindful of this paradox and its generative irresolvability "makes meaningful and beautiful the primary paradoxes that human beings *have* to live with"[30], the "original difficulty"[31] that resides in the issuing forth of new life in our midst.

Children are a reminder of an-archaic debts, reminders of a *real* genealogy and the interlacing of that genealogy with all things.

---

29   David Smith (1988).
30   Gary Snyder (1980). p. 29-30.
31   John Caputo (1987). *Radical Hermeneutics: Repetition, Deconstruction and the Hermeneutic Project*. Bloomington: Indiana University Press, p. 1. See also David W. Jardine (1992). Reflections on education, hermeneutics and ambiguity: Hermeneutics as a restoring of life to its original difficulty. In W. Pinar and W. Reynolds, eds. (1992). *Understanding Curriculum as Phenomenological and Deconstructed Text*. New York: Teachers' College Press.

This genealogy, this generativity, and this deep natural affection (generosity) — the question of cultivating and maintaining the well-being of a "kind-ness" — does not and cannot simply string along a chromosomal thread, but exhales outward into the whole of the Earth, into a sense of place and space, coupled with an attunement to what is needed for a livable future.

The whole Earth is our "kind," our kin. We are human, full of humus, and our natural affection cannot begin with isolating humanity as some substance which needs nothing but itself in order to exist.

Our humanity is not a substance. We are empty of self-existence and only as such — only interlaced with all things — can we be what we deeply are.

> Fixing the pain of the Wound-as-portal
> is asking after
> fixing the pain of generativity itself.
> "Healing the
> wounds,"
> wrongly read,
> works against
> the heartwound of
> pedagogy.

Note the metaphors – the allure of the Earth, the smell of blood, might seduce the celibate Cartesian subject out of its hard-won isolation (little wonder that hermeneutics, linked to Poros and Eros, is so little tolerated and so feared. Every living discipline is full of blood relations. Ghosts. Voices).

Note too, that in the sciences, we speak of despoiled results, contaminated data —both of these caused by illicit, uncontrolled-for "contact" that it struggles to pre-empt.

Here, in the logic of Cartesianism, we have "the almost religious process of self-purification"[32] where methodical doubt purges the unclean.

---

32   Joel Weinsheimer (1987). *Gadamer's Hermeneutics*. New Haven: Yale University Press, p. 9.

The ambiguous, the dubitable, and the agonies of our fleshy inheritance are pathologized into a dis-ease to be cured through a methodical doubt which cuts or burns or washes away. The price of such self-purification is self-isolation (hence the inevitable consequence of loneliness that comes from Cartesianism).

> [Purification rituals work with cleansing water or cleansing fires and crucibles. Boiling things down to their essence, boiling away impurities and eliminating the "so much depends" inessential accidents of interface (nothing *happens*). Descartes' doubt etched away all that was dubitable and he sat in his study by a fire, using its transformative power to melt the honeycomb wax he held, forcing it to give up its essence as extended substance, forcing away its allures of sweetness: "You can still smell something of the flowers from which it was made. But notice... ."[33]

>> [the same fire burning away the Earth lore and the same alluring smell of meat drooped down. Descartes' approaching the fire until the honeycomb wax is no longer alluring: no smell, no taste, no sweetness of flowers, no sting of beebuzzing, not even nourishment. The wax become a mere "extended substance."[34] It now just takes up space, like the animals that have nothing to say, the children that babble and the women who talk all the time and say nothing.[35]]

Husserl's "eidetic variation" and "eidetic reduction" boils down the accidental to its essence. It is no coincidence that precisely the metaphor of purifying fire (and cleansing water) is used in Husserl's example:

> "This apple-tree in bloom, in this garden, and so forth". In the phenomenologically pure experience, we find, as belonging to its essence indissolubly [fully cleansed], the perceived as such, and under such titles as "material thing," "plant," "tree,"

---

33   René Descartes (1955). p. 213.
34   René Descartes (1955). p. 213. See also David W. Jardine (1988). Piaget's clay and Descartes' wax. *Educational Theory. 38*.
35   Ursula LeGuin. (1987). Introduction. To *Buffalo Gals and Other Animal Presences*. Santa Barbara: Capra Press, p. 11.

"blossoming," and so forth. The *inverted commas* are clearly significant; they express that change of signature. The *tree plain and simple,* the thing in nature . . . can burn away. But the meaning — the meaning of this perception, something that belongs to its essence — cannot burn away.[36]

The rendering into a phenomenologically pure experience has metaphorically "burned away" those features of the "tree plain and simple" that can burn away.

With the essence, we need no longer suffer the possibility of loss and the agonies of facing this *real* tree as something that will fade, whose blossoms will fall, whose passing will echo our own real passing, the etching of age on the skin. We are supposed to take human comfort in the heavenly persistence of its essence.

> We do not have to *live through* such suffering. Or living through it purges our fleshy attachments to it.

>> —the parallel between the burning of witches/Cartesianism and the events of Husserl's Germany and his own Jewishness are Unspeakable: Judaism from which he converted in a religious experience involving the New Testament and visions of philosophy as a Rigorous Science of Being. The pathologizing of doubt rings in Husserl's words:

>>> I can only think that you have sensed some of the sustaining ethos through the laconic sobriety and strict concentration on the matters at hand in my writings. You must have sensed that this ethos is genuine, because my writings. . .are born out of a need, out of an immense psychological need, out of a complete collapse in which the only hope is an

---

36   Edmund Husserl (1969), p. 260-261.

> entirely new life, a desperate, unyielding resolution to begin from the beginning and to go forth.[37]
>
> The decisive influences, which drove me from mathematics to philosophy as my vocation my lie in overpowering religious experiences and complete transformations. Indeed, the powerful effect of the New Testament on a 23-year-old gave rise to an impetus to discover the way to God and to a true life through a rigorous philosophical inquiry.[38]
>
> We shall be drawn into an *inner transformation*.[39]

Husserl lost his son in World War I.

Perhaps it will become manifest that the total phenomenological attitude and the epoche belonging to it are destined in essence to effect, at first, a complete personal transformation, comparable in the beginning to a religious conversion.[40]

---

37 Edmund Husserl (1964). Edmund Husserl: A letter to Arnold Metzger. *Philosophical Forum. 21,* p. 54.
38 Edmund Husserl (1964). p. 56.
39 Edmund Husserl (1970). p. 100.
40 Edmund Husserl (1970). p. 137.

CHAPTER EIGHT

We need to go deeper into the logic of univocity upon which Cartesianism hinges. Of identity.

The "I am" has a parallel after-image in the world, formed, like the "I am," out of the logic of univocity: "It is."

[Heidegger disassembled this Logico-univocal "It is" into *Es Gibt*[1] — this unwinds the "It is" from the logic of presence into the ana-logic of "it gives." The Earth as a gift, freely given (the definition of "generosity" — rooted with generativity). He disassembled the Logico-univocal "I am" in a-like way with "facticity" and "historicity."[2]]

"I am"*
* the "meaning of the Being of the *sum*"[3] (of the "I am" in *cogito ergo sum*) is this:
    Univocal Self-Presence.

"It is"**
** the meaning of the Being
of the World
is the same:
Univocal Presence to the Self.

1   Martin Heidegger (1977a) Letter on humanism. In *Basic Writings*. New York: Harper and Row.
2   Martin Heidegger (1962).
3   Martin Heidegger (1962).

Thus meet the purified, worldless subject

                           and the purified, subjectless world.

                         [The ironic bewilderment at the appropriateness of citing Heidegger after talk of burning and witches and purification and Husserl's fate must never be lost. He converted to Christianity, but his Jewishness was a matter of blood, not beliefs]

Lurking under the affirmation of the "I am" is a parallel affirmation regarding the univocity of the world. The world has only one true Logos. All signs point this way.

                         [note below the threads of the Second Council of Nicaea in this parallel]

For not to have one meaning is to have no meaning and if words have no meaning, our reasoning with one another, and indeed with ourselves has been annihilated; for it is impossible to think of anything if we do not think of one thing; but if this is possible, one name might be assigned to the thing.
Aristotle, Metaphysics, 1039a[4]

"It is impossible to think of anything if we do not think of one thing": this is an expression of the principle of non-contradiction and its correlative, the principle of identity:
A=A.
It expresses a simple assumption we make about the world and objects in the world: things are, so to speak, identical with themselves.
That is to say, when we speak of an entity, or attribute something to it, that entity either *is* or *is not* what is so attributed: the third principle of excluded middle (an entity cannot, at the same time and in the same respect, both be and not be attribute "x").

---

4   Aristotle. *The Basic Works of Aristotle*. New York: Random House.

CHAPTER EIGHT

> [The Jewelled Net of Indra violates this Trinity of Principles. Deep ecology violates this Trinity of Principles. The interpretive disciplines violate this Trinity of Principles. Their violations are on behalf of dependent co-arising and relatedness as the living reality of our Earthly being]

However unclear, ambiguous or blurred our understanding, experience or language may be, entities in the world clearly, unambiguously and precisely *are* what they *are*.

"The essence of truth is identity"[5] and, "taken as a negative expression of the principle of identity, the principle of non-contradiction is the basic principle of all cognition, of all truths as identities."[6]

The logic involved in this line of thought is relentless and inevitable:

> Descartes' emphasis on clear and distinct ideas . . . served to canonize the Aristotelian principle of non-contradiction. Since the Cartesian paradigm recognizes no self-contradictions in logic, and since logic (or geometry), according to Descartes, is the way nature behaves [as it must, since the behaving of nature is knowable only through those ideas *about it* which are clear and distinct], the paradigm allows for no self-contradiction in nature.[7]

Whatever things are, they are what they are and they are not what they are not.

Since a basic assumption of all cognition is thus that things are the way they are (what could be called the "univocity of reality", A=A), to speak about such things, our speech must reproduce such singularity.

To bespeak the self-sameness or univocity of reality ("The world is all that is the case"[8]), speech itself must be univocal if it is to give a voice to the real.

---

5   Martin Heidegger (1978). p. 39.
6   Martin Heidegger (1978). p. 52.
7   Morris Berman (1983). p. 23.
8   Ludwig Wittgenstein (1961), p. 7.

Since "it is impossible to think of anything if we do not think of one thing" (A=A), "one name might be assigned to the thing" in order to give a voice to this self-identical nature.

Irrespective of whether we "locate" this self-identical nature in "things themselves" to which thought must submit, or in the essence of cognition (which then "constructs" objects according to its own demand for self-identity), "identity is the basic criterion of all truth" and therefore a basic criterion of all true discourse.

To speak truly is to adhere to the univocal frontiers of things themselves (or to adhere to the univocal frontiers of reason itself which reproduces its own frontiers by constructing objects of knowledge in light of those frontiers).

Discourse claiming to be *about* the world must revolve around "one name" because the world is singular in its utterance.

The deep-seated belief in the univocity of reality and its unwavering belief in an isolatable self-identity of things (what Husserl described as the *Urdoxa*[9] —a belief in the self-existent "being out there" of entities) requires that speech *about* such univocal entities must itself be univocal. In the face of this, the arising of ambiguity, equivocity, metaphorical speech, analogy, rhetoric, poetry —all of these are taken as quite literally contra-dictions, i.e., peculiarities of speech which do not reflect the nature of things themselves.

In order to properly signify this univocal nature, we find that:

> the notion of signification requires a univocity of meaning: the definition of the principle of identity, in its logical and ontological form, demands it. Univocity of meaning is ultimately grounded in essence, one and self-identical.[10]

To speak truly about things is to submit speech to the univocal character of the thing itself.

---

9   Edmund Husserl (1969), p. urdoxa
10 Paul Ricouer (1970). *Freud and Philosophy*. New Haven: Yale University Press, p. 23.

[Or, under the auspices of Kant's Copernican Revolution, to speak truly is to submit experience to the univocal core of Reason itself; or, more closely following Descartes, to speak truly is to speak with clarity and distinctness, a clarity and distinctness which "matches" those things which are clear and distinct (i.e. self-identical in themselves). In Kant, one imposes the clarified, *a priori*, categories if reason itself on the myriad of things. They must submit because Reason demands it. We can hear in this echoes of the long history of the notion of "substance" as that which stands by itself and rests within its own frontiers, that which requires nothing except itself in order to exist.[11]]

How are we to gain access to such a univocal character? It becomes necessary to assure the adherence of speech to the univocal character of things themselves. Since "a single truth alone is acceptable when we are dealing with a problem of knowledge in the strict sense"[12], signification which makes claims to be true must orient to univocity, to "one voice." We must secure ourselves in those techniques or methods which will promote such a singularity of voice (this being what Jurgen Habermas named the "monological" character of scientific discourse [13]). Discourse becomes formalized,[14] orienting to precision, definition and repeatability, orienting, in a sense, to "form" or "essence," to that which is self-identical. The desire to define becomes warrantable as a correlate of the definite character of the things which are to be designated by such definitions. The methodical purging of discourse of its ambiguities operates under the desire to match up discourse with the unambiguous (i.e., self-identical, A=A) character of things themselves.

---

11   René Descartes (1955). p. 255.
12   Jean Piaget (1965). *Insights and Illusions of Philosophy*. New York: Meridian Books, p. 216-217.
13   Jurgen Habermas (1973).
14   James B. MacDonald (1975). Curriculum and human interests', in W. Pinar (ed.), *Curriculum Theorizing: The Reconceptualists,* McCutchan Publishing Corporation, Berkeley, p. 283.

[This is why formal logic tends to form the backdrop of such discourse because, as Jean Piaget demonstrates, such discourse perfectly adheres to this deep, presumptive univocal correlation between discourse and things themselves. Formal logic is perfectly "equilibrated" since the structures of thought/language in terms of which we do logic and the object of such doing *are precisely the same*. Formal logic "proceeds by the application of perfectly explicit rules, these rules being, of course, the very ones that define the structure under consideration."[15] In formal logic, the frontiers of discourse and the frontiers of the object of discourse are identical. The lines that have been drawn are identical, because the matters under consideration in formal logical operations have become matters of method (i.e., matters regarding the ideal, formalized *operation* of discourse itself). Formal logic becomes paradigmatic of discourse because it exquisitely displays "that which needs nothing but itself in order to exist" — it is an exquisite example of the Scholastic notion of "substance" inherited by and then from Descartes. It does not even need a "knower," or one who "operates," because its indigenous operations are exactly those which an operator would use to "know" it.]

Method gains a primacy to the extent that it begins to determine which matters are warrantable objects of investigation. We have come upon an age where the *matters* of inquiry have become matters of method.[16] Method becomes the means whereby Descartes' clarity and distinctness becomes, so to speak, "operationalized." That is, method becomes the way in which clarity and distinctness *operates* and following the meticulous methods of the sciences becomes cast in Descartes' shadow.

Our interpenetrations with the world are now proper, formal, Civilized according to our higher nature.

15   Jean Piaget (1970). *Structuralism*. New York: Harper and Row. p. 15.
16   Martin Heidegger (1972a). The end of philosophy and the task of thinking. In *On Time and Being*. New York: Harper and Row, p. 55.

> [This is why Piaget's stages are always portrayed as going *up* — old tales of ascendancy, old metaphors for "growing up" in the literalness of heights grown]
>
>> [This is why the "higher" stages of the development of knowledge in Piagetian theory are defined by their *operational* character. The highest level of the development of knowledge, for Piaget, is logico-mathematical knowledge, i.e., knowledge of the operation of knowledge itself, in short, a knowledge of matters of method. Objectivity is defined as adherence to such methods, since it is precisely such methods which *constitute* an object of knowledge in the first place. Through a peculiar convolution, then, Piaget's notion of "schemata" or "structures," defined as systems of transformations of operations, comes haunting close to Descartes' scholastic notion of substance as that which need nothing other than itself in order to exist. His structuralism operates under:
>>
>>> an ideal (perhaps a hope) of intrinsic intelligibility supported by the postulate that structures are self-sufficient and that, to grasp them, we do not have to make reference to all sorts of extraneous elements.[17]

Connected with this turn to method, and perhaps equally inextricable in our image of inquiry, is the "relentless passion for quantity"[18] as a paradigm of self-identical clarity and distinctness.

In discussing Gottfrid Leibniz's notion of adequate knowledge, Martin Heidegger states:

> An adequate knowledge is thoroughly clear knowledge, where confusion is no longer possible, where the reduction into marks and moments of marks (*requisita*)

---

17 Jean Piaget (1970). p. 4-5.
18 Thomas Merton (1965). *Gandhi on Non-Violence*. New Directions Books, p. 2.

can be managed to the end. Of course, Leibniz immediately adds regarding *cognitio adaequata:* "I am not sure that a perfect example of this can be given by man, but our notion of numbers approximates it."[19]

The paradigm of univocity and identity is *numerical identity* and its various statistical permutations. (It is no coincidence that the dreamer of Descartes' dream was most deeply and passionately a mathematician). Number, quantification, becomes paradigmatic to the extent that even unclarity and indistinctness become quantified into designations of the possible frequency of error in one's results.

---

19   Martin Heidegger (1978), p. 62.

CHAPTER NINE

Hill and rivers, the Earth plants and trees, tiles and stones, all of these are the self's original part.[1]

The true mode of being of a thing as it is in itself, cannot be a self-identity in the sense of a substance. Indeed, this true mode must include a complete negation of such self-identity, and with it a conversion of the standpoint of Reason.[2]

Interpretively speaking, each thing that comes to meet us already is all that it is not. As am I. I bring the tree's oxygen and it brings the sun. Simple, really. When we meet, we are already full of each other.

Interpretation plays with the principle of identity, the principle of non-contradiction and the principle of excluded middle. It is, to *this* extent "illogical."

However, this "illogic" reveals the deep *ana-logic* of the Earth.

This gate was opened by Husserl (but re-closed by his essentialism.[3] Husserl required that we not begin with the *assumption* that the world follows the principle of non-contradiction, but that we take the world just as it comes to meet us.

> Phenomenology is not a method of reconnection to what is separate. *This* is the plaint of objectivism, beginning as it does with the *fantasy* of disconnection — the *fantasy* of a subject isolated from the Earth and an Earth isolated from the subject which, thus formulated, poses the problem of re-connection as insuperable.

---

1 Nishitani Keiji (1982). p. 108.
2 Nishitani Keiji (1982). p. 117.
3 "Like many a pivotal thinker, Husserl is an ambiguous figure, and thus the beginning he inaug
   urated is ambiguous also." (Madison, 1988, p. xi).

> Phenomenology, *in its founding gesture*, is a form of recollective, reflective inquiry that wishes to disrupt this forgetfulness and the ensuing "fear and hatred of what [has] been denied."[4]

Phenomenology, in its founding gesture, is a form of inquiry which requires a "letting be"[5] of things just as they give themselves in our experience, and a profound and meticulous attentiveness and care in attempting to speak, to say, to save this wild integrity of experience.

As Husserl maintains: "phenomenological explication does nothing but *explicate the sense this world has for us prior to any philosophizing. . .a sense which philosophy can uncover, but never alter.*"[6]

The difference of phenomenology's interest in the sense and experience of the world prior to any philosophizing / theorizing centers around its relation to the notion of the univocity of reality and the correlative notion of univocal discourse. These notions are captured in Husserl's description of the "thesis of the natural attitude."

It is this attitude that Husserl called an *Urdoxa* or "grounding belief" to the world that undergirds Cartesian logic, for it implicitly pronounces the deep belief in the univocal character of the world, and, thereby, the univocal character of true speech.

It is this attitude which phenomenology "puts out of play" in its own vocation:

> I find continually present and standing over against me the one spatio-temporal fact-world to which I myself belong, as do all other men found in it and related in the same way to it. This fact-world, as the word already tells us, I find to *be out there*, and also, take it just as it gives itself to me as something that exists out there. All doubting and rejecting of the data of the natural world leaves standing the general thesis of the natural standpoint. The world is as fact-world always there; at the most it is at odd points "other" than I supposed; this or that under names such as "illusion" or "hallucination" and the like must be struck *out of it*, so to

---

4   Ursula Le Guin (1989). p. 47.
5   Martin Heidegger (1962).
6   Edmund Husserl (1970a). p. 151.

speak; but the "it" remains ever, in the sense of the general thesis, a world that has its being out there.[7]

It is a natural *assumption* about the world that it has its being "out there." That is to say, independent of experience, language, etc., the world is what it is ("the 'it' remains"). We may run into various difficulties in understanding that world — under names such as illusion, hallucination, ambiguity, unclarity, equivocation and the like. But these difficulties do not affect the fact that the world has its being out there, totally independent and out of relation to us.

Such difficulties must be struck out of discourse if it is to be true to this "being out there." Even in such striking out, the "it" remains, ever self-identical, ever calling for univocal discourse to give it a voice.

It is precisely this thesis that undergirds Cartesian logic because it is precisely this thesis that is first *negated* and then *reclaimed* by Descartes methodical doubt. The question persists in Descartes' work, of how it is that I might move from the ideas I have, the thoughts I have, to some understanding of that which is "out there" — how do I know that these ideas that I have are ideas of things "out there?" The fundamental *problem* in Descartes' meditations becomes one of how the self-present subject can touch something outside of itself, thus keeping in force the desire than undergirds the thesis of the natural attitude by *beginning with* a subject which dreams that it is worldless, out of touch. Correlative to this, of course, is beginning with a world with which we are out of touch, such that the contact between this "subjectless world" and this "worldless subject" becomes a desperate *epistemological* problem that can be simply stated thus: once the subject contacts the world, it is no longer the world that is as it is out of relation to the subject but is the world as *representation,* the world as *picture* (for a subject). Democratize this one further step, and we quickly move from the late 19th century notion of *Weltanschauung* — "world views," which bespeaks a particular relativity of "perspectives" — to our current, "floating" state of "everyone has their own experience and who is to say who is right?"

---

7   Edmund Husserl (1969), p. 106.

As we have seen, Descartes concludes that this subject can make this contact only through precisely the clarity and distinctness of those ideas that participate in such self-presence — these are (*via* God's assurance) ideas *of* the world "out there." It is these ideas that provide such a desired transcendence. If it clearly and distinctly *appears* to be an idea of some object "out there," it *is* an idea of an object "out there."

> [As we shall see below in an explication of the work of Immanuel Kant and Jean Piaget, very different provisions are at work in this regard. Descartes still retains a hesitancy about clarity and distinctness, needing some guarantor of such clarity and distinctness. Of course, Descartes reverted to God as guarantor. But he proved God's existence as benevolent (and thus non-deceiving and thus my clear and distinct ideas are not deceptive because God would not deceive me in this way) through the ontological argument[8] which relies upon a trust of the clarity and distinctness of logic and thereby *assumes the veracity of clear and distinct ideas* (in particular, the veracity of the idea of God utilized in the ontological proof) in order to prove the existence of the guarantor of that veracity. In the work of Immanuel Kant, this proof was invalidated[9] and, more pointedly, *what this proof was after* was shown to be unnecessary. Reason is, to use Piaget's term "self-regulating" and needs no external guarantor of its veracity].

---

8   Roughly put, we begin with the *idea* of God as that entity than which no greater entity can be conceived ("can be conceived" leaves us in the realm of ideas). It is greater to exist than to not exist. Therefore, by definition, God exists.

9   Simply put, Kant demonstrated that "existence" is not a predicate which adds to or makes greater that which it predicates. If existence was a predicate which adds to that which it predicates, we would find ourselves in a peculiar dilemma. For example, if we define a triangle as a figure with three sides whose internal angles add up to 180 degrees, and then we come upon an object in the world with three sides whose internal angles add up to 180 degrees, we could not say that this thing in the world is a triangle, because this thing in the world *also exists* and therefore (according to the logic of the ontological proof), this real, existing triangle has an extra property ("existence") which makes it somehow "more" than our definition of a triangle which did not include this property. Because of this obvious absurdity, Kant maintains that existence is not a predicate/property of a thing.

Once encapsulated in its own self-presence, only the clarity of that self-presence will do. The thesis of the natural attitude is thus not disrupted or put out of play in Descartes' nightmare, but simply negated and then regained through its mathematization. Descartes retains the belief in the "being out there" of the world, but simply transforms this sense of being in light of the *cogito* — to *be* out there is to be clear and distinct. All of the ambiguous ways in which things were *experienced* to be out there that cannot withstand his methodical doubt are suspended in the face of this loud, brazen voice of clarity.

Only those ways of the Earth able to "object" remain *and even then*, objection often simply increases the violence. Since the subject declares for itself the conditions under which objections will be heard (i.e., a clarity and distinctness *produced by severance*), all that can "object" is that which presents itself as clear and distinct.

Again, all of this is a perfect fit for the metaphor used by Immanuel Kant of Reason being a judge which compels witnesses to answer questions that he himself has posed.[10] Phenomenology begins by "putting out of play" our tendency to *assume* such a principle as that to which experience must submit in order to be admitted into the boundaries that inquiry has drawn for itself.

It puts out of play our tendency, in inquiry, towards univocal foundations, i.e., towards causes or explanations or suppositions or declarations that will *found* this experience in something not present in the delicate contingencies and contours of the experience itself.

It puts out of play the desire, in inquiry, to finally and definitively and unambiguously and univocally *name* our experience of the world once and for all. It puts out of play an image of understanding as domination, control and prediction.

Correlatively, it puts out of play our belief in the univocal, non-contradictory *being* of the Earth.

[*all of this can be said of
phenomenology only in its*

---

10   Immanuel Kant (1964). p. 20.

> *founding gesture. The eidetic reduction of experience to its fixedness inverts this gesture.* Phenomenology *begins* with refusing "the suppreptitious substitution of a mathematically substructured world of idealities for the only real world, our everyday life world."[11] It begins with refusing. Phenomenology:
>
>> "leaves no room for 'metaphysical' substructurings of being *behind* the being intentionally constituting itself in actual and possible achievements of consciousness."[12]
>
> Any yet, through the eidetic reduction, we have, instead of a world substructured with mathematical idealities, we have a life-world *infrastructured by essences.*]

The act of "putting out of play" this natural attitude that leads to substructuring is the *phenomenological reduction.*

> If we miss the meaning of the reduction, everything is lost. The temptation to misunderstand is almost irresistible.[13]

If we miss the meaning of the reduction, phenomenology becomes lost in quarrels with scepticism, subjectivism, idealism and psychologism,

---

11 Edmund Husserl (1970). p. 48-9.
12 Edmund Husserl (1974). Kant and the idea of transcendental philosophy. *Southwestern Journal of Philosophy.* 5(#3). p. 12.
13 Edmund Husserl (1960). Phenomenology and anthropology. in R. M. Chisholm (ed.), *Realism and the Background of Phenomenology.* Illinois: The Free Press, p. 163.

and it is none of these. It is none of these, not because of peculiar distinguishing features which make its "standpoint" different. It is none of these because it is not a standpoint at all: "we start out from that which *antedates* all standpoints."[14]

Phenomenology is not some version of how we might make Descartes' dream come true — how we might make a defensible, foundational stand in relation to the world and our Being-in-the-world. It is, rather, an attempt to express how things *already stand* with us in the world, how we are *already* right in the middle of things. It wishes to re-enliven the objectifications and boundaries with which we are *already living* (that which "antedates all standpoints" is not some pristine, untouched "experience," but the full complexity of our lives, with all its hidden, undeciphered signs[15]) and win back the surging, delicate life that both enforms such boundaries and slips between the cracks, frustrating the desire for *stasis*, foreclosure and clarity. It does not see (except through the cowardice of the eidetic reduction to essences) such fluidity and ambiguity as an error, as a lack of vigilant clarification, but as an indication that we "have continuously anew the *living truth from the living source.*"[16]

In order to free us to give a voice to how we already stand, to voice life as it is actually lived, Husserl formulates the phenomenological reduction as a way of loosening the hold of the thesis of the natural attitude. This is at once a loosening of the hold of our belief in the univocal character of the world and our Being-in-the-world, waking us from this dream that our lives and the lives of our children and the boundless generativity of the Earth's gifts are best understood under the vigilant stare of the clear and distinct "I am" and the methods it can wield.

It loosens, therefore, the hold of our belief that understanding or being connected or being in touch with the Earth and our Earthly lives requires some special method or procedure that somehow achieves a

---

14   Edmund Husserl (1969). p. 88.
15   But see, for example David W. Jardine (1988b).
16   Edmund Husserl (1969a). *Formal and Transcendental Logic*. The Hauge: Martinus Nijhoff, p. 279.

relationship between two "things' (subject and object) deemed initially unrelated.

> [Phenomenology finally loosens the grip of the *epistemological problematic* of the relation between subject and object and all the hysterical solutions that erupt from this, including the bizarre and paranoic version of "constructivism" that somehow the believe that the world is chaotic without us. It was left to Heidegger and Gadamer to fulfill this promise.]

By unearthing the *intentionality of experience* (this notion goes back through Franz Brentano[17] to St. Thomas Aquinas), the reduction shows that experience is always already an experience *of* something which is *not* me.

> [All of this business about intentionality is what teacher narrative tends to miss about phenomenological research. Phenomenology does not place the individual experiencing subject at the core of things in isolation from the concatenations of the world-horizon. It does not mean subjective *intent*, but how any experience breaks out beyond subjectivity to an object, a topic, a world, a language beyond the intent of the subject but implied, implicated, related, hidden, in the experience that might seem simply one's own.]

We are always and already connected to things, to the Earth, to each other, to our children, albeit in ambiguous and multivocal ways. Thus, in response to Descartes' methodical doubt, Husserl's own *Cartesian Meditations* shows that even if I methodically doubt everything that can be doubted and I am reduced solely to "my experience," that experience is always an experience *of* something.

---

17 Franz Brentanno (1971). *Psychology from an Empirical Standpoint*. London: Routledge and Kegan Paul.

> [This is the portal for teacher narrative and autobiography. To the extent that my "personal practical knowledge" includes a knowledge *of children,* that *of which* I have knowledge is suddenly "beyond me," a "transcendence within [the] immanence"[18] of my experience. I find myself encountered by worlds of relations and must try not to withdraw from the infinite ensuing dances that are invited by such encounters. Sometimes I'm overwhelmed and must withdraw for a time, to find my measure again. I find that writing helps.]

Thus, even in the logic of Cartesianism, if I search my present experience I find, "in" that experience, this pine tree outside my window as an object *of* that experience.

What is needed is not a method to achieve a relation to this thing, but a delicate way of re-collecting those relationships in which we already dwell, which already pertain.

Through the revealing of the intentionality of experience, the phenomenological reduction sets us into relation with the thesis of the natural attitude such that "we make no change in our convictions."[19] We do not go from believing that the world has its being "out there" to denying this thesis. The reduction is not a matter of "a transformation of thesis into antithesis, of positive into negative"[20] but a suspension of all position-taking about the being of the entities which transcend our experience of them, our life with them — phenomenology wishes to "see" what our place, our life, our lived-experience (of the world) *is*. We are to faithfully document the interweaving meanings of our experience-of-the-world just as it gives itself to be, without (as the thesis of the natural attitude would require) asking of that experience whether it is or is not indicative of some univocal world which has its being "out there."

---

18   Edmund Husserl (1969). p. 178.
19   Edmund Husserl (1969), p. 108.
20   Edmund Husserl (1969). p. 108.

This is why phenomenology can be so very annoying to those who remain within the non-phenomenological orientation, because it refuses to ask or answer the very questions that give that orientation its impetus.

Where does the phenomenological reduction take us, then? Well, it doesn't take us anywhere. It doesn't move us from our actual lives on this Earth to some other-worldly realm; it does not wish to pretend, as science must, that it knows nothing of (i.e., has no relation to) life until its methods are enacted (the Cartesian pretence of "starting anew" with no debts); it doesn't desire to substitute idealized modes of rationality, discourse and action for the actual ways in which our lives are conducted. It doesn't take us away from the world outside into the "moist gastric intimacy"[21] of subjectivity and "personal experience". It doesn't move from considering objects to considering "experiences" in some psychological sense since it has shown that all experience is intentional and therefore, part of the work of explicating "experience" is explicating the meaning of that *of which* we have an experience, the meanings in which our experience is interwoven.

This point is essential because some versions of phenomenology often lose this ambiguous "objectivity-as-experienced," pulling back too far into singular " personal voices," reducing that which is experienced to the additive sum of "experience*s*." Phenomenology often becomes a form of impotent self-enamourment with one's own "inner experiences," (or the collected and "shared" [as the buzz word goes] experiences of oneself and others) forgetting that that experience has a living "intentional object" which *prevents* such (individual or collective) self-enamourment. This enamourment can, in some cases, turn phenomenology into a vicious democratization of Cartesianism where everybody has their own experience and the integrity of that which is experienced, say this pine tree, is violated in favour of a multiplicity of *human* voices. The thing itself falls silent, silenced now not by the singular and oppressive voice of logico-mathematical clarity (univocity), but by the collective babble of experiencers each cocooned in themselves (equivocity).

---

21 Jean-Paul Sartre (1970). p. 4.

CHAPTER NINE

> [Part of the reason for such Democratic Cartesianism is that through the revealing of multiplicity and ambiguity and differences and controversies and dilemmas in our experiences of the world, we cannot let ourselves believe that *the world* is multivocal and ambiguous and different and controversial and full of lemmas — that *the world* is full of multiple daimons, voices, that haunt here and here, this and this. In the face of the revealing of such multiplicity and difference, we tend to locate the differences "back" *in us* and thus save the world in its (presumed) univocity. We *presume* that the world is One.]

Part of the work of phenomenology must include explicating how the text of my experience interweaves with the texture of human life as a whole, and how this happens in such a way that I do not reduce the texture of human life to "my experience" and, at the same time, I do not reduce "my experience" to simply a silenceable instance of "human life in general." This is the bizarre confusion of "psychological immanence."

> The moist gastric intimacy of one's own experience is always bursting out, veering out into the world, finding itself there, experiencing this warm sun which is not an *experience* but rather *something experienced*. This "something that is experienced" is a peculiar thing. It is not an *object* cut off from experience and the experiencer. But it is not an *experience*. It retains an irreducible integrity. It has an "otherness." It is not reducible to *me* (or *us*). And it isn't simply the attaching of these two things together. Phenomenology breaks out of these vicious options, both extremes of which rely on the natural attitude. This pine tree outside my window is deeply interlaced with me, with my breath, with my thoughts and words, with the moisture

> of my eyes, squinting as they must in the sunlight backlit yellowgreen standing out from the bluegreen spruces. But it is not experienced this way as an object that stands over and against me as separate and cut off. But again, it is not *me*.]

And here is the rub that is so hard to take: phenomenology will pursue this epistemological puzzle no further than to allow this resonant and vibrant and irresolvable tension *to be as it is*, as problematic or unproblematic as it is actually experienced to be over the course of each of our lives.

It is thus and to this extent that phenomenology is akin to ecology which will also leave alone this irresolvable paradox that this pine tree is part of us and apart from us. It is not blessed by human dominion, yet it is intimately part of me, part of my breath and bone.

In this way — in living with this tension of experience / experienced — phenomenology does not provide us with a new standpoint, new methods, a new framework, a different model, an alternate theory, another perspective, a better picture, a clearer view. Things are *exactly* what they were before *except for this one blessed difference* — the intramundane desire to redeem the world through the wielding of the weapons of clarity, objectivity, truth, univocity, has been "let go." The desire to resolve this ambiguous tension — a tension that Descartes despised so much — has been forfeited. It leaves us right where we always already were, with the actual play and interplays of life, with all its difficulty and ambiguity, unredeemed or, better, not in need of redemption.

> [and yet all of this crashes down around the eidetic reduction which some see as the redemptive gesture of phenomenology].

Humanity is not the redemption of the Earth. We may be the moment that the Earth "comes to," but we climb too easily up into our heads, draining consciousness out of the bowels and out of the muscle ache breath short here, full of the very chickadee giggle chirp song changed for spring.

CHAPTER TEN

Textus: perhaps the hermeneutic interest in text is feminine. Perhaps hermeneutics is "the feminine science."[1]

Text as full of generative power. Interpretation as the spinning of a good yarn.

But there is also the interest in *inscription* — leaving marks by pissing on posts, sniff left there like the helplessness of the written word, *open* to interpretation.

Lyotard's "point" about the pen prick on white paper and writing as masculine urge to inscribe.

But then the blood trails of Ellen Bass, leaving a history of yourself again and again and again.

Writing as production. Blood trails as signs of reproduction.

> [What is the relation between the trace of writing *itself* and the traces we find *in* language itself?]

Consider:

Gary Snyder: If you travel over central Alaska, there is virtually no trace of human habitation. Yet there have been people living there for 8000 years. One way to look at it — the way nineteenth century Europeans would have looked at it — was to say that these people had absolutely nothing going for themselves. They haven't even left a trace. From another standpoint. . .the fact that they could live there for 8000 years and have a very complex and rich intellectual and spiritual culture and yet not leave a trace is a considerable monument.

---

1 Anne Davies (1989). Freedom within bounds. *Applying Research to the Classroom,* 7(3), p. 2. Davies is citing David G. Smith.

> *Catherine Ingram:* Do you know the Chuang Tzu poem called "When Life was Full There Was No History"?
> *Snyder:* Exactly, yes. Same kind of thing. We have to re-think what that means.[2]

> *Consider:* writing that leaves no trace, writing that blends in to the landscape and its indigenous tracings and passes away again without notice, infinite in its effects, but all of its effects *proper* to its place.
>
>> If people acknowledge their membership in the fabric of the whole, acknowledge that they are part of the habitat, part of the network, part of the web, and feel that the welfare of the web is their welfare, and their welfare is the welfare of the web — in other words, not be mindlessly but mindfully one with the whole — that is an extraordinary thing right there, and it dumps the cartridges out of the weapons.[3]

Consider writing as a form of trace that begins with an acknowledgement of its responsibility to that of which it speaks. Part of this responsibility is the *inability* of writing to encompass its topic. (This is its Phaedrus-helplessness and the interpretive refusal to declare [itself]).

The portal of writing is found in its moment of weakness, where it breaks, down into the belly laugh of its topic.

Interpretive-Interpretable writing is full of weakness and frailties, open-textured, leaving room for the new eruption of meaning, leaving room for the new, leaving room in anticipation of the agonizing, re-generative and fucking dangerous arrival of the young.

This courage to not see the arrival of the young as a matter of self-denial but the affirmation of a broader, more ecologically sane sense of self.

---

2   Gary Snyder (1990). In conversation with Catherine Ingram. In Catherine Ingram (1990). *In the Footsteps of Gandhi.* p. 237-8.
3   Gary Snyder (1990). p. 238-9.

CHAPTER ELEVEN

> In the dreadful self-isolation of the Church, that soul-fortress towering over the dark abysms of the bestial/mortal/World/Hell, for St. Francis to cry out "Sister sparrow, brother wolf!" was a great thing. But for the Buddha to be a jackal or a monkey was no big deal. And for the people that Civilization calls "primitive," "savage," or "undeveloped," including young children, the continuity, interdependence, and community of all life, all forms of being on the earth, is a lived fact, made conscious in narrative (myth, ritual, fiction). This continuity of existence, neither benevolent nor cruel itself, is fundamental to whatever morality may be built upon it. Only Civilization builds its morality by denying its foundation.
> By climbing up into his head and shutting out every voice but his own, "Civilized Man" has gone deaf. He can't hear the wolf calling him brother — not Master, but brother. He can't hear the earth calling him child — not Father, but son. He hears only his own words making up the world. He can't hear the animals, they have nothing to say. Children babble, and have to be taught how to climb up into their heads and shut the doors of perception. No use teaching women at all, they talk all the time, of course, but never say anything. This is the myth of Civilization, embodied in the monotheisms which assign a soul to Man alone.[1]

The war of paradigms between interpretive work and more traditional, quantitatively based work is a religious war. The metaphor of war does not befit what we wish. It does befit what we face: a facade of angry dominion over the Earth and a fear of the lividness and tenuousness and fragility and heat of a life actually lived.

A bloated image of ourselves as in-dependent, without dependence, without dependents.

A fear of "it depends."

This fear is the root of essentialism and essentialist pedagogy.

> [When phenomenology speaks about pedagogy, it implicitly recommends its own way of speaking as "good speech."
> When interpretation speaks about pedagogy, it doesn't

---

[1] Ursula Le Guin (1987). p. 11.

know *who* to listen to: how should we speak to speak well? phenomenologically? mythically? poetically? intimately and personally? high-handed and fully of theory? like a Piagetian? hot and sexual? cold, mathematical, precise? with the odd disciplines of method? describing evoking telling a story about explaining mathematizing full of footnotes rich and scholarly? full of the wild blood muses head cracked open ooze? Interpretation does recommend itself, but what it thereby recommends is standing in the middle of the wild rush of competing voices and singing, loud, clear, in harmonies or in full mindfulness of discord, sometime revery, sometimes phenomenology, sometimes the clear cascades of scholarship and the accuracies of text, sometimes a tale about a tender moment, sometimes "the fecundity of the caress," sometimes a shriek of pain from just this life. It recommends mindfulness in the midst of multiplicity. It recommends not falling prey to the lures of fundamentalism, *including* the essentialism and normativity of phenomenology. Perhaps I should say *especially* the essentialism and normativity of phenomenology — *especially,* since these two are close kin and perhaps we expect more sometimes from those closest to us. What is the best way to speak? Such an essentialist question cannot stand the interpretive answer — *it depends*. "It depends" is not immorality nor "situational morality" but the deep ethos, the deep *ecos*, the deep *pedagogy* of *dependents*. The deeply immoral is the ignoring of dependency. A form of speech that recommends itself without qualification is immoral.]

[Books like this one are not always best. Phenomenology is not always called for, and in its loud demand for essence, it cannot hear this call. It depends. If phenomenology recommends itself for a specific task, it must become conversant with the multiplicity of voices each of which have a voice in who gets to decide what tasks are best for it. If it decides of itself, it again recommends that it does not depend.]

This fear is the root of monotheism and its fruits as well.

CHAPTER ELEVEN

[God promised us that we would never die. That deep within us there is a soul which does not depend on this Earth, that has no fleshy countenance.]

[This promise is the deep haunt of objective science. Objective science is borne out of a religion *already* convinced of man's dominion over the Earth (i.e., over the flesh) and a Continent *already* convinced of its moral and cultural dominion over others. Objective science is simply the systematizing and methodologizing of what is already taken for granted.]

It is, in part, a war between, on the one hand, the monotheism and inherent abstractness and "other-worldliness" (unanimalness, in-animism) of mathematics/Christianity/ Platonic Essentialism (and Husserlian, too) and the twirl of the Cartesian logic and, on the other hand, the polytheism and inherently fleshy animism of interpretation / Paganism / Earthy Kindness:

Foundation	Finding/Losing
Christianity	Paganism
Platonic	Earthy
Essences	Kinds
Univocity	Ambiguous Tales Re-told
One	Many
Literalism	Metaphoricity
Bounded/sealed	Porousness
Reprimand	Evocation, Allure
Normativity	Similitude and Resemblance
Proselytizing	Inviting, Seducing
Method	Discipline

Interpretation proceeds out of the belly and the breath and, because of this, it lives in the midst of multiple interdependencies which it cannot fully name. There is no single naming, [*uni voce*], that would name once and for all, not even its own naming. It is not foundationalist or fundamentalist.

Interpretation turns away from the Logic of Cartesianism, not by ignoring it (none of us have that luxury) but by deeply reading this Logic out into its multiple interdependencies, out into its bloodlines and kin.

Interpretation reads Cartesianism as a form of Desire. It reads Cartesianism as *being possessed* by the desire for mastery and ground (Cartesianism cannot utter its own desire because it falsely believes that its founding gesture is not its own *desire* for ground but rather the *denial of all desires*. It takes for first what is in fact second. It does this because what in fact is first is not a ground but a breath iteration, air-gulped at the nicklespittle fear of fleshy demise: the vibrancy of coming and going, Woundagony and *then:* denial of all desires).

Interpretation has no dominion but rather is dominated by the patterns that already pertain *before* and *in spite of* its utterances. Interpretation *depends*. It has *dependents*. Kin.

We are "founded," but not on solid ground but shifting, generative ground.

> [surrounded by many gods that it is eminently sensible to fear, for they are not there just for me. We lose our dominion and at once lose the childish belief that the world is there simply for us]

We are founded in intimate tales, not in clear and distinct knowledge held in hoards.

There is youth in the age of these tales, and wisdom in how each, youth and age, can atrophy in its own way:

> The negative senex is the senex split from its own puer aspect. He has lost his "child." The archetypal core of the complex, now split, loses its inherent tension, its ambivalence. Without the enthusiasm and eros of the son, authority loses its idealism. It aspires to nothing but its own perpetuation, leading but to tyranny and cynicism; *for meaning cannot be sustained by structure and order alone.* Such spirit is one-sided, and one-sidedness is crippling. Being is static, a pleroma that cannot become. Time — euphemistically called 'experience' but more often just the crusted accretions of profane history — becomes a moral virtue and even witness of truth, *'veritas filia temporis'*. The old is always preferred to the new.

CHAPTER ELEVEN

Sexuality without young eros becomes goaty; weakness becomes complaint; creative isolation becomes only paranoid loneliness. Because the complex is unable to catch on and sow seed, it feeds on the growth of other complexes or other people, as for instance the growth of one's own children [telling words for essentialist pedagogy]. Cut off from its own child and fool the complex no longer has anything to tell us. Folly and immaturity are projected on to others [see Immanuel Kant's "overcoming of immaturity" and Descartes' "repudiation of childhood"]. Without folly it has no wisdom, only knowledge — serious, depressing, hoarded in an academic vault or used as power. The integration of personality becomes the subjugation of personality, a unification through dominance, and integrity only a selfsame repetition of firm principle.[2]

There is matter to the patterns that pertain

[But consider:

...a strong bias of the spatio-spiritual grain in favour of domination and division. The tell-tale terms...: mind *over* matter, men *over* women, and consciousness *over* body. The male allies himself with, and defines himself according to, consciousness, and defines consciousness as that which imposes its form on what is *other* than it — matter, matrix, mother. The male, *pater*, imposes the *pure pattern* on the mere stuff, the matter [*mater*]. The male feels he must impose order on the inchoate and the *base,* the *lower* matter. So powerful has been this engrained bias that even after the manufacture of the microscope, a few hundred years ago, observers were convinced that they perceived miniature humans already formed within sperm, the full human within the human sperm, fully-formed horses within horse sperm. They hallucinated. Women were mere incubators and feeders.[3]

"imposes the *pure pattern* (*pater*) on the mere stuff, the matter (*mater*)," Old Story

...God's face over the waters, without form and void.

---

2 James Hillman (1987a). p. 20-21.
3 Bruce Wilshire (1990). p. 259.

> ...Re-told, as the young child in Jean Piaget's genetic epistemology imposes cosmos on the chaos and in-flux of experience.[4]]

The aim of interpretation is to sustain its dependency on this generative, Unsayable "already" in its very act of interpretive saying. It turns away from the pretense to full namings of objectivism and fundamentalism towards hidden consequence, opaque corners and the irresolvably unfinished and unfinishable character of human life.

The "essential character" of, say, pedagogy is always "yet-to-be-decided,"[5] not because of some lack of effort or lack of moral courage, but because children keep coming.

Interpretation is a keeping open and it is a profound form of *weakness*:

> My soul is opened by admitting my weakness and my need, for these needs make me a human creature, dependent in my creatureliness upon the whole of creation. Or, to say it another way: as Tao is "weakness," so the way (Tao) to Tao is through our needs, our continual state of dependency. And we cannot meet these needs ourselves, self-enclosed, tight-lipped. Abandoned child [as the Logic of Cartesianism abandons our kinships with children in favour of knowing/ controlling them as "object"] and abandoned old man [the sadly isolated "I am," full of knowledge but alone] together, in need of nursing *caritas*...find that love for which they long only when control and knowledge and laid away.[6]

[Essence/fundament and its normativity has no room in it, no play in it. Bony tongue cluck seriousness. Language drained of its meat and drool. This is why phenomenology, in the midst of its very strength, can be so humourless, because it cannot admit its weakness and frailty and the tension that comes from the irresolvability of life as it is actually lived, "unfixable" once and for all.]

---

4   Jean Piaget (1971a). *The Construction of Reality in the Child*. New York: Ballantine Books, p. xiv.
5   Hans-Georg Gadamer (1989). p. 112.
6   James Hillman (1987a). p. 40.

"A longing for the complete cessation of tension"[7] — this is the coupling of a death instinct with an instinct for everlasting life, the promise of monotheism providing we can renounce the Flesh and its inherent "tension." It is also the instinct of Romantic Ecologism, longing to be consumed by the Mother. Such Romantic Ecologism is as dangerous as the severances of Cartesian Logic:

> Fantasies of this kind seek to dissolve the tension between the desire for union and the fact of separation, either by imagining an ecstatic and painless reunion with the mother or, on the other hand, by imagining a state of complete self-sufficiency, and by denying any need for others at all. The first line of defense encourages a regressive symbiosis; the second, solipsistic illusions of omnipotence. Neither solves the problem of separation; each merely denies its existence in different ways.[8]

"Neither solves the problem of separation": but also, neither solves the problem of union either. Taken together, neither solves the problem that I am what I am not.

De-pathologized version: that I am what I am not *is not a problem* to be solved. It is my "original face," un-envisaged.

---

7   Christopher Lasch (1979). *The Culture of Narcissism*. New York: W. W. Norton, p. 241.
8   Chistopher Lasch (1979), p. 242.

CHAPTER TWELVE

The saying and the re-saying, the naming and the unnaming, go on,[1]
   ...pouring out of the inexhaustibility of the Unsayable (Whole),
   ...emptying like the issuance of Creation in Meister Eckhart's mystical rumblings[2] There is an undeniable parallel here between this ever-absent issuance in the work of Eckhart and Martin Heidegger's notion of "it gives," and the withdrawing character of Being (See Martin Heidegger [1968]. *What is Called Thinking?* New York: Harper and Row). See also John Caputo (1985). *The Mystical Element in Heidegger's Thought* wherein he compares Eckhart and Heidegger in great detail.
   ...emptiness[3] like the *sunyata* of Buddhist mystical rumblings, possessing no "essence," no self-existence (*svabhava*) (thus the holiness of each thing, each stubborn particular bearing the whole of things, emptying out into what it is not), each entity exquisite, re-newing the whole of things, *livid* in this tension,
   ...genealogies like the Old Testament and the endless lessons passed from lip to lip, groin to groin, to this son and this[4], each one taught to tell and re-tell (genealogies as the heart of Torah, with the specific tales mere interruptions of the deep, livid cascade, breath to breath) (the young child at Bat Mitzvah or Bar Mitzvah required to ingest a piece of Torah, read it

---

1   Hence David Smith's, notion of pedagogy as a mindfulness to the conditions under which life can go on. See David G. Smith (1988). Children and the gods of war. *Journal of Educational Thought.* 22(2A).
2   see Meister Eckhart. (1986). *Meister Eckhart: Teacher and Preacher.* New York: Paulist Press, and (1981). *Meister Eckhart: The Essential Sermons, Commentaries, Treatises and Defense.* New York: Paulist Press.
3   see Kato Bunna (ed.) (1987). *The Threefold Lotus Sutra.* Tokyo: Kosei Publishing Co.
4   See Dahlia Beck (1991). A case of speculative audacity. Presented at the Bergamo Conference on Curriculum Theory and Classroom Practice, Dayton, Ohio, October, 1991.

back out into the flesh of the family and friends, re-reading, re-telling, re-membering the genealogical traces, re-saying what can never be Uttered, these words issued from the Unutterable, living in "the tension between tradition and innovation"⁵ Interpretation arises, as Fishbane suggests, from breakdowns in understanding, not from licentious toying with text, fiddling to see if we get aroused. But the structure of the recovery of understanding, when the "individual talent" (re-)enters into the tradition/text does have the character of a player entering a game in which the game itself "maintains its generative and often determinative hierarchical preeminence" even in the case where the new player may fecundly transform the game itself.)

... repeating the genealogies of the Old Testament is a breathing exercise, a sonorous exercise.⁶ Note that Gadamer uses metaphors of the

---

5   Michael Fishbane (1986). Inner Biblical exigesis: Types and strategies of interpretation in ancient Israel. In G. Hartman & S. Budick, eds. *Midrash and Literature*. New Haven: Yale University Press, p. 29-30.

> For inner biblical exegesis there is no merely literary or theological playfulness. Exegesis arises out of a practical crisis of some sort — the incomprehensibility of a word or a rule, or the failure of the convenantial tradition to engage its audience. There is, then, something of the dynamic of "tradition and individual talent" here. In all cases the "tradition" maintains its generative and often determinative hierarchical preeminence, even as "individual talent"... clarifies or transforms tradition in light of present-day ignorance or other exigencies. (p. 34)

However, even though contemporary "Christian" hermeneutics such as Gadamer's emphasise the "play-like" character of interpretation, such playfulness is not the mood or motivation of exegesis but it *structure*.

6   Christian preachers had to rely, when interpreting scriptures and revealing their hidden meanings, mainly on the ideonic side, the implications of the content of the verse. Jewish preachers could use a total text, hermeneutically discussing not only the meaning of terms and words, but also their sound, the shape of the letters, the vocalization points and their shapes and sounds, the *te'amim* (the musical signs added to the Hebrew words), the *tagin* (the small decorative additions to the letters), the frequency with which words and letters appear in a verse or a chapter, the absence of one of the letters from a biblical portion, the variety and number of divine names included in

CHAPTER TWELVE 131

musicality and sonorousness of language. It is these (unlike the "newspeak" of Orwell's dystopia) that are the songs that dogmatism cannot abide, relying as dogmatism does on an unambiguous text.

> [but still here the eschatological hope (and disappointment) of a Messiah who will *put an end to this* ongoing genealogical agony. Hope of the last days. It may be that the "interpreter [is the] successor of the great prophets,"[7] but what is now prophesized

> the text, the numerical value of letters, words and whole verses, the possible changes of letters (*etbash, temurah*), the new words formed from the initial or final letters of a biblical section (*no-tarikon*), and the countless ways other than ideonic content and meaning by which the scriptures transmit a semiotic message. (Joseph Dan [1986]. Midrash and the dawn of Kabbalah. In George Hartman & S. Budick, eds. (1986). p. 128).

Dan goes on to make an interesting point regarding literalism and dogmatism. He speaks about the necessity in translations to flatten and clarify the text:

> A translator has to choose between all possible interpretations and present one of them, losing in this way the richness, as well as the profundity of the original. The translated text thus conveys a sense of clarity which is completely missing from the original. (p. 129).

> This is one of the reasons why the Roman Catholic Church could develop a set of dogma. Dogmatic thinking must rely upon an unambiguous text. (p. 129).

One could characterize contemporary hermeneutics as an effort, against dogmatism, to read texts into their full ambiguity and thus to read texts *generatively,* out into the open. This is why hermeneutics tends to become focussed on occasion on etymologies and semantic plays and cross-figures.

But the problem of translation remains:

> Here [the translator] must resign himself. He must state clearly how he understands. But since he is always in the position of not really being able to express all the dimensions of his text, he must make a constant renunciation. Every translation that takes its task seriously is at once clearer and flatter than its original. Even if it is a masterly re-creation, it must lack some of the overtones that vibrate in the original. (Hans-Georg Gadamer [1989], p. 386).

7   James Kugel. (1986). Two introductions to Midrash. In Geoffery Hartmann, ed. *Midrash and Literature.* New Haven: Yale University Press, p. 84.

in contemporary hermeneutics is that prophecy will go on. Hermeneutics is not eschatological. It lives neither for the Second Coming nor the First — the time when interpretation and genealogy will end and our hearts can rest. It does not desire this. Hermeneutics as the restlessness of the breath.[8] Gadamer's hermeneutics seems to suggest an image of hermeneutics *without such foundationalism:* without "author(ity)" but fully and solely *in* the cascade of historicity. Gadamer thus suggests a notion of "the whole" and the problematic relation of this "whole" to the part or piece of text (not only *this portion* of a given text in relation to the whole of the text, but *this* reading of this portion brought to bear upon *this*, in relation to the whole of the text, the whole of the cascade of readings and the whole of those things upon which this text has been brought to bear), but it is debatable the extent to which this "whole" is still conceived as constituting a "unity and univocality."

> Better, for hermeneutics, this interruption of the genealogies *happens* all the time, in the most insignificant of events — "the gods" are *always* afoot, "*this* and *this*,"[9] *without* the comfort and assurances of original or eventual "unity and univocality" — messages everywhere, each from different, conflicting, inter-related, multiple voices:

---

8   It is difficult to determine the extent to which hermeneutics still lives in the belief of the "unity of one meaning" (Edmund Husserl, [1970], p. 111):

Midrash:

> the very act of exegesis celebrates the canon, the unity and univocality of all Scripture, and allows it to speak directly to Judaism in its present situation. (James Kugel [1986]. p. 78)

> ...in the midrashic view divine words have an existence independent of circumstance and immediate intention, that, in short, a text is a text, and whatever hidden meaning one is able to reveal in it through "searching" simply *is there,* part of the divine plan. (p. 79)

Of course, the unity and univocality of Scripture rests against the unity and univocality of God himself: meaning may be "hidden deep in the heart of the text" (Joseph Dan [1986]. p. 128) but it *is there.*

9   Bronwen Wallace (1987). p. 111.

> *Kai enthautha,* "even there," at the stove, in that ordinary place where every thing and every condition, each deed and thought is intimate and commonplace, that is, familiar, "even there" in the sphere of the familiar, *einai theous,* it is the case that "the gods themselves are present."[10]

...emptying out into the harmonies of its Earthly place of Ecological rumblings, belonging just here and no where else, but having such belonging utterable only in ongoing genealogical tales of the Earth that transfigure and compost in the re-telling, full of kind-ness and generosity/generativity of this place, not utopian (no-place), normative (law rather than kind) essences.

A Refusal of the Platonic Essentialist question "What is Pedagogy?" as itself an anti-pedagogic question.

Pedagogy requires that we give up the hope and disappointment of essence (the hope and disappointment of self-possession, the hope and disappointment of dreams of immortality, the hope and disappointment of the "I am" uttered without dependents — a soul free of its fleshy kin).

> [Gadamer's "yet-to-be-decided" is still caught within the spell of "desired or feared."[11] "Desire" and "fear" as colons. So compare Trungpa's suggestion that we must give up hope[12] to VanManen's notion of pedagogic hope.[13]]

Hope as the arousal of the Will to Power. Disappointment as the feeling of resistance. Neitzsche's fearful finalizing of the Desire for foundations: once that Desire is loosed from its objectifications, we are left with just that Desire Desiring its own perpetuation, Desiring to feel its Desire.

---

10   Martin Heidegger (1977a). Letter on humanism. In *Basic Writings.* New York: Harper and Row, p. 234.
11   Hans-Georg Gadamer (1989).
12   Chogyam Trungpa (1991). Trikaya and Hopelessness. In *Crazy Wisdom.* San Francisco: Shambala Press.
13   Max VanManen. On pedagogic hope. *Phenomenology + Pedagogy.* 1(2).

Neitzsche finally freed the desire and will to power from its slavish attachment to the "ground" that it created, from its "objectifications." The desire in philosophy, to discover a foundation, to respond to the question "what is the nature of reality, what is first, what is most real, most basic, what is the ground?" are all manifestations of the will to dominate that ground, to possess it, to "have" it. God, substance, sense data, fact, transcendental consciousness — none of these are names for entities determined in themselves of which we have simply become conscious. They are, rather, determined by the will to power, determined by the need to give ourselves a ground of which we then forget our creation.

> . . .it is the highest degrees of performance that awaken belief in the "truth," that is to say reality of the object. The feeling of strength, of struggle, of resistance convinces us that there is something that is here being resisted.[14]
>
> . . .the criterion of truth resides in the enhancement of the feeling of power.[15]

> Will to truth is a making firm, a making true and durable, an abolition of the false character of things, a reinterpretation of it into beings. "Truth" is therefore not something there, that might be found or discovered — but something that must be created and that gives a name to a process, or rather to a will to overcome that has in itself no end — introducing truth, as a *processus in infinitum*, an active determining — not a becoming-conscious of something that is in itself firm and determined. It is a word for the will to power. Man projects his drive to truth, his "goal" in a certain sense, outside himself as a world that has being, as a metaphysical world, as a 'thing-in-itself', as a world already in existence. His needs as creator invent the world upon which he works, anticipate it; this anticipation (this 'belief' in truth) is his support.[16]

> The will to power can manifest itself only against resistances; therefore it seeks that which resists it. Appropriation and assimilation are above all a desire to overwhelm, a forming, shaping and reshaping, until at length that which has been overwhelmed has entirely gone over into the power domain of the aggressor and has increased the same.[17]

---

14   F. Nietzsche (1975). *The Will to Power*. New York: Random House, p. 290.
15   F. Nietzsche (1975). p. 290.
16   F. Nietzsche (1975). p. 298-9.
17   F. Nietzsche (1975). p. 346.

CHAPTER TWELVE 135

Interpretation does not proceed out of the desires emanating from already having climbed up into our heads and already having become "visionaries,"[18] bent on bending the Earth to our will, with the world before us as a display, a picture[19] purveyed with the omniscience of God, or the (so it hopes) eventual control prediction and manipulation of the methods of objective science (objective science as eschatological), or the (so it pretends) essentializing and thus eventually encompassing

18   Once cultures are no longer prefigured visually — as objects theatres, texts — it becomes possible to think of a cultural poetics that is an interplay of voices, of positioned utterances. In a discursive rather than a visual paradigm, the dominant metaphors...shift away from the observing eye towards expressive speech and gesture. (James Clifford [1986]. p. 12)

Once the visual metaphor is released, the whole idea of reality as a picture with pieces to be filled in (and therefore the fantasy of having the whole *given*), is also released. Also released is the idea of cumulative knowledge, even the Husserlian notion of the cumulative character of phenomenological "visions" (Husserl always encouraged us towards "seeing"). With the slippage of such cumulative visions, the *Wesenschau* is also released.

There are links buried here between the visionary, images, iconoclasm, Nicea and the normative reprimand, all tied up with images of purity:

The metaphor under which the critic operated was that of a preacher-moralist...who oversees, who separates the impure from the . . .transcendent zone. This zone, or consecrated site, marked that point where the church had collapsed into the bank: the silent, sanctified museum where the contemplation of the optical, freed of all kitschy imagery, recalls the silent prayer of the iconophobic Protestants of the country's past. The high cultural had to be separated from the everyday, and image from language, artist from critic, the empiricist-optical-formal-pure experience from the impure jabber of talk. Abstraction was the cardinal rule, and it continued the attachment to a teleological program of reduced conventions as it strove towards metaphysical purity.

Robert Morris (1989). Words and images in modernism and postmodernism. *Critical Inquiry. 15* (Winter, 1989), p. 343.

19   Martin Heidegger (1977b). The age of the world picture. In *the Question Concerning Technology*. New York: Harper and Row.

reflectiveness of a transcendental subject (essentialist phenomenology as eschatological).

> [Even the turn of phenomenology to "lived-experience" can too easily place our lives before us in an array to be meticulously described "up" into its essence, away from the contingencies of the flesh]

> ["flesh" as phenomenological *topic*, not phenomenological *resource*]

> Phenomenology need not = essentialism.

But it is so haunted, age-old and German and Greek and Christian, full of precedents of a tendency towards essence, "climbing up into our heads" — the realm of the transcendental subject, the realm of Heaven, the realm of Platonic Ideas, all disembowelled from the flesh and its unavoidable generativity and de-generativity. Perfect Ideas do not need renewal. The flesh needs renewal. Essences are not renewed by instances. Kinds need kin.

> [But for kind to need kin, we can no longer deny this "relentless clock of meat" Allen Ginsberg, somewhere].

CHAPTER THIRTEEN

Interpretation breeds in an irresolvably generative world that pulses beyond the single voice (univocity/monotone), a world full of kindness and kin who keep coming, full of willing and wanting beyond my own.

Animals.

Trees.

The breath of my son, longing to be told the tales.

Cold snow wind pitched pines breath long hard deep steep cliff climb body heat.

Things *happen*[1] in such a world.

And the multiplicity of such happenings does not gain its integrity or Reason from some singular exogenous source or from some singular indigenous source.

> [such happenstances can never be directly and fully named because they *just happen,* and no essence names such a happenstance. We can spin out into the webs of what each is *like.* We can greet each happenstance as *kin,* but we can never utter That (Whole of things) out of which just this thing erupts "in kind."

> [this is why Hannah Arendt places the heart of pedagogy in the *fact* of natality,[2] the fact that children are *borne* into the world].

> [This is the irresolvable tension of pedagogy:

---

1   see Joel Weinsheimer (1985). *Gadamer's Hermeneutics.* New Haven: Yale University Press, p. 7 for the notion of "hap." Wonderful to compare this to James Hillman's (1987a) notion of "opportunity."
2   Hannah Arendt (1969). *Between Past and Future.* New York: Penguin Books, p. 177.

> The child requires special protection and care so that nothing destructive may happen to him from the world. But the world, too, needs protection to keep it from being overrun and destroyed by the onslaught of the new that bursts upon it with each new generation.[3]

>> [A love of generativity cannot become pedophilic: we must equally love the conditions under which generativity is possible. A love of the conditions under which generativity is possible cannot become androphilic: we must equally love the agonizing transformation of the old, the *changing of those conditions.* Loving one without the other creates "monstrous states of seige."[4]

> Interpretation stands between these two numb extremities — Hermes standing between, swinging gate-keeper (Hermes as the tightening and loosening of the *tanden* in Pranayama Yoga.[5])]

Generativity, generosity, this gift — this child, my child — just happens and all we can do is (at)tend to the conditions of its happening.

"The conditions under which life can go on."[6] The conditions can only be known "in kind." We never can know these conditions exactly and essentially because these conditions are not *some thing* exact (A=A) but a whirl of interlacing possibilities and parallels and implications and innuendos and evocations and suggestions and half-truths and hints: things, beings, are moving and living in this interlacing whirl, coming and going, always *right in the midst of being different in kind, being transformed.* We

---

3   Hannah Arendt (1969). p. 186.
4   David G. Smith (1988).
5   See Katsuki Sekdia (1976). *Zen Training: Methods and Philosophy.* New York: Weatherhill, especially chapter 7. See also Andre van Lysebeth (1983). *Pranayama: The Yoga of Breathing.* London: Unwin Paperbacks.
6   David G. Smith (1988).

CHAPTER THIRTEEN 139

can learn the ways of the Earth but these ways are not univocal and set before us, because, in being brought to bear on *"this* and *this,"*[7] *it depends.*

> [These conditions always have to be intimately known *in place.* Their *full* truth is always only *in place,* they are *real* only ever *in place.* This is why Heidegger[8] uses the image of *alethia* to describe truth: it is always an uncon-cealing, but, as such, it always also conceals. Seeing the truth from here always requires *not* seeing it from there (the truth is what it is not) — truth thus always has a darkness, a blindness, a *lethalness* to it, and an tensive need to *go on,* unable to fully consume what is yet-to-come. It is not simply *presence:* somehow having the whole matter *given.*

Its "truth" is always veiled: The truth is thus pursued when we pursue the ongoing character of its veiling and unveiling.

> [This may be Heidegger's and Gadamer's *eventful character of truth*]

> ...that we live within order and that this order is both greater and more intricate than we can know. The difficulty of our predicament: Though we cannot produce a complete or even adequate description of this order, severe penalties are in store for us if we presume upon it or violate it.[9]

Unlike monotheism, there is no urge to declare that there is only one true Logos and that all signs point this way (As Descartes had the world point to the self-presence of the "I am" or Wendell Berry might, as, I presume, a Christian, have this order he describes above suggest an Orderer.) Such monotony denies the power of the word, the power of speech, the power of evocation, the power of instruction to the "pan[daemon]ium of images"[10] (Daimons everywhere — an *anima mundi*) that a living world

---

7   Bronwen Wallace (1987). p. 111.
8   Martin Hediegger (1968).
9   Wendell Berry (1987b). Two economies. In *Home Economics.* San Francisco: North Point Press, p. 55.
10 James Hillman (1983). Chapter Two.

invites — the fecundity of this breath, and this, quick inhale at the sudden scatter of nightbirds full moon howl.

The centre of such a pandemonium is empty. Each supposedly self-existent thing empties out into its interdependencies (just as each supposedly self-existent text/sign empties out into interpretive webs of interdependencies) *and I* (this supposedly self-reliant "I" who lusts to emulate the imagined self-reliance of essences by having an eternal, UnEarthly soul), *I am one of them.*

We cannot say what some thing (text/sign) essentially *is,* because it *is* what it *is not* (so it is not just that we can never describe/understand/know the totality of things but we somehow *can* describe/understand/know individual things):

> To say *that a thing is not itself* means that, while continuing to be itself, it is in the home-ground of everything else. Figuratively speaking, its roots reach across into the ground of all other things and help to hold them up and keep them standing. It serves as a constitutive element of their being so that they can be what they are, and thus provides an ingredient of their being. *That a thing is itself* means that all other things, while continuing to be themselves, are in the home-ground of that thing; that precisely when a thing is on its own home-ground, everything else is there too; that the roots of every thing spread across into its home-ground. This way that everything has being on the home-ground of everything else, without ceasing to be its own home-ground, means that the being of each thing is held up, kept standing, and made to be what it is by means of the being of all other things; or, put the other way around, each thing holds up the being of every other thing, keeps it standing, and makes it what it is.[11]

I *am* of the Earth.

> [This whole passage must also be read as occurring *over time* — each Jewel grows and breeds and falls and decays, and in each sliver of time, in each sliver of its passing, *the whole thing must be re-read all over again.* Children are a sign of such comings and goings.]

> [None of us will be the same after this reading, after this breath. Essence as a desire for death, for a redeeming *ending.*

---

11   Nishitani Keiji. (1982). p. 149.

CHAPTER THIRTEEN   141

Children as the frustration of essence, but a frustration still lovingly held in kind. "All the children are wild," but this is not the chaos feared by the one True Logos].

The Earth of breath and belly, (below the severed head, blinking, *thinking* that it is) is an *anima mundi* — a *living* web, fully of wanting and willing beyond my own wanting and willing — with no pervading mono-logic that would set it all straight and save us from the crashing cascade of a life actually lived and breathed and walked.

[This paper from which you are reading does not simply
announce itself,
announce what it "is."
It is not exquisitely this piece of paper because it requires nothing but itself in order to exist; it is not a *substance* in the Scholastic sense. Rather, it is what it is because it is what it is not
— it announces sun and sky and earth and water and trees and loggers and the meals they eat and chainsaws and gasoline and pulp and the dioxin produced by the bleaching of this paper and the effluent and the poisoned fish near pulp mills, and the cancer and the pain and the death and the sorrow and the tears and the Earth and the trees growing up out of it, full of sun and sky and earth and water. It announces all things without exception. This piece of paper, in all its uniqueness and irreplaceability, requires
everything else
in order to exist.
Pulling out this piece of paper tugs at the fabric of all things without exception. Thus, to paraphrase
Nishitani Keiji[12],
the fact that this stubbornly particular piece of paper is just this paper is a fact in such a way as to involve at the same time the deliverance of
all things in their original, Earthly countenance and inter-dependency.
And this deliverance is
a deliverance *in kind:* there is a Dharma to such belonging-together of all things.

This is why it makes a literally humiliating sort of sense to say that if this particular piece of paper did not exist,

---

12   Nishitani Keiji (1982). p. 156.

nothing would exist,

for with the non-existence of this paper, a constitutive element of all other things would be missing such that none of those things would *be* what they now are *with* the existence of this paper — without this piece of paper,

everything would be changed.

This is also why there is a peculiar
Dis   ori   e   n   t   a
tion
involved in suddenly realizing that *any* object, even the most trivial of things, is in the center of this inter-dependency, with all things ordered around it. There is nothing special about this particular piece of paper *and* it is the absolute center of all things without exception.

Re-citation:

> *"the center is everywhere.*
> Each and every thing
> becomes the center
> of all things
> and, in that sense, becomes an absolute
> center. This is the absolute uniqueness of things,
> their reality."[13]

Re-membered:

> That a thing *is* — its absolute autonomy — comes about only in unison with the subordination *of* all other things. It comes about only. . .where the being of all other things, while remaining to the very end the being that it is, is emptied out. Moreover, this means that the autonomy of this one thing is only constituted through a subordination *to* all other things. Its autonomy comes about only on

---

13   Nishitani Keiji (1982). p. 146.

a standpoint from which it makes all other things to be what they are, and in so doing is emptied of its own being.[14]

In short, and against the Scholastic notion of "substance" (where a substance is something that needs nothing except itself in order to exist) we have a simple, ecologically sane insight: every entity needs *everything else* in order to exist.

This is not a metaphysical insight. It is a physical insight, an insight of the flesh. It cannot be known only in the head, for it is the very insight that the head resists. Edmund Husserl is right when he suggests that transcendental experience — that heady realm — cannot easily imagine its own passing away.

The body feels this resistance as fear for its own injury, but such fear comes and goes or the body cannot function. The head makes this into the metaphysics of self-identity and self-existence.

---

14   Nishitani Keiji (1982). p. 148.

CHAPTER FOURTEEN

Interpretive work flies in the face of centration, foundation, singularity, foreclosing authority, definiteness, finality, essentialism. It acts with a certain wildness, a certain anarchy that is deeply laced into the entrails of the Earth, full of heat and blood, sexual, physical, moving and momentary, deeply fearful of fundamentalism.

> [We must haunt the woods with the deer's blood, and stay out of sight, having learned to well the consequences in North American/European culture of being caught out in the open, loving the Earth, howling at the Moon and pulsing with the smell of wildness: "interpretive research" must be done outside of the boundaries of "Civilization":
>
>> "'Civilized' man has gone deaf. This is the myth of Civilization, embodied in the monotheisms which assign a soul to Man alone."[1]
>
> Interpretation breeds the very paganism and wilfulness that Christianity despises.
>> Hermes' Pagan Heart.
>>> "Pagan" has come to mean so very little. The word's roots are far different. "Pagan" comes from the Latin *paganus,* which means a country-dweller (*paganus* is derived from *pagus,* Latin for rural district). Likewise, "heathen" originally meant someone who lived on the heaths. After Christianity won its victory over the older polytheistic religions, often the last people to be converted were those who lived in the unpopulated rural areas, the Pagans and the Heathens.[2]
>>>> [Consider the *urban(e)* character of much philosophizing/theorizing, losing as they often do

---

1 Ursula LeGuin (1987). p. 11.
2 Margot Adler (1989). The juice and the mystery. In Judith Plant (1989). *Healing the Wounds.* Toronto: Between the Lines Press, p. 152.

> a sense of the inviolable Earthen-physical sources of human life.³ It be life up on the hills of Rome, whereas sub-urban is below them.]

Interpretive work breeds against the will of a desire for a "unity of one true meaning." This new one that comes to meet us has something of its own to tell us about our kind, a whisper beyond our longing to tell it about its essence. Essentialism makes the mutterings of kind inaudible.

3   What we call the modern world is not necessarily, and not often, the real world, and there is no virtue in being up-to-date in it. It is a false world, based upon economies and values and desires that are fantastical — a world in which millions of people have lost any idea of the materials, the disciplines, the restraints, and the work necessary to support human life, and have thus become dangerous to their own lives and to the possibility of life. The job now is to get back to that perennial and substantial world in which we really do live, in which the foundations of our life will become visible to us, and in which we can accept our responsibilities again within the conditions of necessity and mystery.

>   Wendell Berry (1983). *Standing by Words*. San Francisco: North Point Press, p. 13.

What is the real work? I think that it is important, first of all, because it is good to work. And that all of us will come back again to hoe in the ground, or gather wild potato bulbs with digging sticks, or skin a pole, or scrape a hive — we're never going to get away from that. We've been living in a dream that we're going to get away from it, that we won't have to do it again. Put that out of our minds. We'll always have to do that work. It might be stapling papers, it might be typing in an office. But we're never going to get away from that work, on one level or another. So that's real. The real work is what we really do. And what our lives are. And if we can live the work we have to do, knowing that we are real, and that it's real, and that the world is real, then it becomes right. And that's the *real work:* to make the world as real as it is, and to find ourselves as real as we are within it." (Gary Snyder [1980]. p. 81-2).

We live in a world that is fully alive, full, not of lifeless objects and objective mechanisms, but of voices and signs and intent, living, fleshy *kinds*[4] to which each case adds an irreplaceable, fecund *difference*.[5]

---

4   See Jean Piaget's (1965) semi-autobiographical *Insights and Illusions of Philosophy*. New York: Meridian Books, where he discusses the shift in the sciences, noted by Henri Bergson, away from questions of kind towards questions of law.
5   David W. Jardine (1992a). "The fecundity of the individual case": Reflections on the pedagogic heart of interpretive work. *Journal of Philosophy of Education*.

CHAPTER FIFTEEN

Relations of Kind. Full of the kinships that bind our lives to each other and to the life of the Earth.

Full of "analogical integrities."[1]

Articulations of "that anciently perceived likeness between all creatures and the earth of which they are made."[2]

There is, here, an issue of the nature of writing and the nature of breath and the arcs of family resemblance that bind text and breath and author and topic and the semantic-etymologic buzz and bump and humus, "winding around forgotten syntax"[3]:

> The rhythm of a song or a poem rises, no doubt, in reference to the pulse and breath of the poet. But that is too specialized an accounting; it rises also in reference to daily and seasonal — and surely even longer — rhythms in the life of the poet and in the life that surrounds him. The rhythm of a poem resonates with these larger rhythms that surround it; it fills its environment with sympathetic

---

1 Wendell Berry (1988). The profit in work's pleasure. *Harper's Magazine,* March, 1988, p. 138.
2 Wendell Berry (1983). *Standing by Words.* San Francisco: North Point Press, p. 76.
3 I'm farming all the time: cutting six cords of firewood for the winter, planting fruit trees, putting in fencing, taking care of the chickens, maintenance on the car, and maintenance on the truck, doing maintenance on the road. There's an enormous amount of physical work to be done.
   That's a kind of work rhythm to be sure. . .which is just good old rural life work rhythms. Though I think probably the rhythm I'm drawing on most now is the whole of the landscape of the Sierra Nevada, to feel it all moving underneath. There is the periodicity of ridge, gorge, ridge, gorge, ridge, gorge at the spur ridge and tributary gorges that make an interlacing network of, oh, 115-million-year-old geological formation rhythms. I'm trying to feel through that more than anything else right now. all the way down to some Tertiary gravels which contain a lot of gold from the Pliocene. Geological rhythms. I don't know how well you can do that in poetry. Well, like this for example. Have you ever tried singing a range of mountains?" Gary Snyder (1980), p. 48.

vibrations. Rhyme, which is a function of rhythm, may suggest this sort of resonance; it marks the coincidences of smaller structures with larger ones, as when the day, the month, and the year all end at the same moment. Song, then, is a force opposed to speciality and to isolation. It is the testimony of the singer's inescapable relation to the earth, to the human community, and also to tradition.[4]

But these arcs of resemblance, anciently perceived, root down even further into the ecological crisis we now face.
First:

Rhyme leads one no doubt to hear in language a very ancient cosmology. Rhyme is not only an echo from word to word. Arrangement for arrangement, the order of language, being an order in language, evokes and mimes a cosmic order. In realizing itself, rhyme. . .is tune in to [this cosmology]. Rhyme and meter are praise. An indirect theology.[5]

Second:

There are lots of sounds that we haven't heard that the birds know about. There are lots of rhythms that we haven't heard that the trees know about. It's not only the sounds in *your* environment.[6]

Third:

We must suspect that Amish horse-powered farms work well, not because — or not just because —they are energy efficient, but because they are living creatures and therefore fit harmoniously into a pattern of relationships that rhyme analogically from ecosystem to crop, from field to farmer. In other words, ecosystem, farm, field, crop, horse, farmer, family and community are, in certain critical ways, *like* each other. It goes without saying that tools can be introduced into this agricultural and ecological order without jeopardizing it — but only up to a certain kind, scale and power. The tractor has been so destructive, I think, because it is *unlike* anything else in the agricultural order and so it breaks the essential harmony.[7]

4   Wendell Berry (1983), p. 17.
5   Henri Meschonnic (1988). p. 93.
6   Obo Addy, from the liner notes to the Kronos Quartet (1992). *Pieces of Africa*. Elektra/Nonesuch CD 979253-2.
7   Wendell Berry (1983). p. 75.

Fourth:

> The light, the textures, the colours of Africa and the African landscape and the sounds of the birds and the insects are totally different from Europe. It's not so much cultural as environmental. You can switch cultures in a way but you can't deny your environmental background.[8]
>
> This book is based on a disturbing collapse of language and the Earth.

It is based on the collapse of discourse into the flesh of things — that speech breath writing hold(s) echoes of harmonies that are Earthly. Consider:

> Unlike all other living creatures, man's relationship to the world is characterized by *freedom from environment*. This freedom implies the linguistic constitution of the world. Both belong together. To rise above the pressure of what impinges on us from the world means to have language and to have "world." This freedom from the environment is also freedom in relation to the names that we give things, as stated in the profound account in Genesis, according to which God gave Adam the authority to name creatures.[9]

This is vitally important. This *freedom from the environment*, from the immediate "pressures of what impinges on us from the world," allows the world to be named and *loosens* the bond between word and thing. It does *not* loosen my flesh from the pull of sunlight, but does let me experience it and ponder it, not just undergo it. It just may be the locale where the path often forks

But this loosening is not a *severance* of signifier and signified (evident also in the licentiousness of the tail-ends of Post-Modernism).

The impingements of the Earth have *their own* analogical integrities, *their own* kinds which our words do not make up all by themselves.

And neither do our words simply "represent" (the language of "this is that").

---

8   Kevin Volans (1991). From the liner notes to Kevin Volans/Kronos String Quartet performing
9   Hans Georg Gadamer (1989). p. 444.

> [Analogical —"this is like that" — integrities are not representational but obedient (*ab audire* —to listen, to give heed, to be attuned)].

Words and things "belong together" in relations of kind, in relations of breath and bone. Words are earthen things as much as is that ravencall. Our freedom, here, is not licentiousness but the "give and flexibility,"[10] the "open-texture"[11] of kinds.

> [Expressions of affinities:
>
>> "Understanding is the expression of the affinity of the one who understands to the one whom he understands and to that which he understands."[12]

The song and words and breath of the poet are linked. The Earth is part of us and apart from us. Speech, well-versed, resonates with the anciently perceived likeness between all creatures and the Earth of which they are made.

Ecology is a type of writing-on-the-edge.

> The true poem is walking that edge between what can be said and that which cannot be said. That's the real razor's edge. The poem that falls all the way over into what can be said can still be very exciting, but the farther it is from the razor's edge the less is has of the real magic. It can be very well done but the ones that make your hair stand on edge are the ones that are right on the line. And then some of them fall too much in the realm of what can't be said. Then they are no longer poems; they are meditation themes like the koan, or they are magical incantations, or they are mantras. Mantras or koans or spells are actually superelliptical poems

---

10 W. Norris-Clarke (1976). p. 188.
11 Ludwig Wittgenstein (1968).
12 Hans Georg Gadamer (1983). *Reason in the Age of Science.* Boston: MIT Press, p. 48.

that the reader cannot understand except that he has to put hundreds of more hours of meditation in toward getting it than he has to put in to get the message of a normal poem. Haiku has something of this quality. The haiku of Basho and his immediate disciples have the quality of the poem pushed as far as one can push it. "The words stop but the meaning goes on."[13]

It is a demand of memory, of re-membering the echo of "this is like that" — "tales," not as skittered *across* language from word to word in kind, but as stuttering out into the Earth's kindness, ancient cosmologies that we did not invent — *logoi* of the cosmos, not ego-logics imposed on a spread-legged Earth.

> [But still these ego-logics are akin to the cosmologics because we are *like* the bios we are in. The Cartesian ego-logic severs its kinship to eco-logics under the warrant of clarity (the kinships between mathematics and the Earth are not clear unless we *begin* with mathematics and *impose* these logics on the Earth), and the Earth cannot live up to this demand, because it doesn't fit together as an objective array of univocal objects/ substances, but fits together laterally in relations of kind.]

The an-archaic linking of tale to tale is *like* the an-archaic linking of crop to field to farmer, of breath to bone to rhyme to rhythm to song, of etymological thread to epistemic kinship to and understanding of our kind.

One way that this memory of an-archaic kind is lost is the flattening of discourse into the "duckspeak" of current education talk. Such flattening, in the service of objectivity and repeatability and accuracy, siphons off the warm, difficult resonances of things that makes speech stumble, that makes speech alluring:

> In Orwell's dystopia, emphasis was placed upon short, clipped words "which could be uttered rapidly and which roused the minimum of echoes in the speaker's mind." In other words:
> Ultimately, it was hoped to make articulate speech issue from the larnyx, without involving the higher brain cells at all. This aim was frankly admitted in the

---

13   Gary Snyder (1980). p. 21-2.

Newspeak word *duckspeak,* meaning "to quack like a duck." Applying this ideal of political language to the realm of sexual politics we note the similarities between duckspeak and male obscenity: Words like *fuck, prick, cock, cunt, slut,* illustrate the point.[14]

Applying this ideal of political language to the realm of educational language, we note the similarities between duckspeak and our unintended curricular obscenities. "Time on task ratios," "studenting behaviours," "career and life management," "displays a mastery of appropriate management skills geared to the perceived needs of individual students." Quack.

14   Mary Daly (1985). p. 331-2.

CHAPTER SIXTEEN

Interpretation as Anarchism. This is not quite right in the image of anarchy we have inherited.

The hairs on the back of the neck bristle, Rationalism's nighttremors.

Jack Weatherford traces *an-archon*. He describes how French ethnographer, Louis Armand de Lom d'Arce, Baron de Lahontan, working around 1690, used the term "anarchy" to describe the forms of social organization of the Huron who lived "without a government separate from their kinship system"[1] and who retained an "orderly society, but one lacking a formal government that compelled such order."[2]

An-archon means "no leader," no *arche* over and above this implicit, interweaving, interdependent system of kinships and family resemblances. Things "fit together" with no "supervisor" with "supervision" left over above the fray. Implicit in such "fitting" is a sense of individual responsibility — *my* responsibility to my son — that cannot be deferred to or demanded by a "governor."

> [note how "essences" provide a anonymous, unaddressable "governor" for instances, deferring the immediacy that I must kindly negotiate with my son — *arche*/essence as wrapped up in the crisis of intimacy[3]]

> [crisis of intimacy: Intimacy is lost *both* when children are oppressed under the weight of gericentric univocity ("the authority of age, tradition"[4]) *and* when they are abandoned

---

1   Jack Weatherford (1988). *Indian Givers*. New York: Fawcett Columbine, p. 123.
2   Jack Weatherford (1988). p. 123.
3   see David G. Smith. Teacher education and the notion of global culture. Presented at the American Association of Colleges of Teacher Education, San Antonio, Texas, February, 1992.
4   David G. Smith (1988).

> under the licentiousness of pedocentric equivocity ("child-centered pedagogy[5])]
>
> > [the numbness of the extremities: "kindly negotiation" is neither of these numb extremities]

An-arche as a recovery of the irreplaceability of the stubborn particular in the make-up of the kind.
    Anarchy is not chaos.
        Anarchy as kind-ness and generosity.
           Pedagogy as an-archaic.

    Wittgenstein's *Philosophical Investigations* can be read as a response to the crisis of intimacy between signifier and signified: "Family resemblance" as an analogue to how our breath is a fitting, inevitable response to our Earthliness, how our utterances of "kinds" instead of hard edged locutions of "all that is the case" is an *ecological breakthrough at the level of language*. Thus, family resemblance is not only a metaphor for the belonging together of word to word, but a metaphor also for the belonging together of words to thing.

    Post-modernism as a hyperdistention of the crisis of intimacy. It falls for essence and then rejects it and embraces its inverse. The inverse skips over kindness all over again.

---

5   David G. Smith (1988).

CHAPTER SEVENTEEN

Such a living, animate world demands of us a generative response which is at once ecological and pedagogic at its heart.

Interpretation must be resolved to tell the children the full richness of the tales of the Earth, but it must also be resolved that children must be *brought into the telling.*

Hermeneutics is this standing between, at the boundary between the old and the new, the young and the old, puer and senex.

When we tell the tales, these tales must not be simply repeated identically. These tales must be *re-membered* by children, this one and this.

In his "Introduction" to the collection *Writing Culture: The Poetics and Politics of Ethnography,* James Clifford addresses the problem of collecting these tales in an ethnographic study and cites a parallel between the way in which such knowledge is held *in* the culture and what an "ethical" and appropriate presentation of that knowledge might be:

> Using techniques of deliberate frustration, disgression, and incompleteness, old men impart their historical knowledge to younger kinsmen, preferably at cock's crow, the hour before dawn. These strategies of ellipsis, concealment, and partial disclosure determine the transmission of stories between generations. A person's knowledge is supposed to grow only in small increments, and in any aspect of life people are deliberately told only a little bit more than the speaker thinks they already know. It soon becomes apparent that there is no "complete" corpus of First-Time knowledge [and] that no one can know this lore except through an open-ended series of contingent, power-laden encounters [it depends]. The ethical questions raised by forming a written archive of secret, oral lore are considerable. Part of [the] solution [can be] to undermine the completeness of [my] own account (but not its seriousness) by publishing a book that is a series of fragments. The aim is not to indicate unfortunate gaps remaining in our knowledge [this would pathologize the incompleteness against the background of an inappropriate hope in the possibility and desirability of a complete — i.e., dead — corpus]

but rather to present an inherently imperfect mode of knowledge, which produces gaps as it fills them.¹

Such fragmentariness of the account alone is not enough, because it is still imaginable that the "incompleteness" only works laterally. The incompleteness is also deeply temporal and oral and auditory: those yet to be here amongst us will generatively add on to what has already been said, re-telling and re-membering the stories, thus transforming the stories by adding their own breath and bone and blood to the corpus of their being understood. So the corpus is *essentially,* not *accidentally* incomplete.

It also requires "a special effort of memory"² because the corpus does not collect like pieces added to a puzzle, but accretes like new musical motifs which are always vaguely familiar transmutations of the songs of birds and the rhythms of trees.³

There is, of course, the deeply ethical question, as Clifford suggests, as to whether one might produce a written corpus of this lore: perhaps one should not, unless, somehow, the written traces can take on the heat and fluidity of that flesh, transmuting and, especially, requiring the reader of the written text to take up the written account in a power laden encounter which adds the reader to the corpus — which makes *that depth of demand* on the reader.

Part of this ethical question is deeply pedagogically disturbing: attempting to produce a complete corpus proceeds *as if* "the new ones" were not essential; *as if* "passing on" were an accidental feature; *as if* the new ones had nothing new to say about the "already produced complete corpus"; *as if* the corpus could be complete without children, and children again, and again, and the passing away of the old ones who told the tale just this way, to these children, in that deep winter.

1 James Clifford (1986a). Introduction. To James Clifford & George Marcus (1986). *Writing Culture: The Poetics and Politics of Ethnography.* Berkeley: University of California Press, p. 8.
2 Hans-Georg Gadamer (1989). p. 434.
3 Obo Addy (1992).

In such a tell-tale world, there is no one member that has all the information. In this way, the "Corpus" of knowledge is literally that: full of "members," each one irreplaceable.

Each old man would have a slightly different tale to tell about the world and its workings and would have to tell that tale slightly differently to each child, according to their age and to what they already know.

This is an "imperfect mode of knowledge" only if it fails to go on within the conditions of necessity and mystery. Better, it is not imperfect in the sense of failing to be a complete corpus. It is imperfect in the sense of being incapable of the finality and stasis inherent in the notion of perfection. It is, rather, ek-static knowledge, knowledge with an inherent self-transcendence built in. This transcendence is not to some "otherworldly realm," but a transcendence into the future and into the past, winding out into forgotten syntax.[4] It transcends any one individual, not simply by being quantitatively more than this one now, but by extending *before* this one and *after* — better, *by extending this one now out into the cascade in which they live.*

It is not only that none of the old men have all the knowledge, but also that it must "go on," this knowing. The whole matter, then, is not just epistemic but a deep moral commitment to pedagogy — there are always "new ones in our midst" and therefore the story is still going on and the whole truth is never just given[5] but is always "yet to be."

No center, no arche; no one of them could stand in for all the others — non-representational:

> This work consists of the accumulation of local knowledge *in place,* generation after generation, children learning the visions and failures, stories and songs, names, ways, and skills of their elders, so that the cost of individual trial-and-error learning can be lived with and repaid, and the community thus enabled to preserve both itself and its natural place and neighbourhood.[6]

---

4   Diane DeHovanessian (1986).
5   Hans-Georg Gadamer (1989). p. 77.
6   Wendell Berry (1983). Poetry and marriage. In *Standing By Words*. San Francisco: North Point Press, p. 100.

> There is much that we need that we cannot get from our contemporaries — even assuming that the work we have from them is the best that is possible: they cannot give us the sense of the longevity of human experience, the sense of the practicable, of *proven* possibility, that we get from older writing. Our past is not merely something to depart from; it is to commune with, to speak with.[7]

That is to say, in the telling of the tales, new members are brought in and these new members transfigure the tales, adding themselves and their flesh to the corpus of the Earth, keeping it going, not essentially/identically, but in kind.

But then again:

> Men live there whole lives within the Dominant area. When men go off hunting bears, they come back with bear stories, and these are listened too by all, they become the history and mythology of that culture. So the men's "wilderness" becomes Nature, considered as the property of Man. But the experience of women as women, their experience unshared by men, that experience is the wilderness or the wildness that is utterly other — that is in fact, to Man, unnatural. That is what civilization has left out, what culture excludes, what the Dominants call animal, bestial, primitive, undeveloped, unauthentic — what has not been spoken, and when spoken, has not been heard — what we are just beginning to find words for, our words, not their words: the experience of women. For dominance-identified men and women both, that is true wildness. Their fear of it is ancient, profound and violent — the wild country.[8]

But the bear story is not the wilderness. The bear story is a story *of* the wilderness, and this "of" must be understood in its dual aspect: this story is *about* the wilderness in the sense that this is what the story *heeds,* and this story *belongs to* the wilderness in the sense that this is the story's source and its limit.[9]

---

7   Wendell Berry (1983). p. 14.
8   Ursula Le Guin (1989). p. 163.
9   Compare with Martin Heidegger (1977a):

> Thinking is the thinking of Being. The genetive says something twofold. Thinking is of Being inasmuch as thinking, coming to pass from Being, belongs to Being. At the same time thinking is of Being insofar as thinking, belonging to Being, listens to Being. (p. 196).

Thus:

> A man would go or be forced to go into the wilderness and measure himself against [it], recognize, finally, his true place within it, and thus be saved from both pride and despair. Seeing himself as a tiny member of a world he cannot comprehend or mastery or in any final sense possess, he cannot possibly think of himself as a god. And, by the same token, since he shares in, depends upon, and is graced by all of which he is a part, neither can he become a fiend; he cannot descend into that final despair of destructiveness. Returning from the wilderness, he becomes a restorer, a preserver.[10]

This is why so much theorizing can go insane, losing this unnameable measure against which to place our urban(e) words:

> When they forbid their prophets to go into the wilderness, they lose the possibility of renewal. And the most dangerous tendency is modern society, now rapidly emerging as scientific-industrial ambition, is the tendency toward encapsulation of human order — the severance, once and for all, of the umbilical cord fastening us to the wilderness [Kant's "leading strings"[11]] The threat is not only in the totalitarian desire for absolute control. It lies in the willingness to ignore the essential paradox: the natural forces that so threaten us are the same forces that preserve and renew us.[12]

10   Wendell Berry (1986). p. 99.
11   Immanuel Kant (1964). p. 21.
12   Wendell Berry (1986). p. 130.

CHAPTER EIGHTEEN

We should not be disappointed if what we have to say, here, now, about the essential characteristics of pedagogy, gets turned under like fertile soil, providing the undergrowth for the new.

This should be an ecstatic moment of witness and joy.

The worry of Edmund Husserl in his *Crisis of European Science* is unnecessary:

> Can the world, and human existence in it, truthfully have a meaning if... history has nothing more to teach us than that all the shapes of the spiritual world, all the conditions of life, ideals, norms upon which man relies, form and dissolve themselves like fleeting waves, that it always was and ever will be so, that again and again reason must turn into nonesense, and well-being into misery? Can we console ourselves with that? Can we live in this world, where historical occurrence is nothing but an unending concatenation of illusory progress and bitter disappointment?[1]

This bespeaks the hope and disappointment of essentialism and rationalism — life as actually lived cannot be fixed and to the extent that we stake our consolation, our morality and our lives on such fixity, to that extent, disappointment is inevitable.

As we have come to expect from the history of Western philosophy, the response has always been to *deny* this concatenation, to "hold on" at all costs, closing the colon and demanding that all things pass regulated by Reason, by Human Experience, by Mathematics, by God, by the separation of those Chosen and those not, by *some* resolving center/essence/fundament (Nietzsche's "will to power" is simply another one: his work is fundamentally Cartesian because, with the collapse of the fundaments, he was still looking *inwards*).

---

[1] Edmund Husserl (1970). p. 7.

It is telling that the hope of the West to hold fast in the midst of the concatenation of life is understood in Buddhism as an illusion which is precisely the cause of human suffering. Note how easily colonialism fits here: the hope of the West is the cause of suffering for the world.

Epistemologically, culturally, ecologically, economically, spiritually and from the viewpoint of gender, this point is sadly undeniable.

Even phenomenology, which finally allowed us to burst out into the open and begin to finally live and breath beyond the monotheistic agonies of hope and disappointment still contains such denials in its lingering essentialism.

Put the other way around, Husserl and his old European essentialism could not contain his own insight.

> "The notion of the "life-world" has a
> Revolutionary
> power
> that
> explodes
> the framework of Husserl's transcendental thinking."[2]

The only alternative that essentialism can see is chaos. Essence or Chaos. Kindness and anarchy and wildness live in the crack between these worlds.

Pedagogy lives in the cracks between these worlds.

Phenomenology got out of hand and climbed down below the severed head when Husserl wasn't looking.

When daddy isn't watching, we fuck. And we hate his harsh and certain voice, full as it is of calm and confidence regarding what essentially is and what essentially is not, unrelenting in its demand. *Univoce.*

When daddy isn't watching, we fuck.

---

2   Hans Georg Gadamer (1977). p. 196.

CHAPTER NINETEEN

"We cannot see how, in the [reduction], the "Heraclitean flux" of constituting life can be treated descriptively in its individual facitity."[1]

> Not even the single philosopher by himself, within the [reduction], can hold fast to anything in this elusively flowing life, repeat it with always the same content, and become so certain of its this-ness and its being-such that he could describe it, document it, so to speak (even for his own person) in definitive statements. But [such] full concrete facticity can be...grasped in another good sense, precisely because...the great task can and must be undertaken of investigating the...fact... as belonging to its essence, and it is determinable only *through* its essence.[2]
>
> The life-world does have, in all its relative features, a *general structure*. We can attend to it in its generality and, with sufficient care, fix it once and for all in a way equally accessible to all.[3]

Husserl's work fell prey to the old options of inquiry, the old numbness of the extremities — on the one hand, we have the facticity and particularity of experience which, in and of itself and taken up in isolation, offers us only *differences,* only minutiae all speaking with equal, different voices — Chaos. The flow of human experience offers us only *equivocity-*"individual facticity."

On the other hand, we have *essences* which can be fixed once and for all. We have *univocity*. Given the task of voicing life as it is actually lived, it is *assumed* by Husserl that this voice must either be the single, isolated voice of difference (such that lived-experience turns out to be idiosyncratic

---

1   Edmund Husserl (1970) p. 177.
2   Edmund Husserl (1970). p. 178.
3   Edmund Husserl (1970). p. 139. What Heidegger (1977a) calls "the uniform accessibility of everything to everyone" (p. 197). The positiveness of such accessibility is wound around notions of oppression, suppression and denial. The negativeness of such accessibility is a loss of a sense of uniqueness and place and responsibility and individuality.

and subjectivistic), or the clear and foreclosing voice of identity (such that lived-experience turns out to be nestled in its general structure).

The option Husserl took was that of the search for essences: to our lived-experience of something we must ask the question of the meaning of that experience-of-something in such a way that we perform what he called an "eidetic reduction," a reducing of a lived-experience to its essence.

What Husserl lacked — what, in fact, he did not even seek, since fixed essences served his desire for philosophy as a Rigorous Science of Being[4] —was a deeper, more difficult, nebulous, interweaving, alluring voice that refused such a resolution of life into this either/or of equivocity and univocity. Of mine or yours.

Such a courageous refusal is found in the later work of Ludwig Wittgenstein. He sets forth, in regards to language, the same entreatment that Husserl set up regarding "experience":

"Philosophy may in no way interfere with the actual use of language; it can in the end only describe it. For it cannot give it any foundation either. It leaves everything as it is."[5] And yet he couldn't leave it as it is.

Re-citation. Re-membering. What follows are three already-cited passages from Wittgenstein's *Philosophical Investigations*. Wittgentstein is describing an everyday situation in which several phenomenon are all given the "same" name — in this particular case, they are all called "games." He playfully explores whether this giving of the same name indicates that each of these different examples has some one thing in common that would make them all *identical* in some particular respect. If so, that would make them all able to be named *univocally* with this word "game" (and would therefore fulfill Husserl's requirement for a search for the "essence" of "games" as something univocally nameable and therefore able to be "fixed once and for all."

Wittgenstein finds, instead, that this word names a belonging together of these different examples that is *neither* an identity / univocity, nor is it simply a difference / equivocity. Fixed essences and the "Hericlitian flux" are not the only options.

---

4   Edmund Husserl (1965).
5   Ludwig Wittgenstein (1968). p. 49.

CHAPTER NINETEEN

Re-citation:

> As in spinning a thread, we twist fibre on fibre. And the strength of the thread does not reside in the fact that some one fibre runs through its whole length, but in the overlapping of many fibres.[6]
>
> Don't say: "There *must* be something common" [some essence, some univocal core of meaning]... but *look and see* whether there is anything that is common to *all*. For if you look at them you will not see something that is common to *all*, but similarities, relationships, and a whole series of them at that. To repeat: don't think but look![7]

Again, almost the same call as Husserl in his *Idea of Phenomenology:*

> No inclination is more dangerous to "seeing"...than to think too much, and from these reflections in thought to create supposed self-evident principles [which then] implicitly determine and unjustifiably limit the direction of investigation.[8]

But also again, Husserl's desire to render phenomenology into a Rigorous Science of Being unjustifiably limited his *own* "seeing."
Wittgenstein:

> we see a complicated network of similarities, overlapping and criss-crossing: sometimes overall similarities, sometimes similarities of detail. I can think of no better expression to characterize these similarities than "family resemblances." (*Familienahnlichkeiten*).[9]

These passages portray the deeply *dialogical* and *analogical* character of lived-experience, the deeply *conversational* nature of life as it is actually lived, with its irresolvable and potent "family resemblances" and "kinships." They hint at the practical, lived struggle for communication and meaning which is not solved through univocal definitions and declarations, no matter how clear and distinct, no matter if they are the severed

---

6   Ludwig Wittgenstein (1968). p. 32.
7   Ludwig Wittgenstein (1968). p. 32.
8   Edmund Husserl (1970b). p. 50.
9   Ludwig Wittgenstein (1968). p. 32.

objectivities of Cartesianism or the fixed and given essences of Husserl's phenomenology.

Regarding our Cartesian desire to draw univocal boundaries (this could also be a comment about Husserl's essentialism), Wittgenstein rather playfully says "that never troubled you before when you used the word."[10] Descartes' dream of clarity and distinctness, his dream of dispelling the rich, interweaving ambiguity of the Earth and our lives on the Earth, does not trouble the lived usage of language, the lived character of experience:

> If someone were to draw a sharp boundary I could not acknowledge it as the one that I too always wanted to draw, or had drawn in my mind. For I did not want to draw one at all. His concept can then be said to be not *the same* as mine, but akin to it. The kinship is just as undeniable as the difference.[11]

[Compare:

> What the specialist never considers is that such a boundary is, in itself, profoundly disruptive. Its first disruption is in his mind, for having enclosed the possibility of control that is within his competency to imagine and desire, he has become the enemy of all other possibilities. And secondly, having chosen the possibility of total control within a small and highly simplified enclosure, he simply abandons the rest, leaves it totally out of control [chaos]; that is, he foresakes or even repudiates the complex, partly mysterious patterns of interdependence and cooperation, controllable only within limits, by which human culture joins itself to its sources in the natural world. This attempt at total control is an invitation to disorder. And the rule seems to be that the more rigid and exclusive the specialist's boundary, and the stricter the control within it, the more disorder rages around it.[12]]

[the more it rages]

---

10   Ludwig Wittgenstein (1968). p. 33.
11   Ludwig Wittgenstein (1968). p. 36.
12   Wendell Berry (1986). p. 71.

As Wittgenstein documented so well, if we look at language as it is actually used, it is more fluid, flexible, lively and risk-laden than the Cartesian Logic of clarity would have us imagine. In the ordinary course of our lives:

> we are not *striving after* an ideal, as if our ordinary vague sentences had not yet got a quite unexceptionable sense, and a perfect language awaited construction by us.[13]
>
> In philosophy we often *compare* the use of words with calculi which have fixed rules, but cannot say that someone who is using language *must* be playing such a game. But [even] if you say that our languages only *approximate* to such calculi you are standing on the very brink of a misunderstanding. For then it may look as if what we were talking about were an *ideal* language. But here, the word "ideal" is liable to mislead, for it sounds as if these languages [such as mathematics and logic] were better, more perfect that our everyday language; and as if it took the logician to show people at last what a proper sentence looked like.[14]

Again, *almost* Edmund Husserl:

> The trader in the market has his market-truth. In the relationship in which it stands, is his truth not a good one, and the best that a trader can use? Is it a pseudo-truth, merely because the scientist, involved in a different relativity and judging with other aims and ideas, looks for other truths — with which a great many more things can be done, but not the one thing that has to be done in a market? It is high time that people got over being dazzled, particularly in philosophy and logic, by the ideals and regulative ideas and methods of the "exact" sciences — as though the in-itself of such sciences were actually an absolute norm for objective being and for truth.[15]

Wittgenstein even takes a pointed swipe at Descartes' notions of doubt:

---

13   Ludwig Wittgenstein (1968), p. 45.
14   Ludwig Wittgenstein (1968), p. 38.
15   Edmund Husserl (1969a). *Formal and Transcendental Logic*. The Hauge: Martinus Nijhoff, p. 278.

> It may easily look as if every doubt merely *revealed* an existing gap in the foundations; so that secure understanding is only possible if we first doubt everything that *can* be doubted, and then remove all these doubts. [But, for example] the signpost is in order — if, under normal circumstances, it fulfills its purpose.[16]

Descartes' methodical doubt, therefore, rips holes in the delicate and ambiguous fabric that langague and thinking already have because of the peculiarity of its demands. It does not *reveal* gaps which we then must remove. It *creates* gaps in what is, prior to such doubt, reliable and unbetraying, albeit not without some risk.

Wittgenstein's notion of family resemblances is thus deeply alluring and suggestive. It suggests that the alternative to clarity, distinctness and identity is *not* chaos, meaningless facticity, individualistic personal opinion or idiosyncrasy, but rather is analogical kinship, a belonging together without being identical or simply different. The alternative to Descartes' nightmare of identity (*and* the alternative to Husserl's drastic alternatives of Heraclitean flux and fixed essences) is *conversation,* a mutual reading of the signs in which the "others" voice is an essential, not accidental moment in my own understanding of myself and my understanding of this thing which is the topic of our talk. (Everything is what it is not) Attending to how others may read the signs allows me to see that *my* reading does not encompass this thing, nor does our mutual reading. (Conversation as the prevention of literalism) Our conversation "keeps the object, in all its possibilities, fluid."[17]

It keeps open the possibility that the conversation can go on. Hermeneutics thus protects the Earth from the violence of univocal naming and its consumptive desires.

Wittgenstein's notion of "family resemblances" is deeply pedagogy at its heart. It provides a way to attend to the ambiguous and difficulty interrelationships that pertain between our lives, as educators, and the

---

16   Ludwig Wittgenstein (1968). p. 41.
17   Hans-Georg Gadamer (1989). p. 330.

children all around us.[18] Operating with a notion of "family resemblance" as an image of that relation:

> means living in the belly of a paradox wherein a genuine life together is made possible only in the context of an *ongoing conversation* which never ends and which must be sustained for life together to go on at all. The openness that is required is not a vague licentiousness, but a risky, deliberate engagement of the full conflict and ambiguity by which new horizons of mutual understanding are achieved.[19]

It does not mean living in a conceptual confusion. It means living in the belly.

---

18   see David W. Jardine (1988). "There are children all around us." *Journal of Educational Thought.* 22(2A).
19   David G. Smith (1988). p. 175.

CHAPTER TWENTY

"The consequence of accepting the ideal of logical proof as a yardstick."[1]

> The logical ideal of the ordered arrangement of concepts takes precedence over the living metaphoricity of language. For only a grammar based on logic will distinguish between the *proper* and the *metaphorical* meaning of a word. What originally constituted the basis of the life of language and its logical productivity, the spontaneous and inventive seeking out of similarities by means of which it is possible to order things, is now marginalized and instrumentalized into a rhetorical figure called metaphor.[2]
>
> This changed relationship...is at the basis of concept formation in science and has become so self-evident to us that it requires a special effort of memory to recall that, alongside the scientific ideal of unambiguous designation, the life of language itself continues unchanged.[3]

Wittgenstein is part of this special effort of memory.
Ecology is part of this special effort of memory.

The confrontation of Eastern Wisdom traditions with the univocal hegemonies of monotheism is part of this effort of memory:

> "Metaphoricity: It is the
> memory of
> forgotten
> syntax."[4]

It is also the "memory of ways"[5]

---

1   Hans-Georg Gadamer (1989). p. 432.
2   Hans-Georg Gadamer (1989). p. 432
3   Hans-Georg Gadamer (1989). p. 433-4.
4   Diana DeHovanessian, in Michael Fischer (1986), p. 199.
5   Wendell Berry (1983). p. 73.

It is the disseminated entrails of autobiography, "revelations. . .and recollections. . .of the divine sparks."⁶

". . .turning black into white, giving it wings."⁷

"skilful handling of memory."⁸

"making memory last."⁹

We are not dealing with simply the marginalization of metaphoric speech and its allures under the auspices of univocal, unambiguous designation. In such marginalization, poetry and metaphoricity is imagined to be no longer *about the Earth;* the Earth itself is no longer poetic, alluring; we no longer see the Earth itself as "spontaneous[ly] and inventive[ly] seeking out similarities"¹⁰ — *its own* working itself out in kind, a-kind to our kindly speech.

We are not dealing with simply the marginalization of the Earth and its allures under the auspices of human domination (that "one voice").

We are not dealing simply with the marginalization of relationships of kinship and kind under the rule of law/normativity/essence (the break up of the family/familiarity and the post-modern, urban(e) strangeness/stranger).

We are not dealing simply with the marginalization of women and the Wisdoms of "connectedness" under the auspices of the cleavages and severances of patriarchy.

THIS IS A STORY ABOUT THAT: "Civilized Man has gone deaf." Wittgenstein's *Philosophical Investigations* can be read as a form of ear-cleaning on the linguistic level, howls of family resemblance

---

6   Michael Fischer (1986). p. 198.
7   James Hillman (1983). p. 31.
8   James Hillman (1983). p. 42.
9   Hans-Georg Gadamer (1989). p. 391.
10 Hans-Georg Gadamer (1989). p. 432.

crackling beneath the clean surfaces of essence. Linked with essentialism is univocity.[11]

THIS IS A STORY ABOUT THAT: The "hermeneutic" critique of essentialism is parallel to the Wittgensteinian critique of univocal naming. The ongoing character of hermeneutic understanding is parallel to the Wittgensteinian "open-textured"[12] character of family resemblances and kinships.

THIS IS A STORY ABOUT THAT: the "fecundity of the individual case"[13] Order, essence, tradition: all these are *porous* and *generative*, yet-to-be-decided. *This* is the profound extent to which Martin Heidegger's linking of being and time disrupted the flow of philosophizing. that puts generativity at the center of hermeneutic understanding is parallel to the metaphors of family resemblance and kinship in Wittgenstein.

THIS IS A STORY ABOUT THAT: There is an ecological parallel in each case. The *hubris* of our belief in our dominion over the Earth, leaving us unable to hear what the Earth has to say. We are not the only voice. We are of a kind with the Earth. And twirling in the midst of Ecology is Generativity, the ushering in of the fecund new case into the kindness of the patterns that pertain.

---

11 see David W. Jardine (1990a). Awakening from Descartes' nightmare: On the love of ambiguity in phenomenological approaches to education. *Studies in Philosophy and Education. 10*(1).
12 Ludwig Wittgenstein (1968).
13 The ordering of life by rules of law...is incomplete and needs productive supplementation. At issue is always something more than the correct application of general principles. Our knowledge...is always supplemented by the individual case, even productively determined by it. The judge not only applies the law in concreto, but contributes through his very judgment to developing the law. [Our knowledge] is constantly developed through the fecundity of the individual case. (Hans-Georg Gadamer [1989]. p. 38)

It is interesting to compare this sense of "judge(ment)" to Immanuel Kant's judge who "compels witnesses to give answer to questions of Reason's own determining," (1964, p. 21) irrespective of the individual case. This is the way in which hermeneutics can still retain a sense of order and tradition without reverting to a fixed *a priori* or neo-transcendental essentialism.

THIS IS A STORY ABOUT THAT: Boink. Borne out of this web, children. Pedagogy is not possible without kindness. Essences are celebate, unpenetratable, not to be fucked with.

THIS IS A STORY ABOUT THAT: Kin, hence kindred and *Kinder* and kindness and akin and the parallel Sanskrit root is *gen,* hence generativity and genitals and generosity. Kindness and generosity — kindness defined as "natural affection."

THIS IS A STORY ABOUT THAT: pedagogy as a form of natural affection. The metaphoricity of language as the language that has room for children. Metaphoricity has *play* in it.[14] Things can be other-wise (but in kind). The generative metaphor must add that not only *can* things be other-wise (but in kind). Things *must* be other-wise (but in kind). New, fecund, stubborn, particular instances — full of "it depends": full of non-*identity* to the kind [but not just difference] — are needed to "keep the family [resemblance] alive."

---

14 See Hans-Georg Gadamer (1989) for an exploration of play as a clue to the nature of human understanding. See also David W. Jardine (1988).

CHAPTER TWENTY-ONE

The interpretive voice wishes to be of a kind with the Earth, full of the very fragility and finitude and dependency it bespeaks. It is not full of the "scepticism [and] irrationalism"[1] Husserl feared so much, but it does have hints of the pagan "mysticism"[2] that he (and monotheism generally) despised.

Earth Talk. Belly Laughs, and the breath drawn in and let go — like Hermes, at borders, loosing "a swinging gate."[3]

> [this sketches the sensitivity of interpretation to issues of colonialism, because we are always dealing with passages and transformations in the act of understanding. The critique of colonialism cannot be a critique of passage as such, because such a critique would involve denying our own bodily passage, our own inevitable consumption. This is why it is vital to combine a meditation upon colonialism with a critique of representationalism:
>
>> The critique of colonialism in the postwar period — an undermining of "The West's" ability to represent other societies — has been reinforced by an important process of theorizing about the limits of representation itself.[4]
>
> And this with a mindfulness of eco-biological necessity. That is, the critique of colonialism has an eco-biological limit. We are colons and require the wilfull (and, one hopes, mindful) destruction of "others" for our own sustenance:
>
>> Eating is a sacrament. The grace we say clears our hearts and guides the children and welcomes the guests, all at the same

---

1   Edmund Husserl (1970). p. 3.
2   Edmund Husserl (1970). p. 3.
3   Shunryu Suzuki (1986). *Zen Mind, Beginner's Mind*. New York: Weatherhill.
4   James Clifford (1986). p. 9.

> time. We look at eggs, apples, and stew. They are evidence of plentitude, excess, a great reproductive exuberance. Millions of grains of grass-seed that will become rice or flour, millions of codfish fry that will never, and *must* never, grow to maturity. Innumerable little seeds are sacrifices to the food-chain. A parsnip in the ground is a marvel of living chemistry, making sugars and flavors from earth, air, water. And if we do eat meat it is the life, the bounce, the swish, of a great alert being with keen ears and lovely eyes, with foursquare feet and a huge beating heart that we eat, let us not deceive ourselves. We too will be offerings.[5]

This is where the rhythm or song or breath of the poet bespeaks the arc-rhythms of the body:

> Periodic, repetitive behaviour, to create, recreate, enforce, reinforce certain tendencies, certain potentialities, in the bio-psyche. There is another kind of practice [other than the practice of meditation, or the song and breath of the poet] which also is habitual and periodic, but not necessarily as easily or clearly directed by the will: that's the practice of necessity. We are six-foot-long vertebrates, standing on our hind legs, who have to breath so many breaths per minute, eat so many BTU's of plant-transformed solar energy per hour etc. I wouldn't like to separate our practice into two categories. Practice simply is the intensification of what is natural and around us all the time. Practice is to life as poetry is to spoken language. So as poetry is the practice of language, "[meditative, mindful] practice" is the practice of life. But from an enlightened standpoint, all of language is poetry, all of life is practice.[6]

Interpretation as a tough discipline aimed at enlightenment — the moist, green, unfounded, fictional, coming-and-going breath halation Earthly enlightenment that Western aspirations tend to look down upon. Interpretation as a mystical way, but not upwards and away, but *through the world, in the world* — "here, too the gods are present,"[7] "*this* and *this*."[8]

---

5   Gary Snyder (1990a). p. 185.
6   Gary Snyder (1980). p. 134.
7   Martin Heidegger (1977a). p.
8   Bronwen Wallace (1987). p. 111.

CHAPTER TWENTY-TWO

We need to read our psychic life not theologically but mythically. When something appears — a voice, an image, a dream — you respond to it. If [a particular image] comes in, you respond to it. But a Christian has to ask, Is this from God or the Devil? Is it real or did I make it up? Do I believe in this figure, and if I believe, then what are the grounds of my belief? [This may be an argument for Christianity as the foundation of our contemporary images of epistemology. It *is* an argument for the evacuation of the *anima mundi* of its spooks and spirits — all of them are immediately refere(e)d to a mono-logic. We do not have to and are not allow to *pass through* the spooks and spirits that come to meet us, because none of them have *their own* message. This is why there *is* a sort of interpretive work going on in Christianity, but it is "anchored," finally, in the one True Logos. Eco-interpretation and the vittles of the flesh are unanchored, but the sea has a way to it, the wind has a way to it. Things *happen* in such a world]. This [normative order of acceptance or renunciation] disturbs the natural relationship with phenomena. The very act of believing, of declaration of "I believe" is subjectivism. It cuts one off from what's there. If cuts one off from imagination, from one's animal reality.[1]

But what is animism? It's *esse in anima*. It's living in the world. . .feeling the world as personified, as emotional, as saying something. Christianity can't abide [this] because it has "overcome" animism, and it has codified all its superstitions into [one] true belief. . .and that move represses your inherent religiosity in relation to the world, your relations to powers beyond you that humble the ego. For Christianity, the world is dead. Ladders aren't alive.

But if you ask "Tell me, Dr. Hillman, do you really believe walking under a ladder brings back luck?" Oh, no, of course I don't *believe* it. I don't give it a reasoned assent. I don't *stand* for it in that Christian sense of Protestant ego. I act superstitious — and don't let "belief" interfere [something deeper than Husserl's consciousness/ego related "Urdoxa"[2]]. Superstitions depend ["it depends"] on the moment; they stay ambiguous [stay "kind" — clearly this does not mean pleasant and nice] and so they keep in touch with our instantaneous feelings, instincts. The

---

1   James Hillman (1983a). *Inter Views*. Dallas: Spring Publications, p. 89.
2   Edmund Husserl (1969).

Christian kind of belief cuts us off from our reactions: it commands them. And then, because we are cut off, we have to be saved, redeemed."³

Christianity has codified the multiplicity of tales into one true belief. Don't listen to the old men and crones as they tell tales of the ways of the Earth or to the ice-hounds howling in the hills to the west or the body burbling up in heavy breath.

> [Because Christianity is not a religion of the flesh, knowledge of the flesh is not considered vital to the *real* vittles' — the soul. Paganism considers Earth knowledge vital because it considers the Flesh to be vital. Denying the flesh results in the denial of Earth knowledge.
>
> > [science doesn't provide Earth knowledge because it is not premised on our ambiguous *dependency* on the Earth but on premises of mastery that slouch toward Nicaea]

---

3   James Hillman (1983a). p. 91.

CHAPTER TWENTY-THREE

Recall Edmund Husserl's "unity of one true meaning"[1] and his torment over the an-archaic multiplicity of kin.

> ...the One joined in battle with...this non-existent multiplicity which stood in opposition to the One by way of defiant contradiction. To create is to condense, to concentrate, to organize, to unify.
>
> Teilhard de Chardin[2]

For Jaspers, Barth, and Teilhard, the daimons are a pandaemonium: by nature they are multiple. And though they are "non-existent" and "have nothing to say," they contradict and require battle. This battle is against the force of multiplicity. Human internal diversity which makes possible our internal conflicts and self-differentiation, the complexities of Know Thyself...is in their view daemonic [as would be the suggestion of the Earth's "external" diversity of spooks and spirits]. Here we begin to see the staggering consequences of denial of the daimons: it leaves the psyche bereft of all persons but the ego, the controller. [It also leaves the Earth bereft of all but the human voice: ecologically the Earth is a pandaemonic place]. No spontaneous fantasy, image or feeling may be independent of this unifying ego. [If we rewrite this as 'no order in the world may be independent of this unifying ego,' we have the paranoia of constructivism]. Every psychic happening becomes 'mine.' Know Thy*self* shifts to Know *My*self. Without images, the imaginative [interpretive] process withers, only reinforcing the ego's literalism. [e.g. "*There is* an essence to pedagogy": without the ability to hear the daemons, humanity begins to take its own understanding *literally* as constitutive of the whole Earth. The ego can't hear its own voice "in kind", because the spontaneous eruption of other voices has already been 'sorted' according to the collapse of diversity into the one True Logos]. It is therefore of little wonder that the Christian tradition continued to blame this same ego which it had fostered for its

---

1   Edmund Husserl (1970). p. 170.
2   cited in James Hillman (1983). p. 64.

sin of pride and chastised it with humility. The images which could teach the ego its limits...have been repressed.[3]

Bereft of all persons but the Ego. Recall that "bereft" involves bereaving. We miss our animals and our gods with genitals. We miss, too, the fear of these gods and animals, for that bodily heat kept our attention alert to the Earth's movements and our dependencies upon it.]

[3] James Hillman (1983). p. 64-5.

CHAPTER TWENTY-FOUR

Now, at Nicaea a subtle and devastating differentiation was made. Neither the imagists nor the iconoclasts got their way entirely. A distinction was drawn between the *adoration* of images and the free formulation of them on the one hand, and the *veneration* of images and the authorized control over them on the other. Church Councils split hairs, but the roots of these hairs are in our heads, and the split goes deep indeed. At Nicaea a distinction was made between the image as such, its power, its full archetypal reality, and what the image represents, points to, means. Thus, images became allegories.

When images became allegories the iconoclasts have won. The image itself has become subtly depotentiated. Yes, images are allowed, but only if they are officially approved images illustrative of theological doctrine. One's spontaneous imagery is spurious, demonic, devilish, pagan, heathen. Yes, the image is allowed, but only to be venerated for what it represents: the abstract ideas, configurations, transcendencies behind the image. Images become ways of perceiving doctrine. They become representations, no longer presentations, no longer presences of power.[1]

The second Council of Nicaea (A.D. 787) was convened to deal with the issue of the veneration and adoration of religious images and icons,[2] but is entrails wind down to us through "forgotten syntax"[3] and "disseminated identities,"[4] "interweaving and crisscrossing."[5] that indirectly have a bearing on phenomenology and its veneration of and cleaving faithfully to our lived experience.

---

1   James Hillman (1987b). Peaks and vales. In *Puer Papers*. Dallas: Spring Publications, p. 56.
2   See for example Edward James Martin (1978). *A History of the Iconoclastic Controversy*. London: MacMillan; L. Barnard (1974). *The Graeco-Roman and Oriental Background of the Iconoclastic Controversy*. Leiden: E. J. Brill; Daniel Sahas (n.d.). *Icon and Logos: Sources in Eight-Century Iconoclasm*. Toronto: University of Toronto Press.
3   Diane DeHovenassien (1986), in Michael Fischer (1986), p. 199.
4   Michael Fischer (1986). p. 198.
5   Ludwig Wittgenstein (1968). p. 32.

[lived experience should mean experience that is fully alive, full of lives that go beyond my wanting and willing, *including* (perhaps *especially* including) my phenomenological want of essence. This want must not come out simply projected (in, for example, the literalism involved in "*There is* an essence to pedagogy"). It must come out *as a want* — as a livid feature of our lives. We all know the old tales of security, safety, boundary, stability, solid ground under our feet. We all have seen the shale slippages under the rock edges and felt our own bellies droop under faint gravities. As phenomenology drained the lividness of experience into essence (preventing itself from hearing what experience asks of *us*), so too Nicaea drained the lividness of the Earth into God (preventing itself from hearing what the Earth has to say].

At Nicea a subtle differentiation was made between *adoration* of images (idolatry) and the *veneration* of images. The eight sessions of statements emphasized the distinction between the image as such with full divine power and the image as signifying or pointing to that power. It concluded that the divine was *not* inherent in the image; images were not repositories of power. Rather, they were useful for didactic purposes. They were not presences or presentations, but representation, illustration and allegories to remind the faithful of abstract theological figuration transcendent to the image.[6]

At this Council, only Church Men conferred. It was decided that the presences and images of the Earth, everything that comes to meet us in our lives (the voices and spooks as spirits of livid-experience) all these have no integrity except insofar as they are *ens creata* — i.e., entities created by God and therefore having no indigenous order or integrity of their own except as the gift of God and the revealing of His handiwork.

[The deep distrust of phenomenology and the interpretive disciplines is rooted right here. Phenomenology — again, loosed of its essentialism == grants back the integrity of

---

6   James Hillman (1983). p. 71.

> what comes to meet us. It re-animates the Earth and our earthy experience. *Lived* experience is not a psychological notion. It means, not that we are in a world "as-lived-by-us," but that we are in an alive world of which our lives and our experiences are but a fragile part —arced vittles pulled in kind. Phenomenology as Paganism: this pine tree has a whispered message, for me, half-heard suggestions of wind rising up the ridge, almost familiar, a-kin to other walks taken but unable to be captured by an essence, this *happening*. This cuts against the grain of Nicaea. And phenomenology's essentialism is precisely a slouch towards Nicaea.]

This stubborn particular becomes an *ens creatum,* a *creature* which is not itself potent and full of powers and messages and hints and allegations — it does not have anything to say *itself.* It only foreshadows, points to or re-presents true presence: the Creator.

> In the infinite, there is only one single thing (*forma*), and one single word (*vocabulum*), namely, the ineffable Word of God (*Verbum Dei*) that is reflected in everything else (*relucet*).[7]

With the intervention of Cartesianism into this Nicean Logic, it remained the case that the entities of the Earth have no indigenous order or integrity of their own, but, after Descartes, they come to gain order and integrity through the gracious bestowals of meaning that come from human consciousness:

> [If the Church once offered the denigration and sacrificial overcoming of incarnate life as a solution to the human condition, now science offers us the control of matter as our rescue.[8]]

Entities now foreshadow, point to or re-present the new true presence: self-identical self-presence.

---

7   Hans Georg Gadamer (1989). p. 438.
8   Susan Griffin (1989), p. 10.

Objective science, even in turning away from the Church and its council and the evidences of revelation, unwittingly kept in place a thread of Nicene Creed.

With its univocity-of-mathematics-as-the-new-monotheism, the Earth's myriad images and demons are denied power and potency. Objective science thus carried forward the same fear (and eventual rage) of multiplicity and ambiguity that the Church had borne.

> [the "ecclesiastical dislike of any ambiguity... that pagan images might be mistaken for Christian ones."[9]

Likewise:

> to make sure that Christian art was explicit, realistic and unambiguous. They reflect an appreciation of the power of images and a desire to safeguard that power against misuse (which might lead to idolatry [the worship of the image itself]) or misrepresentation (which might revive pagan cults [the worship of the wrong images]).[10]

Perhaps even worse, we are left with a God with no Earthly potency. We are left with a God without genitals, without animality and therefore we are left with our own genitals and our own animality as *sins,* unlike our God:

> This extraordinary religion, the religion that we are all in no matter how hard we try to deny it or escape it, has lost its animals. So it is always fulfilling its image of God without genitals.[11]]

---

9   Juidith Herrin (1987). *The Formation of Christendom.* Princeton: Princeton University Press, p. 313.
10 Judith Herrin (1987). p. 314.
11 James Hillman (1983a). p. 92.

CHAPTER TWENTY-FOUR

The wet intimacy between one thing and another is denied, now not in the name of God but in the name of Reason.
Univocity/monotheism/mathematics as the core of the ecological crisis.
Ecological crisis as Nicaean.
Paganism as ecological.
Interpretation as pagan. Ridiculous.

CHAPTER TWENTY-FIVE

Interpretive work, properly understood, entails a deep veneration of the fully multivocity of the world as it comes to meet us, even below the neck. (Husserl opened this door part way but recoiled aghast into essentialism. Phenomenology is beginning to outlive this recoil).

The world is lived/experienced as full of signs and signals, full of potentialities and powers that are not of our own making and that are not reducible to ourselves or our "willing and wanting,"[1] nor to the wanting and willing of a singular *Deus abscondis* (absent or transcendent God) — or to any other singular, univocal "foundation" (mathematics, human experience, sense data, matter, spirit, this story, that).

Such foundationalism and fundamentalism bleeds the Earth dry, allowing nothing to be loose of the reprimanding center, no voice left to challenge its sway. Nothing can happen in such a world to spook the center and get it into play with the Others. Fundamentalism as humourless. De-luded.

Here is the open war. Interpretation may be anti-Christian, or, perhaps, non-Christian:

> One of the ways of depotentiating polytheism by Christian writers was to deny the power of the world (Logos) to inner voices [it is necessary to add that outer voices are also denied such power unless they are aspects or echoes of the voice of God]. The only true Logos was Christ. To open the door to inner [and outer] voices lets in the powers of darkness, the daimons of antique religion, polytheism and heresy. By refusing even the possibility of more than one voice — except the voice of the devil — all *daimones* became demonic and anti-Christian in their message, and in their very multiplicity. [Multiplicity of voices as anti-Christian. This is why Jung faced such opposition, why phenomenology faces such heat and why hermeneutics is always treated with suspicion. This is also why Jung has been rendered into a retentive typology, phenomenology has emphasized is normative aspects

---

[1] Hans-Georg Gadamer (1989). p. xxviii.

and hermeneutics has become a research methodology: each forms of conservative response to the deepest and most dangerous nightmares of each. Typological archetype psychology, normative phenomenology and methodological hermeneutics are, thus, the most popular forms of each because these allow one to get a good night's sleep, each unhaunted, clear, and calm in its confidence]. Introspection's course and limits were set by a consciousness that insisted on unity. To hear the depths not only affronted Christian tradition; it invited what had been declared by the Devil, Hell, and madness.[2]

"Unable to hear the Wolf call him brother."[3]

And, regarding this "consciousness that insisted on Unity," phenomenology slowly folds back into monotheism.

First:

> You will never find the boundaries of the soul, even if you follow every road; so deep is its ground." Indeed, every "ground" [*Grund*] that is reached points to further grounds, every horizon opened up awakens new horizons.[4]

But then, just when we imagine the transcendental project of phenomenology is about to spill its guts out into the Earth, Husserl goes on:

> . . .and yet the endless whole, in its infinity of flowing movement, is oriented toward the unity of one meaning.[5]

And even though Husserl then goes on to admit that this whole cannot ever be grasped, this ungraspable still somehow orients our lives towards a unity of meaning: towards "an infinite totality,"[6] "a universal reason,"[7] "a universal form,"[8] "the essential order."[9] The phenomenologist becomes

---

2   James Hillman (1983a). p. 64-5.
3   Ursula le Guin. (1987).
4   Edmund Husserl. (1970). p. 170.
5   Edmund Husserl (1970). p. 170.
6   Edmund Husserl (1970). p. 170.
7   Edmund Husserl (1970). p. 170.
8   Edmund Husserl (1970). p. 170.
9   Edmund Husserl (1970). p. 170.

"the bearer of a teleology"[10] bound by a "unity of purpose"[11] of which phenomenology is the "final form."[12]

The courage to "plumb the depths of the soul" thus comes from the hope of one meaning (phenomenology as monotheism). Essences are produced by hope and all the holding on and waiting that hope requires (essence as anal retentiveness, closed sphincters — the reprimand always begins with "now hold on just a minute"). Once produced, essences produce despair in those who fail to live up to them (and also produce a hope to be *elsewhere,* living like *them,* doing like *that over there:* the colonized are never "at home" and the colonizers always bring the "home office" with them).

Normativity as a weapon of colonialism. Hope and despair as the moods of colonialism.

This is precisely the same sort of hope (and despair) that guides the normativity and essentialism of phenomenological pedagogy.

---

10   Edmund Husserl (1970). p. 70.
11   Edmund Husserl (1970). p. 70
12   Edmund Husserl (1970). p. 70

CHAPTER TWENTY-SIX

Cartesian logic still called upon God to guarantee the clarity and distinctness of his ideas. Through the ontological proof, Descartes produced a God full of love and beneficence who would not deceive us. Clear and distinct ideas are true.

After Kant the guarantee is no longer sought in God. *It is no longer sought at all.*

Immanuel Kant's so-called "Copernican Revolution"[1] in philosophy re-claimed at the *epistemological* level what was lost in the *cosmological* level in the work of Copernicus.

Copernicus displaced the Earth as the center of Creation and placed the sun at the center of the visible universe, thus decentering humanity from its special cosmological place. Kant reclaimed the center by putting human Reason at the center of the *knowable* Universe: anything knowable refers back to the conditions of knowability which are determined by the essential character of Reason. But there is an extra step to watch for in this re-claiming.

Human Reason, as a synthesizing faculty, bestows order upon the Universe, turning the chaotic in-flux of experience into a knowable (i.e., orderly) *cosmos*. Knowledge becomes conceived as *constructive of a world*.

We hear our words making up a world. This additional step profoundly shifts the logic of the Cartesian legacy in which Kant's work stands.

Descartes rendered the subject *worldless* through his methodical doubt and the world was retrieved only through God's benevolent guaranteeing of the objective reality of the clear and distinct ideas that this worldless subject thinks[2]. The subject, in Kant's work, is not *worldless*. But neither has it retrieved the world itself through Divine intervention.

---

1   Immanuel Kant (1787/1964). p. 22.
2   René Descartes (1955). p. 107-126.

Rather, *the human subject lives in a world of its own making*. Given this, the human subject can do with the world what it wishes, since the world as experienced is of its own "doing" in the first place.

Consider, from the "Preface" to Immanuel Kant's *Critique of Pure Reason* (1787):

> A light broke upon the students of nature. They learned that reason has insight only into that which it produces after a plan of its own, and that it must not allow itself to be kept, as it were, in nature's leading-strings, but must itself show the way with principles of judgement based on fixed laws, constraining nature to give answer to questions of reason's own determining. Reason...must approach nature in order to be taught by it. It must not, however, do so in the character of a pupil who listens to everything the teacher chooses to say, but of an appointed judge who compels the witnesses to answer questions which he had himself formulated. While reason must seek in nature, not fictitiously ascribe to it, whatever has to be learnt, if learnt at all, only from nature, it must adopt as its guide, in so seeking, that which it has itself put into nature.[3]

There are two echoes in this passage that are enticing. Both contain implicit images of pedagogy.

One is a clear echo of the Enlightenment call that Kant himself (1784) expressed and which we've already cited above:

> *Enlightenment is man's emergence from his self-imposed immaturity. Immaturity* is the inability to use one's understanding without guidance from another. This immaturity is *self-imposed* when its cause lies not in a lack of understanding, but in a lack of resolve and courage to use it without guidance from another. *Sapere Aude!:* "Have courage to use your own understanding!" — that is the motto of enlightenment.[4]

Kant's Copernican Revolution elevated human Reason to the point of being its own guide, of needing no guidance from another. We therefore find hints in the above-cited passage from the *Critique of Pure Reason* of the pupil turning away from his teachers and their guidance (one

---

3   Immanuel Kant (1964). p. 20.
4   Immanuel Kant (1983). p. 41.

meaning of "leading strings" is "pupilage" or being lead or taught by another). Under the Enlightenment ideal, *any* guidance is ruled out as indicative of childishness or immaturity. We must approach the Earth unindebted, "self-guiding."

Another image buried here is one of the boy cutting the leading-strings (or "apron strings") that bind him to his mother — an implicit denial of any lingering dependency on the one who gives us birth. If we admit that the Earth gives us birth, then Reason remains somehow indebted to another. This again despoils the Enlightenment ideal of a humanity guided by Reason alone, somehow independent of its animate but irrational humus ("leading-strings" names a cord used to lead animals). Once the leading strings are cut, it is we now who take the lead, who can "stand on our own two feet" ("leading-strings" were use to teach children to stand and walk; it is also used as a metaphor for "dependency").

As with Descartes methodical doubt, this metaphor of Kant's embodies the denial that the Earth somehow guides us, sustains us and bears us up. Kant's work stands, to this extent, in the shadow of the Cartesian ideal of a subject who is severed and separate from the Earth. Now separate and alien, the Earth no longer houses us but stands before us as an object. This object can henceforth be subjected to the subject's logico-mathematical demands for clarity and distinctness from all that comes to meet it.

Already cited from Susan Bordo:

> If a kind of Cartesian ideal were every completely fulfilled, i.e., if the whole of nature were only what can be explained in terms of mathematical relationships — then we would look at the world with that fearful sense of alienation, with that utter loss of reality with which a future schizophrenic child looks at his mother. A machine cannot give birth.[5]

---

5   Susan Bordo (1987). p. 37.

But worse than this, worse that schizophrenia, we now begin to believe, under the rubric of the Copernican Revolution, that we give birth to the Earth and not the other way around. Kantianism (and Piagetianism) as the final patriarchal distention. No longer is this to be understood merely epistemologically: the world is there *for us*.

Again, the logic is still Nicaean: all signs point this way, now not to God, but to the *a priori* structure of pure reason.

CHAPTER TWENTY-SEVEN

The bizarre and convoluted horror pronounced so calmly, in the mid-19th century by Arthur Schopenhauer:

> "The world is my representation": This is a truth valid with reference to every living and knowing being, although man alone can bring it into reflective, abstract consciousness. If he really does so, philosophical discernment has dawned on him. It then becomes clear and certain to him that he does not know a sun and an earth, but only an eye that sees a sun, a hand that feels an earth; that the world around him is there only as representation, in other words, only in reference to another thing, namely, that which represents, and this is himself.[1]

At first glance, Schopenhauer's words might seem to foretell a sense of interdependency, but, in the end, it is only a dependency. To understand the sun, the Earth, requires only a reflective understanding of our powers to represent. Between sun and earth there is an interdependency, but such interdependency is a matter of our representing, of our *bestowing* cosmos on chaos (as Jean Piaget so calmly defines the young child's actions on the world) such that interdependency is rooted in a deeper dependency on the one who represents. The Earth is ours to envisage, to make in our own image. Thus "the sickness of the West" begins. In our envisaging of the Earth, all we can see is this facade, and this facade gains its integrity by being linked back to human being — suddenly we, as humans, have no place on the Earth but have become that place in which all other things, the whole Earth, comes forth:

> Man sets himself up as the setting in which whatever is must henceforth set itself forth, must present itself. Man becomes the representative of that which is. What is decisive is that man expressly takes up this position as one constituted by himself...and that he makes it secure as the solid footing for a possible development of

---

[1] Arnold Schopenhauer (1963). *The World as Will and Representation*. New York: Dover Books, p. 63.

humanity. There begins that way of being human which mans the realm of human capacity as a domain given over to measuring and executing, for the purposes of gaining mastery of what is as a whole.[2]

Under the shadow of Western epistemology, "what is as a whole" possesses a singular center which dispenses the possibility of things and thus oversteps its own Earthly possibility with unearthly, transcendental zeal. The human being becomes the condition for the possibility of all things. The world become our representation as we solemnly become the singular representatives of all things. We become, here, the grand colonizers.

[It is at this juncture that the colonial metaphor becomes potent. Humanity, conceived as cleaving to Reason, becomes the home(office) from which orders are given. What comes to meet us is colonized with demands for unequivocal clarity and distinctness. Reason becomes the right of passage (*colon* — the home office is where the colonized must get a "pass") for the Earth. Reason decides what will "pass" and what will not and therefore, since the Earth gains integrity from us, we can colonize it without hesitation. It is not a coincidence that Western epistemological inheritance is European and that it is from Europe that colonization proceeded. It is no coincidence that we might, on the epistemological level, believe that we are the ones that can warrantably savage those we consider undeveloped, disorderly, unorganized, unruly, unmethodical, immature, unreliable, unreasonable, possessing no indigenous integrity, in need of our gracious bestowal of order, needing to be "whipped into shape."]

[Tighten this down one more turn and we find precisely these images operative in what Alice Miller[3] called the "black pedagogies" of the seventeenth and eighteenth centuries: children are the wild and wilful ones who must be made to "mind," who must be

---

2   Martin Heidegger (1971) p. 132.
3   Alice Miller (1989). *For Your Own Good: Hidden Cruelty in Child-Rearing and the Roots of Violence.* Toronto: Collins Books.

"taught a lesson." Another turn and we have the disturbing work of Ashis Nandy[4] who documents how the colonized have been understood as children in need of guidance. And the graciousness of such colonization is always and everywhere done under the most noble of rubrics, so gently understated in the title of Alice Miller's (1987) book: *For Your Own Good.*]

Compare: the colonial urge to "have" the whole of things is accomplished by imposition and holding on. Compare with:

> I found myself doing three months of long, hard physical labor, out on the trails every day, living more or less in isolation, twenty-five miles from the nearest road. We never went out. We just stayed in there working on those trails week after week. At the beginning, I found myself straining against it, trying to exercise my mind as I usually exercise it. I was reading Milton, and I had some other readings, and I was trying to go out on the trails during the day and think about things in a serious, intellectual way, while doing my work. And it was frustrating, although I had done the same thing before, on many jobs. Finally, I gave up trying to carry on an intellectual interior life separate from the work, and I said the hell with it, I'll just work. And instead of losing something, I got something much greater. By just working, I found myself being completely there, having he whole mountain inside of me, and finally having a whole language inside of me that became one with the rocks and with the trees. And that was where I first learned of the possibility of being one with what you were doing, and not losing anything of the mind thereby.[5]

---

4   Ashish Nandy (1987). *Traditions, Tyranny and Utopias: Essays in Political Awareness.* Delhi: Oxford University Press.
5   Gary Snyder (1980) p. 8.

CHAPTER TWENTY-EIGHT

> Whereas a church spire inspires me to lift up my eyes to the heavens above, entering a tearoom inspires in me something different. The entrance to the ceremonial room, by the very way it is built, urges me to incline my body and to bow, bringing me closer to the earth those textured layers of humus allow buds of tea trees to leaf. The savouring of the tea allows me to touch again this earth that cradles and nourishes both my body and soul. During the Tea ceremony, I come to respect the fullness of silence, and I become aware of how silently I participate in the constituting of that silence. And in that silence, I experience being-one-with-the-earth.[1]

We have been schooled into aspirations that draw our eyes upward, or, more horrifying, inward into the seductive Cartesian allure of self-presence.

In *Nausea,* Jean-Paul Sartre's fingertips are no longer flesh of the same Earth as the tree he touches; they are no longer flesh at all. His fingertips are only his reflective self-awareness of that touching:

> *Geneson*: So when Sartre...goes to the tree, touches the tree trunk and say, "I feel in an absurd position. — I cannot break through my skin to get in touch with this bark, which is outside me," the Japanese poet would say...?
>
> *Snyder*: Sartre is confessing the sickness of the West. At least he is honest. The [poet] will say, "But there are ways to do it, my friend. It's no big deal." It's no big deal, especially if you get attuned to that possibility from early in life.[2]

---

1   Ted Aoki (1987). In receiving, a giving: A response to the panelist's gifts. *Journal of Curriculum Theorizing.* 7(3), p. 67.
2   Gary Snyder (1980). p. 67.

Something is awakened here that is beyond the nightmare of self-presence and its ensuing exhaustion. It is a "call to be mindful of our rootedness in earthy experiences."[3]

But more: such a call can best be heard "if you get attuned to that possibility from early in life." Attunement. But also pedagogy. The possibility of touching the Earth, this attunement, is rooted (perhaps also uprooted) early in life.

---

3   Ted Aoki (1987). p. 67.

CHAPTER TWENTY-NINE

Climbing up into our heads: in our heads, we end up with an abstract sense of whereabouts:

> The industrial conquistador, seated in his living room in the evening in front of the TV set, many miles from his work, can easily forget where he is and what he has done. He is everywhere and nowhere. Everything around him, everything on TV, tells him of his success: *his* comfort is the redemption of the world.[1]
>
> In homes full of "conveniences" which signify that all is well, in an automated kitchen, in a gleaming, odorless bathroom, in year-round air-conditioning, in color TV, in an easy chair, the world is redeemed. If what God made can be made by humans into *this,* then what can be wrong?[2]

Such an abstract sense of whereabouts can be the result of "environmental awareness" as easily as it can be a result of Cartesian logic, if we forget that although this place — this foothill of pine and spruce and poplar and ash — is interlacing to all things, it is *nowhere else but here.* This interlacing does not make all things *identical,* but rather keeps everything in place, "*this* and *this.*"[3]

Writ too large, "environmental awareness" gets puffy and woozy about "wholeness" as a *concept* or a dream image.

To be ecologically sane, I do require a huge sense of place (because *in my head, in my car, in my house, in "my story",* I, this small ego-me, looms quite large. In the biography of the bios I am in this distended and bloated Ego-image is impossible), but all this shit hits the fan *here:*

---

1 Wendell Berry (1986). p. 52-3.
2 Wendell Berry (1986). p. 52.
3 Bronwen Wallace (1987). p. 111. And this is the important sense in which this book *is* my autobiography and the responsibility and culpability for the logic *we* are living out *I* cannot defer as not part of my life.

> It is impossible to divorce the question of what we do from the question of where we are — or, rather, where we think we are. That no sane creature befouls its own nest is accepted as generally true. What we conceive to be our nest, where we think it is, are therefore questions of the greatest importance.[4]

During the recent twentieth anniversary celebrations of the first moon landing, one of the former Apollo astronauts was asked how he would sum up what the Apollo program was all about. He replied, "It's about leaving."

It is interesting to speculate as to whether there is any interconnection between the lack of success in generating any great excitement about "further, deeper penetration into the solar system" and "getting it [the program] up again" (and a great deal of other unintentional but still rather blatantly phallocentric talk), and the recent flourishing of ecological awareness.

For ecological awareness is not about *leaving* but about responsibly staying put here on Earth. It has to do with the *logos* of our home, our dwelling, and with how we can come to be at home here in a way that does not overstep the real possibilities of dwelling responsibly, sanely, in a way that does not befoul the very "nest" that houses us.

Ecology is therefore about returning our attention to home. It is about tending anew to where we dwell, to our nest, to the delicate and difficult reliances and debts that intertwine our fleshy lives with the fleshy life of the Earth; it is this moist texture that *bestows* our lives and makes them possible. Becoming attentive to this original bestowal, this "original blessing"[5] requires more than "understanding" and "knowing" as they have come to be. Our issuing up out of the Earth is not a set of objective relations that we can place in front of us for our perusal. Understanding such issuance requires cultivating "the continuity of attention and devotion without which the human life of the earth is impossible. The care of the earth is our most ancient and most worthy and, after all, our most

---

4   Wendell Berry (1986) p. 51.
5   Matthew Fox (1983).

pleasing responsibility. To cherish what remains of it, and to foster its renewal, is our only legitimate hope."⁶

Attention, devotion, care, worthiness, cherishing, fostering, renewal, hope: these are not just any words. They echo a deep sense of place, of remaining, of dwelling, of settling. These words bring with them a sense of memory and continuity and regeneration, a mindfulness of what is needed for life to go on, and a passing on of such mindfulness to the young. Children are already present in these words. These are the tales to be told, the housing of knowledge in memory and ways:

> The community is an order of memories preserved consciously in instructions, songs, and stories, and both consciously and unconsciously in *ways*. A healthy culture holds preserving knowledge *in place* for a *long* time [so that we, hear, must live with the consequences]. That is, the essential wisdom accumulates in the community much as fertility builds in the soil. In both death becomes potentiality.⁷

"Leaving" once described our fanciful hopes for the future. It is now becoming one of the traumatic and painful features of ecological insight — we cannot just *leave*, for the exhaustion left in the wake of such leaving inevitably *returns*, and, just as inevitably, it returns *here*. Even if the ecological consequences of our actions do not return to this specific place, *we* return here slightly more insane, slightly more "out of place," "out of touch" with where we really are. We carry this consequence in our hearts along with the displaced and displacing belief that we live somewhere other than on the whole of the Earth, needing to believe, to protect our sanity, that we have left those consequences "someplace else."

[The false reification of the self is basic to the ecological crisis in which we now find ourselves. We have imagined that the "unit of survival" as (Gregory) Bateson puts it, is the separate individual or the separate species. In reality, as throughout the history of

---

6   Wendell Berry (1986). p. 14.
7   Wendell Berry (1983). p. 73.

> evolution, it is the individual *plus* environment, the species *plus* environment, for they are essentially symbiotic.

> When you narrow down your epistemology and act on the premise "What interests me is me, or my organization, or my species," you chop off consideration of other loops of the loop structure. You decide you want to get rid of the by-products of human life and that Lake Erie will be a good place to put them. You forget that the eco-mental system called Lake Erie is part of *your* wider eco-mental system — and that if Lake Erie is driven insane, its insanity is incorporated in the larger system of *your* thought and experience.[8]

If home is abandoned altogether — if we all get caught up in "leaving" — our care for and devotion to the conditions, sources and intimate dependencies of renewal and generativity are also abandoned. Ecology and pedagogy thus interweave to the extent that separating them or separating our responsibilities for them can be accomplished only at a tragic cost: "No matter the distinctions we draw, the connections, the dependencies, remain. To damage the Earth is to damage your children."[9] Perhaps we will see that pedagogy, too, is "our most pleasing responsibility." It, too, requires the very same love, care and generosity of spirit as ecological awareness. Ecology is silently and inevitably interwoven with pedagogy.

In the face of this interweaving, we cannot just "leave" *even though we can just "leave."*

Para-doxa. Beyond beliefs.

---

8   Joanne Macy (1989). Awakening to the ecological self. In Judith Plant (1989). *Healing the Wounds.* Toronto: Between the Lines Press, p. 205-6.
9   Wendell Berry (1986). p. 57.

CHAPTER THIRTY

Ecological awareness begins and remains within a paradox regarding human life. We can do the impossible:

> The unnoticeable law of the Earth preserves the Earth in the sufficiency of the emerging and perishing of all things in the allotted sphere of the possible which everything follows and yet nothing knows. The birch tree never oversteps its possibility. It is [human] will which drives the Earth beyond the sphere of its possibility into such things that are no longer a possibility and are thus the impossible. It is one thing to just use the Earth, another to receive the blessing of the Earth and to become at home in the law of this reception in order to shepherd the mystery and watch over the inviolability of the possible.[1]

"The inviolability of the possible" here is not commensurate with what we *can* do, assuming "that the human prerogative is unlimited, that we *must* do whatever we have the power to do. What is lacking [in such an assumption] is the idea that humans have a place and that this place is limited by responsibility on the one hand and by humility on the other."[2]

[Compare:

If the application of science were simply the problem of how,
with the help of science,
we might do
everything we can do,
then it is certainly not the application we need
as human beings who are responsible for the future.
For science as such will never prevent us from doing
anything we are able to do.
The future of humanity, however, demands that we

---

1 Martin Heidegger (1987) Overcoming metaphysics. In *The End of Philosophy*. New York: Harper and Row, p. 109.
2 Wendell Berry (1983). p. 54-5.

do not simply do everything we can.³]

Human action, human will, can, so to speak, spiral out of order, out of proportion, breaking the analogical threads of kinship that might delimit our prerogative. Our truly sane, human prerogative finds itself interwoven with the Earth and the fundamental dependencies and reliances that "limit" our actions, not to what is *conceivable,* but to what is *sustainable.*

The problem is, of course, that we *can* act without having a strong sense of where we are, of what reliances and harmonies "house" us (we *can* "leave") and we often believe that this "can" is our freedom. Ecology (and pedagogy) remind us that if what we do despoils the conditions under which our doing can go on (if what we do befouls the Earth which houses the possibility of doing *anything*), then such doings are not freedom but insanity. Such supposed "freedom" is insanity if it undercuts its own continuance, its own possibility. Thus, ecology concerns, not what we can do (in some utopian sense which is literally no-place), but what is proper, what is properly responsive to the place in which we find ourselves, those actions which have propriety, those which are "fitting," and which issue up out of a place as a considerate response to that place (i.e., a response that somehow acts in accordance with the sustainability of that response).

Again, this language contains the notions of family resemblance, and kinship. A sense of being at home in a place. It requires action and thought which preserve the integrity of the place that houses us (of course the integrity of the "whole," but worked out *in place*):

> Some people are beginning to try to understand where they are, and what it would mean to live carefully and wisely, delicately in a place, in such a way that you can live there adequately and comfortably. Also, your children and grandchildren and generations a thousand years in the future would still be able to live there. That's living in terms of the whole fabric of living and life.⁴

---

3   Hans-Georg Gadamer (1977). p. 196-7.
4   Gary Snyder (1980) p. 86.

The ecopedagogical response thus involves, not just the possibility but the necessity of *turning* and *re-turning*, of renewal and re-generativity:

> Reproduction is nurturing, patient, resigned to the pace of seasons and lives, respectful of the nature of things. Production's tendency is to go "all out"; it always aims to set a new record. Reproduction is more conservative and more modest; its aim is not to happen once, but to happen again and again and again, and so it seeks a balance between saving and spending.[5]

5 Wendell Berry (1986). p. 217.

CHAPTER THIRTY-ONE

Thinking is not a means to gain knowledge. Thinking cuts furrows in the soil of Being. About 1875, Nietzsche once wrote (Grossoktav WW XI, 20): "Our thinking should have a vigorous fragrance, like a wheatfield on a summer's night." How many of us today still have the senses for that fragrance?[1]

When the young
retell the tale
the old can learn,
but neither about the young or about the old
but about where they might dwell together, this place.
Familiaris.[2]

All the children are wild[3] and
if we measure ourselves against them[4]
we will learn about the porous[5] limits
of necessity and mystery.[6]

Children's voices cleave deep furrows – all these ideas grow wild. Vigourous fragrances if we still have the sense to live more openly in the metaphoricity[7] of our own boneless tongue.

This is some of us speaking,
echocanyon ridge to gorge to ridge.[8]

---

1   Martin Heidegger (1971) The nature of language. In *On the Way to Language*. New York: Harper and Row, p. 70
2   James Hillman (1987a). p. 161.
3   Ursula LeGuin (1989). p. 47.
4   Against the "wild(er)ness." Wendell Berry (1986). p. 99.
5   James Hillman (1987a).
6   Wendell Berry (1983). p. 13.
7   Hans-Georg Gadamer (1989). p. 432.
8   Gary Snyder (1980). p. 48.

> Literalism is a product of senex turned senile[9]
> Forgetting the wisdoms of youth that lure
> the soul out of moist hollows[10]
> making it sing its breath and pulse
> Newsongs of the breaking open of old soils.
>
> The metaphoricity of language is the puer
> playing, flightyskitter through old edifice
> arcs of dry grey stone, full of Eros,
> porous and blood.
>
> *Familiaris*, daemon[11] child, who can tell
> us what lurks if we listen.[12]

This "return to the Greeks" *is* a cosmological matter.[13] Greece thus offers a "polycentric" (p. 33) world with "innumerable personifications" (p. 33),

---

9   James Hillman (1987).

10 James Hillman (1987b). Peaks and vales. In *Puer Papers*. Dallas: Spring Publications.

11 *Daimon* is the original Greek spelling for these figures who later became *demons* because of the Christian view and *daemons* in a positive contradistinction to that view. Know Thyself means to become familiar with, to open oneself to and listen to, that is, to know and discern, daimones. Entering one's interior story takes a courage similar to starting a novel. We have to engage with persons whose autonomy may radically alter, even dominate our thoughts and feelings, neither. They are we are drawn together like threads into a *mythos*. It is rare courage that submits to this middle region where the supposed surety of fact and illusion of fiction exchange their clothes. (James Hillman [1983], p. 54-5)

12 James Hillman (1987a). p. 161.

13 When the monotheism of consciousness is no longer able to deny the existence of fragmentary autonomous systems and no longer able to deal with our actual state, then there arises the fantasy of returning to Greek polytheism. For the "return to the Greeks" offers a way of coping when our centers cannot hold and things fall apart. The polytheistic alternative does not set up conflicting opposites between beast and Bethlehem, between chaos and unity; it permits the coexistence of all the psychic fragments and gives them patterns in the imagination of Greek mythology. A "return to Greece" was experienced in ancient Rome itself, and in the Italian Renaissance, and in the Romantic psyche during the times of revolution. In recent years it has been an intrinsic part of the lives

but in this cosmos, "here, too, the gods are present"¹⁴ in the simplest of events.

Trick. They also had slaves. Now what? See footnote 373. A "return to Greece" in and of itself and taken literally isn't going to help anything. It is not yet another centre of beliefs we need.

of such artists and thinkers as Stravinsky, Picasso, Heidegger, Joyce and Freud. The "return to Greece" is a psychological response to the challenge of breakdown; it offers a model of disintegrated integration.

James Hillman (1975). *Re-Visioning Psychology*. New York: Harper and Row, p. 26-7.

14 Martin Heidegger (1977a). p. 234.

CHAPTER THIRTY-TWO

We are always educating for a world that is or is becoming out of joint, for this is the basic human situation, in which the world is created by mortal hands to serve mortals for a limited time as home. Because the world is made by mortals it wears out; and because it continuously changes its inhabitants it runs the risk of becoming as mortal as they. To preserve the world against the mortality of its creators and inhabitants it must be constantly set right anew. The problem is simply to educate in such a way that a setting-right remains actually possible, even though it can, of course, never be assured. Our hope always hangs on the new which every generation brings; but precisely because we can base our hope only on this, we destroy everything if we so try to control the new that we, the old, can dictate how it will look. Exactly for the sake of what is new and revolutionary in every child, education must be conservative; it must preserve this newness and introduce it as a new thing into the old world.[1]

Pedagogy stands between invention and tradition,[2] between the young and the old and it is responsible for both. And even invention is both something new and something linked to inventory. It provides for the fecund case to deeply meet that *of which* it is fecund.

> [Therefore, interpretation is fundamentally pedagogic at its heart. Therefore, interpretive studies of pedagogy have an interiority that makes them especially apropos to this task. The disciplines of knowledge in schools are *living*.]

This meeting is transformative of tradition as much as it is transformative of the young.

This meeting is *protective* of tradition as much as it is *protective* of the young.

---

1   Hannah Arendt (1969). p. 192-3.
2   Michael Fishbane (1986). p. 34.

Enamoured of the young alone, pedagogy abandons its responsibility to the world (and falls prey to the "pathos of the new"[3] — the pathos of that which has no sustaining "ethos"). Enamoured of the young, pedagogy, while "worshipping the new,"[4] becomes "afflicted by openness,"[5] caught up in a headlong "flight into the future,"[6] wherein "personal revelation is preferred to objective knowledge,"[7] and "wingedness becomes mere haste."[8] Enamoured of the old alone, pedagogy abandons its responsibility to the young (and falls prey to the uninvigorated, merely replicated "ethos of the old," — turning ethics into dusty, condescending moralizing).

Enamoured of the old, pedagogy becomes "unable to sow seed"[9] and "feeds on the growth of others, as for instance the growth of one's own children,"[10] bearing "no wisdom, only knowledge, hoarded in an academic vault or used as power."[11]

Only together are the young fecund (and not simply "new") and is the world set right anew once again (and not simply "old").

The teacher stands along this sharpedge which must move like moontides, pulled by this child and this, attentive, wary, interpreting the world.[12] And this requires deeply understanding — deeply making

---

3   Hannah Arendt (1969). p. 178.
4   James Hillman (1987). p. 27.
5   James Hillman (1987b). Puer wounds and Ulysses' scar. In *Puer Papers*. Dallas: Spring Publications, p. 113.
6   James Hillman (1987). p. 28.
7   James Hillman (1987). p. 28.
8   James Hillman (1987). p. 27.
9   James Hillman (1987). p. 21.
10 James Hillman (1987). p. 21.
11 James Hillman (1987). p. 21.
12 In education [we] assume responsibility for both, for the life and development of the child and for the continuance of the world. These two responsibilities do not by any means coincide; they may indeed come into conflict with each other. The responsibility for the development of the child turns in a certain sense against the world: the child requires special protection and care so that nothing destructive may happen to him from the world. But the world, too, needs protection to keep it from being overrun and destroyed by the onslaught of the new that burst upon it with each new generation. (Hannah Arendt [1969], p. 185-6)

understandable to children — even those aspects of the world that we might despise, for only to the extent that these aspects of the world become *interpretable* does the possibility of interpreting things differently — "setting right anew" — become "actually possible."

At the heart of "teacher-knowledge" is the knowledge that the world is interpretable. This is equivalent to knowing that each child is fecund in relation to the world and this is equivalent to knowing that the world itself is multiple and generative in its facets. Believing that the child is fecund is not simply believing that interpretation is *possible*. It is believing that the world *needs* interpretation for its own renewal. And this is not simply loving children for their newness and ebullience and uniqueness, but also loving the world in its full multiplicity, its full, agonizing *interpretability*. If we don't help this child's newness and ebullience and uniqueness work its way out into the world, we abandon the child *and* the world — the child will remain isolated in difference with no soils for sustenance

> [thereby remaining "unwhole,"
> wound-severed from the world
> — "puerile," the worst aspect of
> children]

and the world will remain unrenewed

> Arendt goes as far as to suggest that, even in the cases where we may "secretly or openly" (p. 189) wish the world were otherwise, we must, in any case:
>
>> stand in relation to the young as representatives of a world for which [we] must assume joint responsibility although [we] ourselves did not make it." (p. 189)
>
> (And this right in the midst of all the dangers involved in representationalism — us standing in for the world). Thus, even in cases where we despise what the world has become, we, as adults, stand before children as co-responsible for what that world has become. The urgency of envisaging pedagogy as involving a generative interpretation of the world in such cases, all too obvious. To become responsible for the world means to care for the conditions under which it might now be set right anew — one condition of which is caring for children, for they are one of the irrevocable conditions of renewal.

[thereby remaining "unwhole," wound-severed
from the young and the possibility of its own
transformation — "senile," the worst aspect of age.[13]].

[This is true of us just like it is true of
trees
who (hah! Which?)

13 "Education is suffering from narration-sickness," says Paulo Freire. It speaks out of a story which was once full of enthusiasm, but now shows itself incapable of a surprise ending. The nausea of narration-sickness comes from having heard enough, of hearing many variations on a theme but no new theme. A narrative which is sick may claim to speak for all, yet has no aporia, no possibility of meeting a stranger because the text is complete already. Such narratives may be passed as excellent by those who certify clarity and for whom ambiguity is a disease to be excoriated. But the literalism of such narratives (speeches, lectures, stories) inevitably produces a pedagogy which, while passes as being "for the good of children," does not recognize the violence against children inherent in its own claim. Because without an acknowledgement and positive appreciation of the full polysemic possibility which can explode forth from within any occasion when adult and child genuinely meet together: a possibility which resides precisely in the difference of every child, every person, a difference about which one can presume nothing despite the massive research literature (e.g., about children) available to us, and despite the fact that our children come from us, are our flesh and blood. Without an appreciation of the radical mystery which confronts us in the face of every other person, our theorizing must inexorably become stuck, for then we are no longer available for that which comes to meet us from beyond ourselves, having determined in advance the conditions under which any new thing will be acceptable, and thereby foreclosing on the possibility of our own transformation. This radical difference of every child, every other person, renders our pedagogical narratives ambiguous but at the same time hopeful, because the immanent ambiguity held within them opens a space for genuine speaking, holding out the promise that something new can be said from out of the mists of the oracle of our own flesh.

David G. Smith (1988d). Brighter than a thousand suns: Facing Pedagogy in the nuclear shadow. In Terrance Carson, ed., *Toward a Renaissance of Humanity: Rethinking and Reorienting Curriculum and Instruction*. Edmonton: University of Alberta, p. 282-3)

CHAPTER THIRTY-TWO

> need rooting soils
> to which they will each in turn add themselves and soils which need new seeds and
> roots to burst open layers that are sedimented too hard for bearing.]

At the heart of teaching is an agony, not an essence.

So, to make mathematics *liveable* (which is *not* the aim of Cartesian logic, believing as it does that mathematics is a self-enclosed, self-referential system, A=A) is to link mathematics to pedagogy, to the breath of *poesis* — the newfluttersong arises, changed for spring, *familiaris,* full of "analogical integrities"[14] that lurk.

Disciplines and ways *need* those who will take them on.

> The gods which found
> me *desire* my attention:
> this is why I sometimes fear their nearness
> closing in and sometimes feel
> their nearness as self-transcendence.[15]
> The gods need us to believe in them.

[The horror of patriarchal knowledge is the unvoiced belief that this knowledge does not need the young except as identical replicas of itself. These are the "black

---

14   Wendell Berry (1988). p. 138.
15   This is also the root of the turn away from tradition, because the desire of the gods which found me veers along a knife-edge where I can be easily consumed by these gods and their desires and lose the particularity of my own voice.
     This loss would be dual, not single. The gods would lose as well.

pedagogies"[16] of "gericentrism"[17]].

[The horror of the opposite extreme is the unvoiced belief that this knowledge is not necessary at all and that all is uniqueness and difference. "Empowering," "child-centered" pedagogy often slouches into this numb extremity that leaves tradition untransformed and unrenewed…

NOTE: but still at work and still powerful now in its worst, most senile aspect (the consequence of being left unrenewed, i.e., unread, i.e., uninterpreted[18]]

…our attitude towards the fact of natality: the fact that we have all come into the world by being born and that this world is constantly renewed through birth. Education is the point at which we decide whether we love the world enough to assume responsibility for it and by the same token save it from that ruin which, except for renewal, except for the coming of the new and the young, would be inevitable. And education, too, is where we decide whether we love our children

---

16   Alice Miller (1987).
17   David G. Smith (1988).
18   This is the horrible consequence of a phenomenology which will not interpret the world but which moves to an alternate sphere of "lived experience" which it claims is *not* infused by the logic we are living out. Such phenomenology is naive and dangerous. See David Jardine (1988b).

enough not to expel them from our world and leave them to their own devices, nor to strike from their hands their chance of undertaking something new, something unforeseen by us, but to prepare them in advance for the task of renewing a common world.[19]

---

19   Hannah Arendt (1969). p. 196.

CHAPTER THIRTY-THREE

"Here, too, the gods are present,"[1] here, in the simplest of events. "This."[2]: a young child, four years old, runs up full of enthusiasm and declares:"I can count all the way up to 100!" All the way up. Bodily ascendencies pulled by faint gravity.

So: To make mathematics more (for)giving of the lovely metaphoricity of language.

To show mathematics as a having-spiralled-out-of-order distention of a more Earthly discourse.

Pedagogy as a loving way to tell mathematics of its kin.

The interpretive task, the pedagogic task, the ecological task, is not to turn away from mathematics and the logic of Cartesianism but to read this logic out into its dependencies of Earthly grace.

To fail to do this is to turn away from that which needs interpretation (opening) most of all.

To fail to do this is to abandon the kin who need us most.

Mathematics itself is not an *enemy* — it is *us* at our most eloquent. And we are *all* living out this logic that is centuries old —the logic of mathematics uninterpreted, taken literally as if it described the very (assumed to be univocal — this assumption a remnant of monotheism) *Being* of things and needed no other voices as kin to its utterances (no need if Being is univocal — consequent of Heidegger's showing that Being is temporal is the immediate multivocity of the history of Being).

To loose this logic we are living out is to re-introduce mathematics to its kin.

---

1   Martin Heidegger (1977a). p. 234.
2   Bronwen Wallace (1987). p. 111.

[But this book isn't about some
one.
It is not an attempt to demonize René Descartes. It is about daimons that haunt us all. Daimons that lurk in the logic we are living out. The problem with essentialism/mathematics is that it cannot understand itself as one of the threads, "interweaving, criss-crossing."[3]
Essentialism and the monotheism it implies refuses to see itself as one of the daimons, dancing,
dark fire,
among others, having a place, an appropriateness, here and here, telling for this, silent for that. It understands itself as the one and everywhere true God. Univocity is *deaf*. It is not its *existence* but its *deafness* that is dangerous. Descartes and Leibniz and Husserl — these men are *some of us*. They are our kin, our kind, ones in need of interpretation, i.e., in need of *opening*.]

Interpretation as an ecological recovery of the humus of texts.

As a closed, dogmatic corpus,[4] mathematics becomes uninterpretable and as such, it becomes full of the coldblooded brutality that the logic of Cartesianism deems its moral right.

---

3 Ludwig Wittgenstein (1968). p. 32.
4 Joseph Dan (1986). p. 129.

CHAPTER THIRTY-FOUR

Reiteration:

> Thinking is not a means to gain knowledge. Thinking cuts furrows in the soil of Being. About 1875, Nietzsche once wrote (Grossoktav WW XI, 20): "Our thinking should have a vigorous fragrance, like a wheatfield on a summer's night." How many of us today still have the senses for that fragrance?[1]

How peculiar it seems to consider this passage as offering an image of the thinking and language of mathematics. Mathematical language is language at its most civilized, full of rules of order and clear procedures on how to conduct oneself properly, how things (ought to) operate, fully severed from the messes that moisten our lives and give them unruly fragrance — "the juice and the mystery."[2]

Mathematics is considered a serious and exact science, a strict discipline, and such images of seriousness, exactness and strictness often inform how it is taught and how it is understood.

It requires silence and neat rows and ramrod postures held fast in drypale blue and pink and green and yellow chalk dust rooms full of paper and pencil leads broken on purpose, any excuse to move, to breath even this drywhite chalkdust air, pale.

It requires neither joy nor sadness, but a mood of detached inevitability: anyone could be here in my place and things would proceed, identical. I remember wishing, Grade Two, that it could just *be done*, how the time stretched in between held nothing but muffled air and made no difference to me, the "sometimes wicked," *or* to the "undone sums."[3]

---

1   Martin Heidegger (1971) The nature of language. *In On the Way to Language.* New York: Harper and Row, p. 70
2   Margaret Adler (1989).
3   Recalling Dylan Thomas's (1967) Reminiscences of childhood. In *Quite Early One Morning.* London: Aldine Books.

Mathematics is proud of its aloofness and its condescension to any who might deem to enter.

Mathematics, "the foundation of language, The Father Tongue,"[4] a "closed operational system"[5] full of bony architectonics free of madness and the drool of the body.

In the face of such persistent images, mathematics has become simply meaningless for some teachers and some children, producing little more than anxiety, apprehension and the unvoiced belief that mathematics is a matter for someone else, for some "expert" (a mann more civilized) who has abilities and understanding which are "beyond me." It has become inhuman, lacking *humus,* lacking any sense of direct presence in or relevance to our lives as they are actually lived — absently re-presenting with no presence, signifying nothing but itself.

Thinking itself uninterpretable and, as such, no longer needing children to renew it but mere machination-replication.

Recitation:

> A distinction must be at once drawn between the individual subject, centered on his sense organs and on his own actions — and hence on the ego or egocentric subject as a source of possible deformation or illusion of the "subjective" type in the basic meaning of the term — and the decentered subject who coordinates his actions as between them and those of others; who measures, calculates and deduces in a way that can be generally verified; and whose epistemic activities are therefore common to all subject, even if they are replaced by electronic or

Consider how in these images mathematics and wickedness meet:

> The memories of childhood have no order, and so I remember that never was there such a dame school as ours, so firm and kind and smelling of galoshes, with the sweet and fumbled music of the piano lessons drifting down from upstairs to the lonely school room, where only the sometimes tearful wicked sat over undone sums. (p. 13)

4   Ursula Le Guin (1987). p. 10.
5   Jean Piaget & Barbel Inhelder (1972). *The Child's Construction of Quantities.* London: Routledge and Kegan Paul, p. 278.

cybernetic machines with a built-in logical and mathematical capacity similar to that of the human brain.[6]

It seems that mathematics still is, as it was for the ancient Greeks, a divine science that knows no humility, no place in the moist darkness of the Earth.

An effort at re-embodying mathematical discourse into the discourse of everyday life.

Claim: that the Earth and our everyday language and experience resonate with an ambiguous presence of *ma themata* — with the themes, the lessons, eyes for balance and symmetries, for adding up and taking away, for dividing fairly, in a way adequate to the circumstances, the interconnections of which the mathematics curriculum is but a ghostly idealization that has forgotten its origins, its *humus*, its humility.

Something like this was the intent of Edmund Husserl's phenomenology — to describe the deep embeddedness of the "exact" sciences in the life-world, in life as it is actually lived. He maintained that we cannot understand the discourse of the sciences by beginning with the: "surreptitious substitution of [a] mathematically substructured world of idealities for the only real world, our everyday life-world."[7]

If we begin with such a substitution, the resonances of mathematical discourse in the deep winds of metaphoricity that make up everyday life...

> The whole of spoken language surrounding the child snaps him up like a whirlwind, tempts him by its internal articulations. The untiring ways in which the train of words crosses and recrosses itself finally sways the child over to the side of those who speak. Only language as a whole enables one to understand how language draws the child to himself and how he comes to enter that domain whose doors, it is believed, open only from within. The sign has an interior.[8]

6 Jean Piaget (1973). p. 7-8.
7 Edmund Husserl (1970). p. 48-9.
8 Maurice Merleau-Ponty (1970a) *Signs*. Evanston: Northwestern University Press, p. 40-41.

> Speech always comes into play against a background of speech; it is always only a fold in the immense fabric of language. To understand it, we do not have to consult some inner lexicon which gives us the pure thoughts covered up by the words or forms we are perceiving; we only have to lend ourselves to its life, to its movement of differentiation and articulation, and to its eloquent gestures. There is thus an opaqueness to language.[9]

... end up being formulated as simply a blurring of what is in fact clear, a concretizing of what is in fact abstract, a making profane of the sacred, humiliation.

Phenomenologically, the reverse is the case. The idealizations of mathematical discourse appear in the midst of the world of everyday life and they are not despoiled by such appearance, but enlivened by being connected back to their living sources:

> These are *human* formations, essentially related to *human* actualities and potentialities, and thus belong to this concrete unity of the life-world.[10]

Mathematical discourse resonates deeply with our humanity, with our language, with our Earth. It is, in vital and important ways, child's play, with all the joy, difficulty, immediacy and humility that such play invites.

And again, this does not despoil its idealized exactness. Rather, it makes such exactness a *real achievement* that erupts out of life as it is actually lived, rather than seeing such exactness as graciously bestowed "from above." Mathematics is not something we have to look up to — churchspire inspiring eyes so cast.[11]

Mathematics is right in front of us, right at our fingertips, right in the heartmeat beat breath inhaled.

---

9   Maurice Merleau-Ponty (1970a). p. 42.
10   Edmund Husserl (1970). p. 170. From this passage it becomes clear why Seamon's (1989) article misses the point of the task of phenomenology. The sciences "add themselves" to the life-world and therefore are part of the task of the explication of lived-experience — in some ways, they are those threads of the life-world most in need of interpretation, because they are those threads that most deeply *refuse* to understanding themselves *as* threads among others.
11   Ted Aoki (1987). p. 67.

All this is *almost* a re-wording of the fundamental gesture of Jean Piaget's genetic epistemology. He desired to understand "the continuity between life and intelligence"[12] by formulating logico-mathematical operations as a real achievement of development.[13] Eyes well: no children here in these texts which are simply *about* them. These operations were not *a priori* structures given at the beginning of development but were the structural outcomes of a sequence of development oriented by the functional *a priori* of assimilation, accommodation and equilibration.

Reiteration:

> "The *a priori* only appears in the form of essential *structures* at the end of the evolution of concepts and not at their beginning."[14]

What is missing from Piaget's account is the living interrelationships with children which we still bear in our language, in our experience, in our hearts. His formulation of the stages of development as sequential reconstructions offers us little recourse for understanding children except for us to take the operations that we have developmentally achieved and turn them back upon children, turning these kin into an object of scientific discourse (rendering these ambiguous kin[ships] and vague familiarities [resemblances] into the identities and non-contradictions of mathematical

---

12   Jean Piaget (1952). p. 352.
13   see Jean Piaget (1970a). *The Principles of Genetic Epistemology*. (London: Routledge and Kegan Paul) in which he carefully distinguishes his work from a form of Platonism which would take the forms and figures of science to be established at the outset of development, "innate."
     Piaget wanted to place the sciences back into a living continuity with the sucking of nipples and the pissing and passing of food. This is why I find Piaget's work so deeply attractive on the face of it. But the voice given to such placement is *itself* a logico-mathematical voice, not a voice that was itself full of sucking and pissing: his was a *scientific* project and as such the continuity was achieved as a type of *reconstruction* of this continuity according to only one voice in that continuum.
14   Jean Piaget (1952). p. 3.

discourse at its most pristine and "heady"), surreptitiously substituting a mathematically substructured world for the world *of* the child-as-kin[15]

But there they are, right in front of us, different., a world full, just like ours, of animism and metaphoricity as Piaget's own work clearly shows.[16]

---

15 The error often and easily made here is to fall prey to the old *epistemic* notions of "the world of the child" as some sort of "object-domain" that is separate and simply *different* than "the world of the adult."

   The world of the child-as-kin is the world *we* are in, too, *with* them *as* kin (not as "knowers" who have them present before us as an "object").

   We are not thereby identical with them, but neither are they aliens bubbled in "another world" with which we must *subsequently* "make contact" — except, of course, in a wonderful, useful *metaphorical* sense which constructivism takes too literally. Children *are* different than us; we *are not* children.

16 Just like our adult world is also full of animism and metaphoricity, once we give up the strictures of univocity which makes this likeness hide away.

   See for example Jean Piaget (1974). *The Child's Conception of the World*. (London: Paladin Books) wherein, for example, Piaget speaks of children's conceptions of life, of dreams and the like.

   In a pointed example, children speak of dreams "happening outside of me," they are "in front of me," and "come from the night" and are "caused by the night." These statements are strikingly true on an experiential and mythic-animistic level. They say something about dreams that is not captured by Piaget's own interpretation which insists, as a background for asking the question in the first place, that dreams "in fact" happen inside the head, and that they don't "in fact" "come from the night" and that therefore, in Piaget's words, the child has produced "exceedingly suggestive deformations of true conceptions." (p. 50) If the origin and locale of dreams are to become objects of scientific discourse (the discourse characteristic of Piagetian theory), *their origin and locale must needs be univocal*. At once, then, the possibility of taking the child's answers seriously, as profound challenges to precisely our own assumptions about the origin and locale of dreams, is never taken up. Children are thus banished from a certain lively presence in Piaget's work because a certain kinships we have with them are ruled out in advance.

   There is a wonderful flipside parallel to this phenomenon and James Hillman's *The Dream and the Underworld*. In this text, he speaks of Freud's notion of dreams as the "royal road to the unconscious," but he then notes that this road has commonly been, so to speak, a one way street: the effort is always to "raise" the unconscious "up" to the level of consciousness and rarely is it a matter

Consider what would happen to the sciences of pedagogy if they took the final move that Hillman suggests in *The Dream and the Underworld*: dreams are not a place *in which* one dreams *about* the underworld. They *are* the underworld. The substructure become logico-mathematical knowledge as that *against which* the child's understanding (and *our own* animistic tendencies, for example) is reconstructed into "an exceedingly suggestive deformation of true conceptions"[17] (those "true conceptions" being, of course, "reality such as our science imagines and postulates."[18]

Automatically in such turning back, children are banished from a certain presence in Piaget's work because we begin with and remain within precisely that discourse (logico-mathematical knowledge which guides our experimental designs in our Piagetian investigations) which we have *already* determined that children are *not* party to, except as silent prefigurements, prototypes or the like, a royal road leading only one way.

This is why such sciences of children become so humourless, since the child cannot *actually erupt* in these works except as an already-kn own-in-advance-how-it-might-erupt object *about which* we can then glean *information*.

The sciences of children don't *themselves* get flighty and full of the *puer aeternus*.[19] Etymologically, kin, kindness, hence "natural affection."

---

of "lowering" consciousness "down" into its under world, into the body and flesh of its demeanor.

Clearly, in the case of Piaget, he originally believed that we could learn about the concepts and categories of established science by exploring their origins "below."

But by establishing a *science* for such exploration, the concepts and categories of established science cannot come deeply *into* question during the exploration, because they sketch out in advance that "ground plan" *from which* questioning can proceed.

17 Jean Piaget (1974). p. 50.
18 Jean Piaget (1972). *The Child's Conception of Physical Causality*. Totawa: Littlefield, Adams and Co. p. 239.
19 James Hillman (1987). This, of course, has a profound and unexamined effect on the *writing* of such sciences of children. To make children present in this writing, it seems to be enough to simply make them the *object* of this writing. The writing

Writing of kin ought to house a natural affection in which these kin are *present in the writing itself,* not simply its subsequent topic.

They are just *about* it, speaking in a voice that does not belong *to* it.[20]

Claim: prior to such reconstructions of our relations to children, we are
already in relation to them
as "kin,"
as our "kind."
More strongly put, this is the case that must be made in relation to the closed doors of
mathematics:
this mathematics is ours,
loved and savoured and accomplished by some of us,
our kind,
our kin.
And these children and their understandings
are the kin of the very ones who love and savour and accomplish mathematics.
Their understandings of the world are of a kind with mathematics.

Sub-claim: that the language/writing in which children can have a certain presence cannot be the language of the sciences oriented to univocity. And it is not enough to simply add "samples of children's own work" to what we already do (which allows us to simply go on as before). Writing that is full of *logopoesis,* full of the flipflutter of analogical integrities — the living metaphoricity of language — *always* and *already* contains a certain presence of children *even when children are not its "topic."*

itself has already prefigured its own voice and children are simply the accidental occasion for, not the "origin" of, such writing in any deep sense.

20 Teachers and students read the great songs and stories to learn *about* them, not to learn *from* them.

Wendell Berry (1987c). The loss of the university. In *Home Economics*. San Francisco: North Point Press, p. 79.

CHAPTER THIRTY-FIVE

To undergo an experience with language...means to let ourselves be properly concerned by the claim of language by entering into and submitting to it. If it is true that [we] find the proper abode of [our] existence in language — whether [we are] aware of it or not — then an experience we undergo with language will touch the innermost nexus of our existence.[1]

If we may talk of playing games at all, it is not we who play with words, but the nature of language plays with us, long since and always. For language plays with our speech — it likes to let our speech drift away in the more obvious meanings of words. It is as though [we] had to make an effort to live properly in language. It is as though such a dwelling were especially prone to succumb to the danger of commonness. Floundering in commonness is part of the dangerous game in which, by the nature of language, we are the stakes.[2]

Re-iteration:

"Here, too, the gods are present,"[3]
here,
in the simplest of events.
"This"[4]: a young child, four years old, runs up
full
of enthusiasm and declares:
"I can count all the way up to 100!"
All the way up.
Bodily ascendancies
pulled by faint
gravity.

1 Martin Heidegger (1971). p. 57.
2 Martin Heidegger (1968). p. 18-9.
3 Martin Heidegger (1977a). p. 234.
4 Bronwen Wallace (1987). p. 111.

In a recent undergraduate class in Early Childhood Curriculum, I asked the following question: in precisely what sense is 198 a *higher* number than 56? The initial reaction to this question was silence, followed by scattered bewilderment and confusion. Although the students were becoming accustomed to this sort of question, the precise intent in asking it was not clear.

Some took the question as an indirect form of accusation: 198 isn't "really" *higher* than 56, so the fact that they may have been using this language is an error to be corrected. Others simply struggled to make explicit what would be meant by "higher." They found themselves caught up in a swirl of interweaving and interconnecting meanings which seemed to resist being "straightened out" in any definitive manner.

One slipped into the language, common to young children, of numbers being "big" and "little." Far from remedying our situation, it simply multiplied the problem, so to speak.

The question then arose: if we don't know precisely what we mean when we use such language, how is it that we can feel confident when we attempt to teach such aspects of mathematics to young children? Implicit here is the equation of the ability to teach something with knowing what it is that you are teaching. This equation is one which I tend to encourage. However, there is a deeper supposition here that must be addressed.

There is implicit here the equation of "knowing what it is you are teaching" with being able to be precise, to be exact and fully explicit, to provide foreclosed, literal definitions and the like. One of the points I hoped to educe with my demonstration was that we *do* know what it means to say that 198 is "higher" than 56, but that this knowing is not definitional, literal, univocal or clear. It interweaves in unanticipated ways with the young child building a higher and higher tower of wooden blocks, with the fact that we can speak meaningfully of "counting *up* to ten," or with the fact that growing older means growing "up," and growing up means becoming taller, and that the "higher" one's chronological age, the "bigger" one is, and that, for children, importance bears a resemblance to height and age, and so on.

That is to say, the world must needs be *interpretable* (not "literal") if the "teacher's world" is to *include* children. The "teacher's personal practical knowledge" must needs be *interpretive* (not "literal") if it is to *include* children as more than a mere *object* of knowing.

    Step: an interpretable world is a world full of family resemblances and kinships.

    Step: an interpretable world is a world full of children and adults.

    Step: pedagogy is only possible in an interpretable world.

Separating the Earth into the "world of the child" and the "world of the teacher" both takes our experience and understanding and the differences between these *too literally* and *too psychologically* and *too epistemically* and *too much "from the neck up."* Against this (false) assumption of an univocal world, the differences in understanding and interpretation and ability and competence and the like must be located *somewhere else other than in the world itself,* and our literalism forces us to place the difference *inside ourselves* (because we can't easily believe that the world *itself* can be contradictory or ambiguous, full of spooks and spirits wanting and willing beyond our wanting and willing).

    The initial difficulty with such interweavings is precisely this "and so on." Although reflecting on our language can bring forth unanticipated, playful interweavings of experience, it is never quite clear, in following such interweavings, if one has gone too far. It is never quite clear just what the para-meters are. After all, is it too much to say that the progression of higher and higher numbers orients to infinity, i.e., to God, the most High, and that numbers which fall below the "ground" (below where we stand, below "[ground] zero") have a dark and negative character? Or is it too much to say that when counting higher and higher quantities, we must keep track of them by consistently bringing them back to Earth, back to base, so that we use "base ten" as a way of preventing the pile from spiralling upward out of sight, a way of keeping them at our fingertips (our digits)? that we therefore organize higher and higher quantities into groups we can manage or handle, into "handfuls?"

> [When does interpretation move past the lurking *familiaris* into the realm of madness and the drool of the body? We can never know ahead of time whether the flight will end in

> a return or simply flighty loss — "when the falcon cannot hear the falconer."⁵ Which understandings and flights will take root can only be discovered through the effort of understanding itself and the embarrassing and ecstatic trials and errors of experience in a deep, worldly sense

"This separation [between which efforts have been worthwhile and bear fruit and those which simply come to nothing] must take place in the process of understanding itself."⁶ What is *liveable* is found only through the living and the livid tales that tell the truth.

But there are clearer signs for when interpretation moves the other way. It does so, partially, when we falsely believe that interpretation is something we must *do,* when we falsely (and dangerously) believe that we "construct" interpretations. Once we believe we "construct" interpretations, we also believe that we must *make* a boundary for them to prevent madness and drool. Once this happens, Hermes retreats, unneeded, and the sparks stop flying. We have taken interpretation up into our heads.

> Recall: the *puer aeternus,* (who, in one of his aspects, is Hermes) the flighty boy, is known for his *body*].

Clearly these examples "go too far," but they are not altogether meaningless. Something is at play which belies the literalism and foreclosure of the mathematics curriculum guide, and it is this "something" that was at work in our class. We came upon a sort of "an-arche" which was not an univocal

---

5   James Hillman (1987). p. 27.
6   Hans-Georg Gadamer, (1989). p. 296. But this working out of experience does not leave tradition and the old behind, so that each new generation must start again. Avoidance of blithering interpretive work requires learning to follow long-standing disciplines, seeking out resonances which persist and resonance in long arcs.

CHAPTER THIRTY-FIVE 237

cosmos, but neither was it a chaos — lateral relations of kinship, daimons everywhere that made all this talk *familiaris*, telling us of what lurks here.

Although there is indigenous to the discipline of mathematics a form of literalism and exactness of speech (which curriculum guides in elementary mathematics seem to emulate), it is not this exactness and literalism of speech which made it possible for us to understand of each other in this class.

Our mutual ability to understand the young child who can count *up* to a hundred was not founded upon literalism or exactness or definition, but was found to be *already at work*, already *working* and already *working reliably and well* . . .

> [but *working unnoticed*. These students were surprised at themselves, surprised at suddenly *finding* themselves part of a long-since-familiar-but-unvoiced "story" in which they were *already fully culpable players played by the telltale itself.* This class was an exercise in ear-cleaning at the linguistic level; an exercise in mindfulness of what is *already at work* within us and without us; an exercise at letting the new ones re-tell the story that *we already implicitly "know"* (but this makes it sound so "epistemic" only) at some silent, sedimented level]

. . . before and as a condition of any desire for such literalism or exactness or definition.

In this way, even though it *appears* that we must climb up into our heads and shut the doors and do mathematics in the dark, *all this is just appearance* — mathematics veers out into the fabric of things, the warp and woof even of the breath of the poet, rhythmed and rhymed as it is to symmetric comings and goings of orders of which it is tensively (a)part.

Its separateness and disconnectedness and aloofness is only its thin facade of presentability and indigenous self-accountability.

In reality, mathematics is all around us, not always, however, in "presentable" form.

It belongs to the wildness and is borne from it and into it.

Re-iteration:

Wittgenstein:

"we can *draw* a boundary for these concepts:

but I can also use [them] so that the extension of the concept is *not* closed by a frontier."[7]

Regarding the desire we may have to univocally define the term "higher," to draw a boundary or frontier, Wittgenstein rather playfully says: "that never troubled you before when you used the word."[8]

The attempt to bind discourse to a central, singular meaning, to a univocal core, reflects *only* our need for practical exigency. We become troubled only when explicitly *called upon* to produce a boundary around such a center:

> If someone were to draw a sharp boundary I could not acknowledge it as the one that I too always wanted to draw, or had drawn in my mind. For I did not want to draw one at all. His concept can then be said to be not *the same* as mine, but akin to it. The kinship is just as undeniable as the difference.[9]

And, as Wittgenstein further notes, I can *draw* boundaries or frontiers in such matters, but I cannot *give* such matters a boundary.[10]

In its lived, lively usage as a mathematical term, the term "higher" — like counting up to ten or how a pile of more blocks is higher than one with less, or how I believed as a child that the height of adults was related to age because you grow up —resonates in an untroublesome way, beyond the idealized frontiers that we *can* draw, but *cannot* give.

7   Ludwig Wittgenstein (1968). p. 32-3.
8   Ludwig Wittgenstein (1968). p. 33.
9   Ludwig Wittgenstein (1968). p. 36.
10 Ludwig Wittgenstein (1968). p. 33.

CHAPTER THIRTY-FIVE

In its lived usage, we are not troubled by the foreclosed alternatives of identity or difference, but can live in an untroubled way with the ambiguous and fluid *kinships* that language evokes.

Haunts of the principle of identity, the principle of non-contradiction and the principle of excluded middle. This question of whether it "really" is or is not, put a demand on our discourse that we could not sustain if we desired to understand the discourse of children and the experiences they undergo in learning mathematics. Either of these foreclosed options belie the possibility of actually *teaching* mathematics to young children. Of course, many of the students ended this class in anger and frustration.

This was a difficult point for many of these students to understand. They deeply believed that mathematics *began* at the moment that the doors are shut, the moment its exactness, literalism, abstractness and foreclosure began and many of them hate (and fear) mathematics for this very reason. Perhaps this hatred (and fear) originates in the ways in which they were cut off from how mathematics already resonates in their own lives, their own experiences, their own understandings. Perhaps they were never allowed to be the vulnerable initiate, never allowed to explore and savour the fragile and delicate beginnings. Such beginnings *appear* to be left behind as mathematical understanding matures.

Thus, when the young child shouts "I have a millllllllion stickers at home," the stretching out of the arms, the raising of the voice, the stretching out of the woooooord and the wide-eyed face of exclamation are not easily hearable as "ridge to gorge to ridge"[11] — each one an analogue for a really *big* number. They are hearable only as exuberant exaggeration — "exceedingly suggestive deformations of true conceptions."[12]

Another topic that came up in this class was "symmetry." In the mathematics curriculum guides, it has become simply a vaguely incomprehensible theoretical term for an abstract notion of one-to-one correspondence of spatial relations. It has become sealed off in anonymously reproducible definitions that are clear, but that do not touch anything outside of themselves. But symmetry also has to do with the slicing open

---

11 Gary Snyder (1980). p. 80.
12 Jean Piaget (1972). p. 50.

of a orange and finding the pinwheel pattern in the midst of the aroma and sticky, bittersweet juice. It has to do with the fact that when the child (or the adult) claps their hands in steady rhythm out in front of themselves, they are not only involved in a similarity of meter (sym-metry, which itself interweaves with similarities of sound or sym-phonics, both of which come together in phenomena such as nursery rhymes — singing songs with young children is a deeply mathematical activity), but are displaying the symmetrical character of their body. Moreover, when we look at symmetrical objects, we tend spontaneously to put them "right in front of us," unconsciously centering the symmetrical object around our corporeal, symmetrical center. Symmetry is therefore *already* an unnamed feature of the Earth, and an unnamed feature of the young child's experience of the world. The child, prior to our earnest interventions as teachers, prior to the mandates of curricular accountability and reproducibility, has *already* sliced open an orange, or clapped their hands, and has therefore *already* lived in the unnamed, ambiguous presence of symmetry, division, fractions, circular patterning and pattern sub-divisions (both visual and auditory), one-to-one correspondence, numeration, and so on.

> [A student-teacher said recently, when she realized that the topic of her lesson might be one with which the children were already vaguely familiar,
> "— , I'm not ready!"
> This is the beginning of a recognition that life goes on beyond our earnest intentions and actions as teachers. It is a profoundly ecological insight. It is the first glimmerings of a precious realization so essential for prospective teachers to undergo — that understanding erupts out of the wildness of life itself, and not simply as a response to an act of teaching and therefore, that teaching must first and foremost attune itself to what is already at work in our lives and the lives of the children we teach. And to understand

what is already at work means understanding something more than ourselves and children: it involves understanding the world in which we find ourselves enmeshed. And this requires the subtle arts of interpretation.]

[This is what the colonizers could rarely do — attune themselves to what is already at work. What was already at work didn't follow the rules, it wasn't presentable (where Reason prescribes the conditions of presentability). This is what the colonizers could never see the *need* to do: whatever is at work without us is simply wildness that needs to be tamed, disorder that needs to be ordered, childishness that needs maturity, wilderness that needs civilization, savageness that needs refinement, a woman who needs a man.]

Discovering the analogical play of language can initially have a disorienting effect because it begins with the flip-side of these colonizing relations: there is a kinship between the rules and the unruly, between the wild and the tame, between the child and the adult, between the wilderness and the civil, between savageness and refinement, between invention and tradition, and each measures itself against "the other."

Moreover, it is *in* this relationship, at the boundaries or edges, that life erupts, that things get lively. Consider: "life erupts at the boundaries."[13] Consider, Hermes as the messenger between realms, the god of borders and crossings, akin to Poros. Consider, *Dancing at the Edge of the World*.[14] Consider the life of poetry dancing on this knifeedge.[15]

In such analogical play, begin to bump into the limits, contours and interweavings of language itself[16] and the secure, familiar, but deadened ground of literalness and commonness begins to slip and move.

---

13   G. Sessions & B. Devall (1985).
14   The title of a book by Ursula LeGuin.
15   Gary Snyder (1980). p. 21.
16   Ludwig Wittgenstein (1968). p. 48.

> [Re-iteration:
> pedagogy
> can teach
> mathematics
> of its kin
> only when
> mathematics
> becomes
> *interpretable*
> and pedagogy
> becomes
> *interpretive*]

We begin to realize that our well-bound intentions and experiences are always already outstripped by the interplays of discourse itself, that our civility and definiteness is surrounded, lovingly, by a wild country that *sustains* our civility and makes it possible.

> [It doesn't make it possible in the sense of "logically possible" (possible "from the neck up") but makes it possible in the existential sense: For pedagogy to be possible, there must *be* an Earth which can sustain our lives. We cannot befoul the Earth which grants us breath and then, with that very befouled breath, speak of the beauty of mathematics and of our eloquent pedagogical aspirations. Mathematics must be understood in a way that makes it *existentially* possible, and its indigenous logic is not enough, for that indigenous logic has, *at the outset,* put out of play those contingencies of the flesh which might inform that existential possibility of "the limits of necessity and mystery."[17]]

---

17   Wendell Berry (1983). p. 13.

This may be why, when it was noted that one of the students had slipped into the language of one number being "bigger" than the other, she responded with embarrassment, apology and statements like "but I didn't *mean* that," as if she felt somehow culpable for the connections and implications of meaning which she had in fact *stumbled upon,* not *created* or *authored.*

> [Ecology reminds us that she *is* culpable for that *in which* she dwells — as much for the Earth as for the "eco-*logoi,*" "the dwelling of/in/on words"]

With the particular example of higher and lower numbers, then, the task was never to solve or re-solve the inherent ambiguity of this term "higher," but to *recognize it as such.*

We have not discovered an error in our speech which we must, in principle, seek to remedy by rendering our speech univocal and unambiguous (by rendering the wild ones tame). Clearly, such rendering is not only possible (we *can* draw a boundary). It is often precisely what is situationally required of us over the course of teaching young children. We sometimes need the safety of civility; we sometimes need the doors shut. But *this* recognition — that drawing univocal and unambiguous boundaries is often required, often called for; that closing doors is something we *do,* not just the "natural" order of things — is quite different than the claim that there simply "are" such boundaries in all cases, and that our task as teachers is always and everywhere to orient to such boundedness.

This recognition makes literalism, univocity and definition a *practical and localized choice* which saves us from the absurdity of believing that we each situation requires of us that we "give" it boundaries.

> [And this saves us from believing that the pedagogical task is always most basically a matter of effective classroom management.
> Good, rich, evocative materials "have" (porous) boundaries which we do not have to "give." This is as much an ecological insight as it is a pedagogical insight.]

This recognition requires remaining attentive to what particular situations, particular speech, particular children, particular activities call for, what they require, rather than requiring of all situations, all speech, all children and all activities that they live within the boundaries that we have already drawn.

CHAPTER THIRTY-SIX

Analogical thinking involves the development and exploration of likenesses, similarities, correspondences — parallels between (life-)worlds of discourse (*ana logos*). Such parallels resist the collapse of one realm of discourse into another, while also resisting the isolation of such realms. They involve, so to speak, the "conversation" or "dialogue" between such realms, a dialogue which sustains a "similarity-in-difference."[1] Understanding and exploring an analogy, therefore, is not a matter of discovering some discursive, univocal term which makes both sides of the analogy *the same,* which collapses the "network of similarities, overlapping and criss-crossing" into literal terms which can be applied, *univoce* to both sides of the analogy. Rather, understanding analogies involves the exploration of the tension that is sustained between similarity and difference, a tension that *cannot, in principle, be discursively cashed out in just so many words.*[2] Understanding an analogy is a matter of becoming party to the conversation between differing realms of discourse that the analogy opens up, "getting in on the conversation." The example used above of higher and lower numbers, then, was not to be taken literally, as if there were some univocal sense in which numerical quantity and physico-sensori-motoric-metaphoric notions of "higher" and "lower" were *identical*. But neither could it be maintained that they were simply *different*. Rather, they had a kinship which drew them together, yet kept them apart. The compelling and powerful character of analogies is not found in

---

1   W. Norris-Clarke (1976). Analogy and the meaningfulness of language about God. *The Thomist. 40.* p. 66.
2   David W. Jardine & Griff Morgan (1987). Analogical thinking in young children and the use of logico-mathematical knowledge as a paradigm in Jean Piaget's genetic epistemology. *The Quarterly Newsletter of the Laboratory of Comparative Human Cognition. 9*(4).

solving such kinships by resolving them into identity or difference — as if they were "problems" which found their resolution in translating them into literal, univocal discourse; as if they were "accidents" that needed to be "fixed"; as if they were merely "decorative" marginalia to the true text of language. Rather, they gain their power precisely in their *resistance to being "solved."* It is because of this resistance to being solved that potent analogies can always be re-addressed. It is because of this resistance that they remain "alive." The "conversation" that the analogy opens up can always be taken up anew. Clearly, a true conversation requires the seeking out of some common ground of understanding. But such a "common ground" need not entail an *identity of place* which would make both parties to the conversation *the same.* If we were both the same, conversation would not be necessary. Rather, a true conversation seeks out a common ground (if we were both simply different, conversation would not be possible) in the midst of a recognition of difference — it is a dialogue, not a monologue. Because of this sustained tension between similarity and difference, analogies are essentially generative and provocative. They can always draw us in again and provoke us to reconsider what they have to offer. W. Norris-Clarke points out another feature of analogical language that weaves such language into the notion of the "stubborn particulars of grace." Understanding an analogical term requires "running up and down the known *range* of cases to which it applies, by actually calling up the spectrum of *different* exemplifications, and then *catching the point.*"[3] This is a telling point. To deeply and fully understand an analogical term, we must cover the range of its exemplifications, and catch the point of the analogy that cannot be said in so many words. This is not a matter of refusal to be specific. Rather, it is a matter of the *embodiment* of meaning in its diverse instantiations (daimons everywhere, each suggesting the other through relations of kin, with no one true god left over, disembodied, who might prevent the necessity of such running of the range of cases).[4] The meaning of "higher" and "lower" is not separate from

---

3   W. Norris-Clarke (1976). p. 67
4   In this sense, there is not one true Incarnation of the Word, but multiple incarnations, each of which are suggestive, not of the One True Logos *of which* they are

its instances, like some ghostly "idea" that could be offered up independently of its instances. It *is* (analogically speaking) the diverse instances. It is not hovering "above" them (another lovely analogical term). There is no *arche*. The whole image of understanding that analogical discourse requires of us is different from that of the understanding required by singular definition. "There is quite a bit of 'give,' 'flexibility,' indeterminacy or vagueness right within the concept itself, with the result that the meaning remains essentially incomplete, so underdetermined that it cannot be clearly understood until further reference is made to some mode or modes of realization."[5] The extent of this "give" cannot be univocally named. It is itself an analogy to the ecological notion of "sustainability." In an ecosystem, threads of interdependence *can* be severed, but there is an unvoiced limit to such severances. The fact is, however, that this limit is fuzzy and shifting and undulating and *must* maintain an open, porous relationship to what it is not (because an entity cannot be what it is if it is not what it is not). To understand the analogical term, therefore, is not a matter of it "condensing, unifying."[6] We must allow it, rather, "to expand to its full analogous breadth of illuminative meaning."[7] Only in such breadth do all the lines and threads of sustenance come forth. In this way, the profound and essential disorientation begins: the full, "whole" meaning of the analogical term "higher numbers" *is* its full breadth of interweaving meanings and interrelationships. The doors of mathematical discourse are therefore *not shut*. Moreover, "whenever [such an analogical term] tries to become too precise, it contracts to become identical with just one of its modes and loses its analogical function."[8]

      the Incarnations (*ens creata*), but *of each other*. Each suggests all the others, laterally and each stubborn particular is thus "whole" without each being redeemed by some singularity which arches over all.

5   W. Norris-Clarke (1976). p. 67.
6   James Hillman (1983). p. 51.
7   W. Norris-Clarke (1976). p. 72.
8   W. Norris-Clarke (1976). p. 69-70.

> [Rather than condensing, as colonizers always believe, into the One True Logos that stands instead of the multitude. This is why Arendt's notion of the teacher or adult as representing the world to children, standing before them as a representative of a world they did not make, can be potentially dangerous]

Recalling Wittgenstein, we can *draw* a boundary and induce such contraction, but we cannot *give* such identity, *produce* such a loss of analogical functioning once and for all. When we turn our backs and cease our diligence, the term "re-generates," or re-expands into its diverse instances. When we turn our backs, the *themata* of mathematics are all around us. We turn our backs, too, and "there are children all around us,"[9] crackling full of the wild generativity that we cannot bind to something finished. A final feature of analogical thinking which is of interest here is the ability of an analogy to move us from what is known to what is unknown, from what is familiar to what is unfamiliar. The effect of such a movement is not simply that we shed light on an unfamiliar or novel aspect of our experience by relating it to more familiar aspects. Rather, analogies both "make the novel seem familiar by relating it to prior knowledge, [and]...make the familiar seem strange by viewing it from a new perspective."[10] It may be that "a venture into the alien is only possible on the basis of the familiar"[11] but such a venture does not leave the familiar untouched. It allows us to return to the familiar in a new way: renewed through now understanding our dependency upon the wilderness.[12]

---

9   see Jean Piaget (1968). *Genetic Epistemology*. New York: W. W. Norton and Company. See also Jardine (1988a).
10   M. Gick & K. Holyoak (1987). Schema induction and analogical transfer. *Cognitive Psychology*. *15*. p. 1-2.
11   Hans-Georg Gadamer (1977). p. 15.
12   Wendell Berry (1986). p. 99.

CHAPTER THIRTY-SEVEN

A friend of my son came to visit recently, and I told him about the huge pond in our neighbour's field. The spring runoff had created a slough about eight feet deep. After discussing that it would be over his head if he fell in, over my son's head, and even over *my* head, he asked, "If a hundred-year-old man stepped in it, would it be over *his* head too?" I answered, "yes, it's *that* deep."

I told this tale to a mathematics curriculum colleague at the University of Calgary and got the response: "Isn't it cute when children get things mixed up?"[1]

One of the difficulties in student-teacher education is the task of reconnecting students to their own mathematical being, such that they can finally *hear*, not only children, but their own breath and bearing of kinship with the Earth and with children. They have to become at home (*familiaris*) with mathematics which entails become at home with themselves in a deeply bodily sense: *this* is what "sensori-motor knowledge" ought to mean in Piagetian theory. Not merely a portion of a science of children, but a way of walking ourselves.

> Here it is difficult as it were to keep our heads up, — to see that we must stick to the subjects of our every-day thinking, and not go astray and imagine that we have to describe extreme subtleties. We feel as if we had to repair a torn spider's web with our fingers.[2]

---

1   If we lose a sense of the interweaving "kinships" or "family resemblances" inherent in this child's talk, we lose not only a sense of being at home with *them*. We also lose a certain kinship and sense of being at home *with ourselves*.
    Without such a sense of the deep resonances and echoes in a tale such as this one about the pond, without being able in our hearts to *experience* the deep mathematicity of a pond, the curriculum discipline of mathematics no longer issues up out of the life we live, the steps and breaths we take.
2   Ludwig Wittgenstein (1968). p. 46.

> The aspects of things that are most important for us are hidden because of their simplicity and familiarity. The real foundations of [our] inquiry do not strike [us] at all. Unless *that* fact has at some time struck [us]. And this means: we fail to be struck by what, once seen, is most striking and powerful.[3]

[Once seen, this mathematics colleague's response becomes striking and powerful in its over-thought deafness]

> The most difficult learning is to come to know actually and to the very foundations what we already know. Such learning, with which we are here solely concerned, demands dwelling continually on what appears to be nearest to us.[4]

Allowing ourselves in that Early Childhood Education class, to experience the freedom and generativity of language is at once endangering ourselves and the tranquillity that our boundaries provide.

This class was a painful experience for some, and this is no surprise.

> [Hermes is the god of the Wound,
> of the opening and
> of weakness
> and this has two aspects. First is the puer innocence of our exploration, openness "without hurt."[5] But then, running into the world and our culpabilities in and for the bios in which we dwell, we are suddenly "opened in a new way at another place, making one suffer from openness."[6]]

After our exploration of mathematical language in this class, some students have said that they have *more* difficulty with language than before, *more* difficulty in finding comfort in the familiar. The work they did in this class was not meant to make their lives *easier*, but to begin to free them for the real difficulty, the real claim that language makes on

---

3   Ludwig Wittgenstein (1968). p. 50.
4   Martin Hedeigger (1977a). p. 252.
5   James Hillman (1987b). p. 113.
6   James Hillman (1987b). p. 113.

us. Some have described how this experience has made them more careful in their language, more attentive to the lessons and themes that our language and the language of children have to offer. For some, however, it induced a sort of temporary paralysis, rendering them silent, speechless, fearful, in some sense, of the unvoiced and unintended implications of meaning that issue with every word. In the long run, this silence and this "fear of the gods that found me"[7] might be a good sign.

> "One's weakness bears one's future; one's inability is the place of one's potential."[8]

It may be a recognition of how our language, our experiences, our *lives* as adults are always already deeply implicated in the lives of children and how deeply *culpable for the world* we actually are, *even when — perhaps especially when — we don't explicitly know it.*

> The more we persist in misunderstanding the phenomena of life, the more we analyze them out into strange finalities and complex purposes of our own, the more we involve ourselves in sadness, absurdity and despair. But it does not matter much, because no despair of ours can alter the reality of things, or stain the joy of the cosmic dance which is always there. Indeed, we are in the midst of it, and it is in the midst of us, for it beats in our very blood, whether we want it to or not.[9]

---

7   James Hillman (1983). p. 42.
8   James Hillman (1987b). p. 114.
9   Thomas Merton (1972). *New Seeds of Contemplation.* New York: New Directions Books, p. 297.

CHAPTER THIRTY-EIGHT

If the discipline of mathematics were as self-enclosed as it often announces itself to be (if it could *give* itself a boundary, and not merely *draw* one), there could never be any "new ones" among us.

It is precisely a loving attention — generosity and kindness, "natural affection" — to these "new ones" that defines our special task as teachers. It is perhaps teachers who must better understand the living character of what they teach.

It is precisely that understanding of mathematics that makes new ones among us *possible,* that teachers require.

We are not allowed the luxury and comfort and self-absorption that issues from self-enclosure, drawn *or* given.

We are not allowed the luxury and comfort and self-absorption of a world taken literally.

To loop back to Le Guin's words, pedagogy has a special relation to the Father-Tongue.

Rejection of it will not do, because this pretends that it has nothing to offer and worse, it leaves the Father Tongue uninterpreted, unrenewed and *still in force,* but wallowed in its worst, most senile aspect.

Rejection pretends that the ones who have climbed up into their heads and shut the doors are not some of *us.*

But simple acceptance of such patriarchal deafness as what we must now teach our children — this will no longer do either, for it also leaves the Father Tongue uninterpreted, unrenewed and *still in force,* but wallowed in its worst, most senile aspect.

Rejection is uncompassionate and unregenerative.

Acceptance is unsustainable and unregenerative.

And *both of these* are the old options; both of these, even a "balance between them," are in the orbit of the Father-Tongue.

Both of these operate as if the Dominant Area is cut off, as if the doors are shut.

- Reversal: akin to the one found in phenomenology
- and the interpretive disciplines.
- It is not that logico-mathematical discourse is
- aloof and paradigmatic and what all language strives but fails to be (i.e., we all *want* to be civilized, to be European, to be colonized and must overcoming our immaturity, our wildness, our dependencies and kinships [as Kant defined the age of Enlightenment]). Rather,
- logico-mathematical discourse is an unsevered
- instance
- of human discourse, a
- living (i.e., interrelated, connected) *example* of its *themata*. The problem has been that

we have believed that the doors
only
open
from
the *inside* of mathematics. We now see that they only *open* from the outside.
Civilization
needs wildness to remind it that the boundaries it believes it
gives, it only
draws.

CHAPTER THIRTY-NINE

"Grief is not a permanent state; it is a room with a door on the other wall."[1]

    once upon a time ther was a rain drop and it gope on a bird then the sun trd into a watrvapr the radrop fad his bovrsrs and trnd into a fofe white cloud and then it trnd in too a havie plak kloub and then it trd in bake to the sam radrop and gropt on the sam bird.

Name Eric

    (Once upon a time there was a rain drop and it dropped on a bird. Then the sun turned it into watervapour and the raindrop left his brothers and turned into a fluffy white cloud and then it turned into a heavy black cloud and then it turned back into the same raindrop and dropped on the same bird.)

All the talk of exploding autobiography eludes the way that the world signs my own culpabilities:
    "Grief is not a permanent state; it is a room with a door on the other wall."[2]

Surely:

    The very urge to write these tales, though they go unpublished and unread, is itself a telling. For this new form of fiction enters our age driven with fierce compulsion. We want to get it down, there is so much to tell about. This craven trivia is so momentously important because history is now taking place in the soul and the soul has again entered history.[3]

---

1 Robert Bly, *When a Hair Turns to Gold*. St. Paul: Ally Press, p. 11.
2 Robert Bly, *When a Hair Turns to Gold*. St. Paul: Ally Press, p. 11.
3 James Hillman (1983). p. 48.

And surely:

> Writers know that they cannot introspect their characters. Their scenes come of themselves and their figures speak, walk in and out. With few people is a writer more intimate than with his characters and yet they continue to surprise him with their autonomy. Besides, they are not concerned with "me" but with the world they inhabit and which refers to me, the introspector, only obliquely. The relativization of the author — who is making up whom, who is writing whom — goes along with the fictional mode. One wavers between losing control and putting words in their mouths. But introspection will not solve this problem, only the act of fictioning further. The action is in the plot…and only the characters know what's going on.[4]

But just as surely, as a writer, these scenes and characters come back around as kin for whom and to whom I am responsible, just as much as this writing bears the grain of my voice.

In writing, I cannot introspect myself but find myself founded in unsuspecting tales — *my* puerile rants at Husserl my love, and at my own altar-boy Christian fantasies of life everlasting (which Husserl also offered in more palatable disguise — tasty morsels of transcendental subjectivities) — both betraying me in the end, flighty boy come crash.

"Grief is not a permanent state; it is a room with a door on the other wall."[5]

My own breath robbed by asthma as a child and the breathtaking love I have for the adventures of language and the blither of a boneless tongue.

---

4   James Hillman (1983). p. 59.
5   Robert Bly, *When a Hair Turns to Gold*. St. Paul: Ally Press, p. 11.

CHAPTER THIRTY-NINE

"Grief is not a permanent state; it is a room with a door on the other wall."[6]
This book, ["Grief is"[7]]
in the end, *is* ["not a permanent state;"[8]]
about me ["it is a room"[9]]
however obliquely angled ["with a door"[10]]
through this world ["a room"[11]]
for which I am ["Grief"[12]]
culpable beyond revoke.

Bang.

Hence the need to descend: in the flesh, I am no one else. This Wound is mine. Aoki's[13] eyes turned downwards, the flutters of the body and breath, the living metaphoricity of the Earth and the long cool arcs of resemblances, anciently perceived — the first movements are ones of weakness and inability: "One's weakness bears one's future; one's inability is the place of one's potential."[14] And writing, as helpless, bears my future and potential. This writing reads me back to me in ways I could not do alone (and it reads me back to me in ways different than it can with another reader, because, if I am just writing about these issues and not living them, *my* self-deceptions are immediate and inevitable). I find myself, not as an autonomous author that holds private intended meaning as a barricade against multiple interpretations ("That is not what I meant" as a way of protecting the autonomy and invincibility of the

---

6   Robert Bly, *When a Hair Turns to Gold*. St. Paul: Ally Press, p. 11.
7   Robert Bly, *When a Hair Turns to Gold*. St. Paul: Ally Press, p. 11.
8   Robert Bly, *When a Hair Turns to Gold*. St. Paul: Ally Press, p. 11.
9   Robert Bly, *When a Hair Turns to Gold*. St. Paul: Ally Press, p. 11.
10 Robert Bly, *When a Hair Turns to Gold*. St. Paul: Ally Press, p. 11.
11 Robert Bly, *When a Hair Turns to Gold*. St. Paul: Ally Press, p. 11.
12 Robert Bly, *When a Hair Turns to Gold*. St. Paul: Ally Press, p. 11.
13 Ted Aoki (1987).
14 James Hillman (1987b). p. 114.

author [and a way of denying the autonomy of the text]). But neither do I find myself as an autonomous author who, instead, sacrifices himself for the text's own intertwirling ("The author's meaning is irrelevant. The text has its own warp and weave" as a way of denying or suppressing issues of my own living culpability in what I write, or making such culpabilities "private issues.") No, instead of these (both of which preserve the autonomy of the author, one through the salvaging of author's meaning, the other through the releasing of the text from the author altogether), my autonomy and privacy and culpability and sacrifice and life and helplessness and future and potential and lures of self-deception all get pulled to pieces. "Kinships with children" is not just a topic. I have a child and my *living* is at stake in writing *about* such a topic. That stake is not *in* the text, nor is it the measure of the text for the reader (all the appearances of vitality in the writing could be just well-honed rhetoric and craft-iness). Worse, perhaps, than the helplessness of writing is my helplessness in the face of what I have written. Interpretive writing is a form of grieving and lamentation, a particularization, come to bear here and no where else. "This."[15] In grieving and lamentation, I issue outwards, crying out into the Earth, bearing witness to the logic *I* am living out. "Grief is not a permanent state; it is a room with a door on the other wall."[16] "Wounds need to be expanded into air, lifted up on ideas our ancestors knew, so that the wound ascends through the roof of our parents' house, and we suddenly see how our wound (seemingly so private) *fits*."[17] I have had too much of the comfort of the fitting. Such fitting bleeds away from here and makes things too understandable. This room must be passed through alone, red ochre corridor, deep darkwater pools green edged.

Mourning.

This book,

---

15   Bronwen Wallace (1987).
16   Robert Bly, *When a Hair Turns to Gold*. St. Paul: Ally Press, p. 11.
17   Robert Bly, *When a Hair Turns to Gold*. St. Paul: Ally Press p. 13, my emphasis.

CHAPTER THIRTY-NINE

["Grief is"[18]]
in the end, *is*
["not a permanent state;"[19]]
about me
["it is a room"[20]]
however obliquely angled
["with a door"[21]]
through this world ["a room"[22]]
for which I am ["Grief"[23]]
culpable beyond revoke.

This is where hermeneutics catches the breath, wormsquirming: striving to write about being ecologically mindful is *insane* without at once striving to *be* ecologically mindful. I am often insane. The difference between what I have written and how I live can be hidden from everyone else, especially when writing attains a certain gracefulness and cadence.

Grief.[24]

---

18   Robert Bly, *When a Hair Turns to Gold*. St. Paul: Ally Press, p. 11.
19   Robert Bly, *When a Hair Turns to Gold*. St. Paul: Ally Press, p. 11.
20   Robert Bly, *When a Hair Turns to Gold*. St. Paul: Ally Press, p. 11.
21   Robert Bly, *When a Hair Turns to Gold*. St. Paul: Ally Press, p. 11.
22   Robert Bly, *When a Hair Turns to Gold*. St. Paul: Ally Press, p. 11.
23   Robert Bly, *When a Hair Turns to Gold*. St. Paul: Ally Press, p. 11.
24   Robert Bly, *When a Hair Turns to Gold*. St. Paul: Ally Press, p. 11.

CHAPTER FORTY

The *puer aeternus* figure is the vision of our own first nature, our primordial golden shadow, our affinity to beauty, our angelic essence as messenger of the divine, as divine message. From the puer we are given our sense of destiny and mission, of having a message and being meant as eternal cup-bearer to the divine, that our sap and overflow, our enthusiastic wetness of soul, is in service to the Gods.[1]

We came as infants, "trailing clouds of glory," arriving from the farthest reaches of the universe, bringing with us appetites well preserved from our mammal inheritances, spontaneities wonderfully preserved from our 150,000 years of tree life, angers well preserved from our 5,000 years of tribal life — in short, with our 360-degree radiance — and we offered this gift to our parents. They didn't want it. They wanted a nice girl or a nice boy.[2]

"Grief is not a permanent state; it is a room with a door on the other wall."[3]

---

1 James Hillman (1987). p. 26.
2 Robert Bly (1988). *A Little Book on the Human Shadow*. New York: Harper and Row, p. 24.
3 Robert Bly, *When a Hair Turns to Gold*. St. Paul: Ally Press, p. 11.

CHAPTER FORTY-ONE

> [I carry] a general scepticism toward all ideas which are used as sources of legitimacy by the winners of the world. I should like to believe that the task . . .is to make greater demands on those who mouth the certitudes of their times and are closer to the powerful and rich, than to the faiths and ideas of the powerless and marginalized. That way lies freedom, compassion and justice.[1]

So Ashis Nandy ends his "Cultural Frames for Social Transformation: A Credo," (1987) pleading the right to end "on a personal note."

I read this again and again, haunted by the ways in which I myself am a winner of the world: white, male, European descent, high income, well-housed, well-fed, well-educated, well-read, exuding a wellness which unintentionally preys on the weak, which unintentionally *creates* sicknesses to sustain itself at the expense of others.

Everything I have to say issues from this wellness I carry, somehow. Everything I do is rooted in an ease which is easy for a winner of the world.

Mourning. "Grief is not a permanent state; it is a room with a door on the other wall."[2]

This door is not simply mine to open when I will it.

This corridor lengthens as I walk.

The effort and urgency and attention and "grief"[3] that has gone into this book, this laborious and earnest writing and re-writing — all this seems so very *opulent*. Writing of ecological mindfulness while housed on 20 acres in the foothills of the Rocky Mountains. So very *opulent*.

1   Ashis Nandy (1987) Cultural frames for social transformation: A Credo," p. 123.
2   Robert Bly, *When a Hair Turns to Gold*. St. Paul: Ally Press, p. 11.
3   Robert Bly, *When a Hair Turns to Gold*. St. Paul: Ally Press, p. 11.

> How can I, as an educator, fulfill my responsibility to my own people; my own people whom I love yet who, like I do, live under an economic and epistemological dispensation which is the *problem* for most of the world?[4]

Interpretation is a form of contemplative mourning. A form of grief. *Finding* that the world operates beyond my wanting and willing, blessed with spooks and spirits made harmless by my excess. *Opulent*.

---

4   David G. Smith (1988c), cited here from an earlier draft version.

CHAPTER FORTY-TWO

As their grief and fear of the world is allowed to be expressed without apology or argument, and validated as a wholesome, life-preserving response, people break through their avoidance mechanisms, break through their sense of futility and isolation. And generally they break *into* a larger sense of identity. It is as if the pressure of their acknowledged awareness of the suffering of our world stretches, or collapses, the culturally defined boundaries of the self. The grief and fear experienced for our world and our common future is categorically different from similar sentiments relating to one's personal welfare. This pain cannot be equated with dread of one's own individual demise. Its source lies less in concerns for personal survival than in an apprehension of collective suffering — of what looms for human life and other species and unborn generations to come. Its nature is akin to the original meaning of compassion: "suffering with." It is the distress we feel on behalf of the whole of which we are a part. There is immeasurable pain in our society — a pain carried at some level by each and every individual — over what is happening to our world and our future. Given our culture's fear of pain and the high value it sets on optimism, feelings of despair are repressed. Hidden like a secret sore, they breed a sense of isolation. But when one's pain for the world is redefined as compassion, it serves as a trigger or gateway to a more encompassing sense of identity. It is seen as part of the connective tissue that binds us to all beings. The self is experienced as inseparable from the web of life in which we are all intricately interconnected.[1]

---

1   Joanne Macy (1989). p. 204.

"She Unnames Them"[1]

Our conclusion ends in the ambivalence of mythical images. Our tension is unresolved. In the soft light of the dust world we cannot see clearly. It may be day's end and a darkening of the light. The morning star — is it Lucifer? The ape — is he man's fallen angel? The revelation that is at hand, that Second Coming, may be the rough beast of Yeats and Picasso, slouching towards Bethlehem. The beast may be but a beast, the blood-dimmed tide of anarchy, a gibbering ape at nightfall, the princely power, *simia dei,* its hour come round at last, bringing a new reign of Egyptian darkness. Or the soft light may be *Aurora consurgens* of a new millennium, of sun and moon together, *sapientia* and *caritas* conjoined, where wisdom and madness flecitiously embrace each other: an altogether new kind of day that the baboon heralds, and gives us the eye with which to see. Either/or — yet one thing is certain: we cannot go down to the ape... on which the future depends without a metamorphosis of our main God, our own individual enclosed consciousness, sustained in its ego-tension and ego-brightness by the senex-puer polarity. We may leave our transitions of generations in ambivalence. These images from myth and nature may indicate a new relationship that is the oldest: our dependence as humans upon the divine light of natural consciousness. This soft light is pre-conscious, at the threshold always dawning, fresh as milk, at dawn with each day's dream, still streaked with primordial anarchy.[2]

---

1   Ursula LeGuin (1987a).
2   James Hillman (1987). p. 49-50.

"She Unnames Them"[1]

It is not writing. Not poetry, not prose. I am not a writer. Yet it is in my throat, stomach, arms. This book that I am not able to write. There are words that insist in silence. Words that betray me. The words make me sleep. They keep me awake.[2]

---

1   Ursula LeGuin (1987a).
2   Kristjana Gunnars (1989). *The Prowler*. Red Deer: Red Deer College Press, section 1.

A Postscript: *Ganesha's Kiss,* 2022

FIGURE SIX: GANESHA'S KISS

Sanskrit: गणेश.
The god of beginnings.
The remover of obstacles.

A Postscript: *Ganesha Kissed*, 2024

FIGURE SEVEN: GANESHA KISSED

By rain, kissed (obstacles removed).
By my notice, kissed (obstacles removed).
With age comes beginnings.
Kissed.

References

Addy, O. (1992). Liner notes interview in Kronos Quartet, *Pieces of Africa*. Elektra/Nonesuch CD 979253-2.

Adler, M. (1989). The juice and the mystery. In Judith Plant (1989). *Healing the Wounds: The Promise of Ecofeminism*. Toronto: Between the Lines Press.

Aitken, R. (1982). *Taking the Path of Zen*. San Fransisco: North Point Press.

Aoki, T. (1987). In receiving, a giving: A response to the panelists gifts. *Journal of Curriculum Theorizing*. 7(3).

Arendt, H. (1969). The crisis in education. In *Between Past and Present: Eight Exercises in Political Thought*, Penguin Books, New York.

Aristotle. (1971). *The Basic Works of Aristotle*. R. McKeon, ed. New York: Random House.

Bass, E. (1989). Tampons. In Judith Plant (1989). *Healing the Wounds: The Promise of Ecofeminism*. Toronto: Between the Lines Press.

Bastock, M. & Jardine, D. (2005). Children's literacy, the *Biblia Pauperum* and the wiles of images. *Journal of Curriculum and Pedagogy*. 2(2), 65-69.

Beck, D. (1991). A case of speculative audacity. Presented at the Bergamo Conference on Curriculum Theory and Classroom Practice. Dayton, Ohio, October, 1991.

Bergum, V. (1990). The lessons of pregnancy for pedagogy. A paper presented at the first International Invitational Pedagogy Conference, Banff, Alberta, June 1990.

Berman, M. (1984). *The reenchantment of the world*. New York: Bantam Books.

Bernard, L. (1974). *The Graeco-Roman and Oriental Background of the Iconoclastic Controversy*. Leiden: E.J. Brill.

Berry, T. (1988). *The Dream of the Earth*, Sierra Club Books, San Francisco.

Berry, W. (1983). *Standing by words*. San Francisco: North Point Press.

Berry, W. (1986). *The Unsettling of America*. San Francisco: Sierra Book Club.

Berry, W. (1987). A letter to Wes Jackson. In *Home Economics*. San Francisco: North Point Press.

Berry, W. (1987a). Getting along with nature. In *Home Economics*. San Francisco: North Point Press.

Berry, W. (1987b). Two economies. In *Home Economics*. San Francisco: North Point Press.

Berry, W. (1987c). The loss of the university. In *Home Economics*. San Francisco: North Point Press.

Berry, W. (1988). [Sermon] The profit in work's pleasure. *Harper's Magazine*. March, 1988.
Bly, R. *When a Hair Turns to Gold*. St. Paul: Ally Press.
Bly, R. (1988). *A Little Book on the Human Shadow*. New York: Harper and Row.
Bordo, S. (1987). *The flight to objectivity*. Albany: State University of New York Press.
Brentanno, F. (1971). *Psychology from an Empirical Standpoint*. London: Routledge and Kegan Paul.
Bunno, K., Yoshiro, T. & Kojiro, M. eds. (1987) The sutra of Innumerable meanings. In *the Threefold Lotus Sutra*. Tokyo: Kosei Publishing Company.
Callahan, B. (2022). Interviewed by Bob Mehr, *MOJO Magazine*. Online: https://www.discountmags.com/au/magazine/mojo-october-18-2022-digital/in-this-issue/25
Caputo, J (1985). *The Mystical Element in Heidegger's Thought*. Bloomington: Indiana University Press.
Caputo, J. (1987). *Radical Hermeneutics: Repetition, Deconstruction and the Hermeneutic Project*. Bloomington: Indiana University Press.
Chambers, C. (1992). All my relations. A paper presented at the American Association of Colleges of Teacher Education Conference, San Antonio, Texas, February, 1992.
Clifford, J. (1986). Introduction. To Clifford, J. & Marcus, G. (1986) eds. *Writing Culture: The Poetics and Politics of Ethnography*. Berkeley: University of California Press.
Clifford, J. (1986a). On ethnographic allegory. in Clifford, J. & Marcus, G. (1986) eds. *Writing Culture: The Poetics and Politics of Ethnography*. Berkeley: University of California Press.
Clifford, J. & Marcus, G. (1986) eds. *Writing Culture: The Poetics and Politics of Ethnography*. Berkeley: University of California Press.
Daly, M. (1978). *Gyn/Ecology: The Metaethics of Radical Feminism*. Boston: Beacon Press.
Dan, J. (1986). Midrash and the dawn of Kabbalah. In G. Hartman. & S. Budick, eds. *Midrash and Literature*. New Haven: Yale University Press.
Davies, A. (1989). Freedom within bounds. *Applying Research to the Classroom*. 7(3).
DeHovanessian, D. (1986). Transference. Cited in Michael Fischer (1986). Ethnicity and the post modern arts of memory. In Clifford, J. & Marcus, G. (1986) eds. *Writing Culture: The Poetics and Politics of Ethnography*. Berkeley: University of California Press.
Descartes, R. (1955). *Descartes' Selections,* Charles Scribners' Sons, New York.
Deshimaru, T. (1983). *The Ring of the Way*. New York: E. P. Dutton.

Devall, B. (1988). *Simply in Means, Rich in Ends: Practicing Deep Ecology.* Salt Lake City: Peregrine Books.
Devall, B. & Sessions, G. (1985). *Deep Ecology.* Salt Lake City: Peregrine Books.
Diamond, I. & Orenstein, G. (1990). *Reweaving the World.* San Fransisco: Sierra Club Books.
Dudley, R. (2019. Ruffed Grouse Have Built-in 'Snowshoes' and They're Not Made of Feathers. Posted January 7, 2019. Online: https://www.featheredphotography.com/blog/2019/01/07/ruffed-grouse-have-built-in-snowshoes-and-theyre-not-made-of-feathers/
Eckhart, M. (1981). *Meister Eckhart: The Essential Sermons, Commentaries, Treatises and Defense.* New York: Paulist Press.
Eckhart, M. (1986). *Meister Eckhart: Teacher and Preacher.* New York: Paulist Press.
Ernest, P. (2002). Introducing 'Speaking with a Boneless Tongue'. Online: http://socialsciences.exeter.ac.uk/education/research/centres/stem/publications/pmej/pom e16/intro_boneless.htm.
Fischer, M. (1986). Ethnicity and the post modern arts of memory. In Clifford, J. & Marcus, G.
(1986) eds. *Writing Culture: The Poetics and Politics of Ethnography.* Berkeley: University of California Press.
Fishbane, M. (1986). Inner Biblical exegesis: Types and strategies of interpretation in ancient Israel. In G. Hartman and S. Budick, eds. *Midrash and Literature.* New Haven: Yale University Press.
Fox, M. (1983). *Original Blessing,* Santa Fe, Bear and Company.
Gadamer, H.-G. (1970). Concerning empty and ful-filled time. *Southern Journal of Philosophy,* 8 (Winter), 341-353.
Gadamer, H.G. (1977). *Philosophical Hermeneutics,* University of California Press, Berkeley.
Gadamer, H.G. (1983). *Reason in the Age of Science.* Boston: MIT Press.
Gadamer, H.G. (1989). *Truth and Method.* New York: Continuum Books.
Gick, M. & Holyoak, K. (1987). Schema induction and analogical transfer. *Cognitive Psychology. 15.*
Glieck, J. (1987). *Chaos: The Making of a New Science.* New York: Penguin Books.
Griffin, S. (1978). *Woman and Nature: The Roaring Inside Her.* New York: Harper and Row.
Griffin, S. (1989). Split culture. In Judith Plant (1989). *Healing the Wounds: The Promise of Ecofeminism.* Toronto: Between the Lines Press.
Habermas, J. (1972). *Knowledge and Human Interests.* Beacon Books, Boston.
Hartman. G. & Budick, S. eds. *Midrash and Literature.* New Haven: Yale University Press.

Heidegger, M. (1962). *Being and Time,* Harper and Row, New York.
Heidegger, M. (1968). *What is Called Thinking?,* Harper and Row, New York.
Heidegger, M. (1971). The age of the world-picture. In *The Question Concerning Technology.* New York: Harper and Row.
Heidegger, M. (1971a). The nature of language. In *On the Way to Language.* New York: Harper and Row.
Heidegger, M. (1972) The end of philosophy and the task of thinking. In *On Time and Being,* Harper and Row, New York.
Heidegger, M. (1972a) Time and being. In *On Time and Being,* Harper and Row, New York.
Heidegger, M. (1977). Modern science, metaphysics and mathematics. *Basic Writings.* New York: Harper and Row.
Heidegger, M. (1977a). Letter on humanism. *Basic Writings.* New York: Harper and Row.
Heidegger, M. (1978). *The Metaphysical Foundations of Logic.* Indiana University Press, Bloomington.
Heidegger, M. (1987). "Overcoming Metaphysics," in *The End of Philosophy.* (New York: Harper and Row.
Herrin, J. (1987). *The Formation of Christendom.* Princeton: Princeton University Press.
Hillman, J. (1983). *Healing Fiction.* Barrytown, N.Y.: Station Hill Press.
Hillman, J. (1983a). *Inter Views.* Dallas: Spring Publications.
Hillman, J. (1987). Puer and senex. In *Puer papers.* Dallas: Spring Publications.
Hillman, J. (1987a). Notes on opportunism. In *Puer papers.* Dallas: Spring Publications.
Hillman, J. (1996). Healing fiction. Woodstock, CT: Spring Publications.
Hillman, J. (2006). The repression of beauty. In In James Hillman (2006). City and soul. (pp.
172-186). Putnam CT: Spring Publications Inc.
Hillman, J. & Shamdasani, S. (2013). *Lament of the dead.* New York: W.W. Norton and Company.
Hongzhi, Z. (1991). *Cultivating the empty field: The silent illumination of Zen master Hongzhi.* (T. D. Leighton & Y. Wu, Trans.). San Francisco, CA: North Point Press.
Huntington, S. (2003). *The clash of civilizations and the remaking of world order.* New
York: Simon and Schuster Paperbacks.
Husserl, E. (1964). Edmund Husserl: A letter to Arnold Metzger. *Philosophical forum. 21,* 48-68.

Husserl, E. (1965). Philosophy as a rigorous science. In *Phenomenology and the crisis of philosophy*. New York: Harper and Row, 71-148.

Husserl, E. (1960). 'Phenomenology and anthropology', in R. M. Chisholm (ed.), *Realism and the Background of Phenomenology*, The Free Press, Illinois, pp. 154-170.

Husserl, E. (1969). *Ideas*, Humanities Press, New York.

Husserl, E. (1969a). *Formal and Transcendental Logic*, Martinus Nijhoff, The Hague.

Husserl, E. (1970). *The Crisis of European Science and Transcendental Phenomenology*, Northwestern University Press, Evanston.

Husserl, E. (1970a). *Cartesian Meditations*, Martinus Nijhoff, The Hague.

Husserl, E. (1970b). *The idea of phenomenology*. The Hague: Martinus Nijhoff.

Husserl, E. (1970c). *The Paris lectures*. The Hague: Martinus Nijhoff.

Husserl, E. (1972). Husserl's inagural lecture at Freiburg im Briesgau (1917). In Embree, L., ed. *Life-world and consciousness*. Evanston: Northwestern University Press, 3-18.

Ingram, C. (1990). *In the footsteps of Gandhi: Conversations with spiritual social activists*. Berkeley: Parallax Press.

Jardine, D. (1984). The Piagetian picture of the world. *Phenomeology + Pedagogy*.

Jardine, D. (1985). Self-understanding and reflection in Piagetian theory: A Phenomenological critique. *Journal of Educational Thought*.

Jardine, D. (1987). Piaget's clay and Descartes' wax. *Educational Theory. 38*(3).

Jardine, D. (1988). Play and hermeneutics: An exploration of the bi-polarities of mutual understanding. *Journal of Curriculum Theorizing. 8*(3).

Jardine, D. (1988a). "There are children all around us." *Journal of Educational Thought. 22*(2A).

Jardine, D. (1988b). On phenomenology, pedagogy and *Phenomenology + Pedagogy*. *Phenomenology + Pedagogy*.

Jardine, D. (1990). "To dwell with a boundless heart": On the integrated curriculum and the recovery of the Earth. *Journal of curriculum and supervision. 5*(1).

Jardine, D. (1990a). Awakening from Descartes' nightmare: On the love of ambiguity in phenomenological approaches to education. *Studies in Philosophy and Education. 10*(1).

Jardine, D. (1990b). On the humility of mathematical language. *Educational theory. 40*(2), 181- 191.

Jardine, D. (1992). Immanuel Kant, Jean Piaget and the rage for order: Hints of the colonial spirit in pedagogy. *Educational Philosophy and Theory*.

Jardine, D. (1992a). "The fecundity of the individual case": Considerastions of the pedagogic heart of interpretive work. *Journal of Philosophy and Education*.

Jardine D. (1992). Naming children authors. Unpublished manuscript. University of Calgary.

Jardine D. & Field, J. (1992) "Disproportion, monstrousness and mystery": Ethical and ecological reflections on the initiation of student-teachers into the community of education. *Teaching and Teacher Education.*

Jardine, D. (2008). On the while of things. *Journal of the American association for the advancement of curriculum studies.* February 2008. Online: http://www.uwstout.edu/soe/jaaacs/vol4/Jardine.htm

Jardine, D. (2016). *In Praise of Radiant Beings: A Retrospective Path Through Education, Buddhism and Ecology.* IAP: Information Age Publishing.

Jardine, D. (2017). "A hubris hiding from its nemesis": Why does the affirmation of diversity tend towards the proliferation of multiple identities, and to what consequence? In E. Lyle (2017). *At the Intersection of Selves and Subject: Exploring the Curricular Landscape of Identity* (p. 9-18). Rotterdam, NL: Brill/Sense Publishers.

Jardine, D. (in press). *"Why Study for A Future We Won't Have?" Commiserations and Encouragement for Ecologically Sorrowful Times.* Peter Lang Publishing.

Jardine, D., Clifford, P., & Friesen, S., eds. (2003). *Back to The Basics of Teaching and Learning: "Thinking the World Together".* Foreword by William E. Doll, Louisiana State University. Lawrence Erlbaum and Associates

Jardine, D. & Misgeld, D. (1989). Hermeneutics as the undisciplined child. In Addison, R. & Packer, M., eds., *Entering the Circle: Hermeneutic Investigations in Psychology.* New York: SUNY Press.

Jardine, D. & Morgan, G. (1987). Analogical thinking in young children and the use of logico- mathematical knowledge as a paradigm in Jean Piaget's genetic epistemology. *The Quarterly Newsletter of the Laboratory of Comparative Human Cognition. 9*(4).

Jardine, D. & Morgan, G. (1988). Analogy as a model for the development of representational abilities in children. *Educational Theory. 37*(3).

Kant, I. (1964). *Critique of Pure Reason,* Macmillan, London.

Kant, I. (1784/1983). What is enlightenment?. In *Perpetual Peace and other essays.* Indianapolis: Hackett Publishing Company.

Kermode, F. (1979). *The Genesis of Secrecy.* Cambridge: Harvard University Press.

King, T. & Monkman, W.K. (1992). A *Coyote Columbus Story.* Toronto: Groundwood Books.

Kugel, J. (1986). Two introductions to Midrash. In G. Hartman. & S. Budick, eds. *Midrash and Literature.* New Haven: Yale University Press.

LaChapelle (1989). Sacred land, sacred sex. In Judith Plant (1989). *Healing the Wounds.* Toronto: Between the Lines Press.

Lasch, C. (1979). *The Culture of Narcissism.* New York: W. W. Norton and Co.

LeGuin, U. (1968). *The Wizard of Earthsea*. London: Penguin Books.
LeGuin, U. (1987). Introduction. In *Buffalo gals and other animal presences*. Santa Barbara: Capra Press.
LeGuin, U. (1987a). She unnames them. In *Buffalo gals and other animal presences*. Santa Barbara: Capra Press.
LeGuin, U. (1989). Women/wilderness. In Judith Plant (1989). *Healing the Wounds: The Promise of Ecofeminism*. Toronto: Between the Lines Press.
Lowry, L. (2011). The giver. New York: Houghton Mifflin Books.
MacDonald, J. (1975). 'Curriculum and Human Interests', in W. Pinar (ed.), *Curriculum Theorizing: The Reconceptualists,* McCutchan Publishing Corporation, Berkeley, pp. 283-294.
Macy, J. (1989). Awakening the ecological self. In J. Plant, ed., *Healing the wounds: The promise of ecofeminism*. Toronto: Between the Lines.
Madison, G. (1988). *The Hermaneutics of Postmodernism*. Bloomington: Indiana University Press.
Mahdi, L., Foster, S. & Little, M. (1987) eds. *Betwixt and Between: Patterns of Masculine and Feminine Initiation*. LaSalle: Open Court Books.
Martin, E. (1978). *A History of the Iconoclastic Controversy*. London: MamMillan.
Merleau-Ponty, M. (1970). *Phenomenology of Perception,* Humanities Press, New York.
Merleau-Ponty, M. (1970a). *Signs,* Northwestern University Press, Evanston.
Merton, T. (1965). *Gandhi on Non-Violence*. New Directions Books, New York.
Meshchonnic, H. (1988). Rhyme and life. *Critical Inquiry. 15* (Autumn 1988).
Miller, A. (1989). *For Your Own Good: Hidden Cruelty in Child-Rearing and the Roots of Violence*. Toronto: Collins.
Misgeld, D. (1985). Self-reflection and adult maturity: Adult and child in hermeneutical and critical reflection. *Phenomenology + Pedagogy, 3*(3), 191-200.
Morris, R. (1989). Words and images in modernism and postmodernism. *Critical Inquiry. 15* (Winter, 1989).
Nandy, A. (1987). *Traditions, Tyranny and Utopias: Essays in Political Awareness*. Delhi: Oxford University Press.
Neumann, E. (1990). *The Child*. Boston: Shambala Press.
Nhat Hahn, Thich (1986). *The Miracle of Mindfulness*. Berkeley: Parallax Press.
Nhat Hahn, Thich (1988). *The Sun My Heart*. Berkeley: Parallax Press.
Nietzsche, F. (1975). *The Will To Power*. New York: Random House.
Nishitani Keiji (1982). *Religion and Nothingness*. Berkeley: University of Calfornia Press.
Norris-Clarke, W. (1976). 'Analogy and the Meaningfulness of Langauge about God: A Reply to Kai Nielsen', *The Thomist, 40,* pp. 176-198.

Parenteau, J. (2022). Miywasin Moment: Raven tales take flight across generations. *Medicine Hat News.* June 21st, 2024. Online: https://medicinehatnews.com/news/local-news/2022/02/02/miywasin-moment-raven-tales-take-flight-across-generations/
Piaget, J. (1952). *Origins of Intelligence in Children,* International Universities Press, New York.
Piaget, J. (1970). *Structuralism.* Harper and Row, New York.
Piaget, J. (1971). *Insights and Illusions of Philosophy,* Meridian Books, New York.
Piaget, J. (1971a). *The construction of reality in the child.* New York: Ballantine Books.
Piaget, J. (1972). *The child's conception of physical causality.* Totawa: Littlefield, Adams and Co. p. 239.
Piaget, J. (1973). *The pyschology of intelligence.* Totowa: Littlefield, Adams and Co.
Piaget, J. (1974). *The child's conception of the world.* London: Paladin Books.
Pinar. W. & Reynolds, W. (1992). *Understanding Curriculum as Phenomenological and Deconstructed Text.* New York: Teacher's College Press.
Plant, J. (1989). *Healing the wounds: The promise of ecofeminism.* Toronto: Between the Lines Books.
Plaskow, J. & Christ, C. (1989). *Weaving the Visions: New Patterns in Feminist Spirituality.* New York: Harper and Row.
Ricouer, P. (1970). *Freud and Philosophy.* Yale University Press, New Haven.
Ross, S.M. (2004). Gadamer's late thinking on Verweilen." *Minerva -An Internet Journal of Philosophy,* Vol. 8. Available on-line at:http://www.ul.ie/~philos/vol8/gadamer.html. Accessed May 2007.
Ross, S.M. & Jardine, D. (2009). Won by a certain labour: A conversation on the while of things. *Journal of the American Association for the Advancement of Curriculum Studies.* Volume 5. Online: http://www.uwstout.edu/soe/jaaacs/Vol5/Ross_Jardine.htm
Sahas, D. (n.d.). *Icon and Logos: Sources in Eighth-Century Iconoclasm.* Toronto: University of Toronto Press.
Said, E. (1978). *Orientalism.* New York: Penguin Books.
Sartre, J.P. (1970). 'Intentionality: A Fundamental Idea in Husserl's Phenomenology', *Journal for the British Society for Phenomenology, 1,* #2, pp. 3-5.
Schopenhauer, A. (1966). *The World as Will and Representation,* vol. 1. New York: Dover Books.
Seikdia, K. (1976). *Zen Training: Methods and Philosophy.* New York: Weatherhill.
Sheridan, M (1992). The teacher as a reader of the world. Unpublished Doctoral Dissertation, Department of Curriculum and Instruction, Faculty of Education, University of Calgary.
Smith, D. (1988). 'Children and the Gods of War', *Journal of Educational Thought,* 22, 2A, p. 173-177.

Smith, D. (1988a). 'From Logocentrism to Rhysomatics: Working Through the Boundary Police to a New Love.' Presented at the Bergamo Conference on Curriculum Theory and Classroom Practice, Dayton, Ohio, October, 1988.
Smith, D. (1988b) "On being critical about language: The critical theory tradition and implications for language education." *Reading-Canada*. vol. 6, #4.
Smith, D. (1988c). The problem of the south is the north (but the problem of the north is the north). Forum proceedings of the *World Council on Curriculum and Instruction*. 2(2).
Smith, D. (1988d). Brighter than a thousand suns: Facing Pedagogy in the nuclear shadow. In T. Carson, ed., *Toward a Renaissance of Humanity: Rethinking and Revisiting Curriculum and Instruction*. Edmonton: University of Alberta.
Smith, D. (1991). Hermeneutic inquiry: The hermeneutic imagination and the pedagogic text. In E. Short, ed. *Forms of Curriculum Inquiry*. Albany: SUNY Press.
Smith, D. (1992). Teacher education and the notion of global culture. Presented at the American Association of Colleges of Teacher Education, San Antonio, Texas, February, 1992.
Smith, D. G. (2006). *Trying to teach in a season of great untruth: Globalization, empire and the crises of pedagogy*. Rotterdam, the Netherlands: Sense.
Snyder, G. (1979). Poetry, community and climax. *Field. 20* (Spring, 1979).
Snyder, G. (1980). *The real work*. New York: New Directions.
Snyder, G. (1990) An interview with Cathrine Ingram. In C. Ingram, ed. *In the Footsteps of Gandhi*. Berkeley: Parallax Press.
Snyder, Gary. (1990a). *The practice of the wild*. San Francisco: North Point Press.
Suzuki, S. (1986). *Zen Mind, Beginner's Mind*. New York: Weatherhill.
Taylor, C. (1991). *The Malaise of Modernity*. Toronto: House of Ananasi Press.
Trungpa, C. (1991). Trikaya and hopelessness. In *Crazy Widsom*. San Francisco: Shambala Press.
Turner, V. (1987). Betwixt and between: The liminal period in rites of passage. In Mahdi, L., Foster, S. & Little, M. (1987) eds. *Betwixt and Between: Patterns of Masculine and Feminine Initiation*. LaSalle: Open Court Books.
van Lysebeth, A. (1983). *Pranayama: The Yoga of Breathing*. London: Unwin Paperbacks.
van Manen, M. (1983). On pedagogic hope. *Phenomenology + Pedagogy. 1*(2).
Volans, K. (1992). Liner notes interview to Kronos Quartet. *Pieces of Africa*. Elektra/Nonesuch CD 979253-2.
Wallace, B. (1989). *The Stubborn Particulars of Grace*. Toronto: McClelland and Stewart.
Weatherford, J. (1988). *Indian Givers*. New York: Fawcett Columbine.
Weinsheimer, J. (1987). *Gadamer's hermeneutics*. New Haven: Yale University Press.

Williams, W.C. (1963). *Patterson*. New York: New Directions Books.
Williams, W.C. (1991). *The Collected Poems of William Carlos Williams*. Volume 1: 1909-1939. New York: New Directions Books.
Wilshire, B. (1990). *The Moral Collapse of the University*. Albany: SUNY Press.
Wittgenstein, L. (1961). *Tractatus Logico-Philosophicus*. London: Routledge and Kegan Paul.
Wittgenstein, L. (1968). *Philosophical Investigations,* Blackwells, Cambridge.
Young, N. (1979). Thrashers. From *Rust Never Sleeps*. Reprise Records.
Zoppellaro, M. (2014). "I am what I am...". An interview with Lou Reed. In *Mojo Magazine*, Issue 242, January 2014.